THE S1

PETER GABRIEL

CHRIS WELCH

OMNIBUS PRESS
LONDON · NEW YORK · PARIS · SYDNEY

Cover designed by Mike Bell Design
Picture research by Nikki Russell

ISBN: 0.7119.6812.8
Order No: OP 48052

Exclusive Distributors:
Book Sales Limited,
8/9 Frith Street,
London W1V 5TZ, UK.

Music Sales Corporation,
257 Park Avenue South,
New York, NY 10010, USA.

Five Mile Press,
22 Summit Road,
Noble Park,
Victoria 3174, Australia.

To the Music Trade only:
Music Sales Limited,
8/9 Frith Street,
London W1V 5TZ, UK.

Cover pictures by Paul Rider/Retna.

Every effort has been made to trace the copyright holders of the
photographs in this book but one or two were unreachable. We would be
grateful if the photographers concerned would contact us.

Printed by Galleon Typesetting, Ipswich.
Printed in Great Britain by Redwood Books Ltd, Trowbridge, Wilts.

A catalogue record for this book is available from the British Library.

Visit Omnibus Press at http://www.musicsales.co.uk

'A droll, brilliant, single-minded visionary . . .'
– a critic

'Shy, timid . . . and incredibly brave . . .'
– a friend

'Come out Peter . . . we know you're in there!'
– a fan

CONTENTS

I

PETER THE GREAT

"BOO! GET OFF . . . awae with ye!"

A solitary figure fixes his piercing gaze on a baying mob and stands with arms folded . . . waiting. Missiles rain down on the fearless young singer's head, as abuse howls around his ears. The Glasgow crowd have a reputation for being the toughest audience in showbusiness. English comedians – English rock bands. It's all the same to them; they are the object of hostility and derision. The band are Genesis, anxious and impatient to start. But their singer retains his stance, boldly facing out his tormentors and waiting until a semblance of silence falls. Only then does he signal to the band to play and the dramatic opening notes of 'Watcher Of The Skies' hammers the hordes at Green's Playhouse into submission. By the end of the performance the crowd are cheering wildly. Peter Gabriel chose his moment with care. He won them over, just as he would win over a wider public many more times during the years that lay ahead.

Mysterious, sensitive, witty and always seeking new challenges, Peter Gabriel has been an innovative force in rock music for the last thirty years. During that time he has helped launch Genesis, one of the most successful bands of all time; created a stage persona as powerful as Bowie's Ziggy Stardust, then after a dramatic split, gone on to forge a successful and distinguished solo career. Singer, musician, writer and visionary, Gabriel has helped develop many of rock's most crucial elements in the process of creating his own musical environment.

Video, studio technology, special stage sets, audience participation, the use of synthesizers, the big dynamic drum sound and exotic ethnic instruments – all these areas have benefited and developed under his aegis.

After unleashing a series of critically acclaimed albums with Genesis culminating in *The Lamb Lies Down On Broadway*, he quit the group in May 1975 and went on to devise a series of highly personal solo albums that impressed critics and fans alike.

As his writing skills grew and matured he laced his work with such evocative songs as 'Solsbury Hill', 'Humdrum', 'Modern Love' and 'Games Without Frontiers'. Between bouts of self-reappraisal and solitude he returned to receive even greater acclaim in the mid-Eighties with his supremely confident album *So*, the hit single 'Sledgehammer' and its award winning video. Much more great work and hits have followed including the superb 1992 album *Us*, written after the series of emotional traumas that would intrude upon his adult life. Never a hasty, slap-dash artist, Gabriel thinks and works long and hard before unleashing a project that he feels he can be proud of and will command respect.

A poignant, sometimes painful depth of emotion permeates many of his best known works like the powerful 'Biko', written in memory of the murdered South African activist, while the romantic tenderness of his duet with Kate Bush, 'Don't Give Up', ensured it became an anthem of those seeking solace from life's troubles. There is humour too in his sometimes sardonic and cynical asides. He may care deeply about matters social and even political, but he is no mere dreamer and far from being anyone's fool.

Gabriel remains a controversial figure, invariably regarded with affection by fans but sometimes misinterpreted and even disliked. "Peter Gabriel's crap – I've always hated him . . ." spluttered one British music press reviewer recently, representing the drab suspicious minds of the inarticulate.

Yet he has been described by others as "A droll, brilliant, single-minded visionary". How does such a shy and self-effacing man arouse so many conflicting emotions? And how does a man with good intentions and bold ideas find himself struggling in the deep waters that sometimes inundate his personal relations and business affairs? He has been threatened, abused and even at one stage faced ruin at the hands of those he has tried most to help.

The disarming smile and creaky laugh are enough to charm most people around to Peter's way of thinking. And yet this imaginative man who thrives on dreams and visions often finds his way blocked and his schemes thwarted by the pressing demands of the matter of fact and down to earth.

His aim to establish world music as an important force almost ended in disaster when the first World Of Music Arts And Dance Festival he organised in 1982 lost money. Old friends rallied round when Genesis got together for a special reunion concert with Peter back at the helm. Despite torrential rain at their Milton Keynes show, the old Genesis magic returned, the fans rolled up and enough money was raised to rescue Gabriel from insolvency. He lived to fight another day, his career picked up and from then on the WOMAD Festivals have become regular international events and a continuing success.

Buffeted by the fates, often ill-used, Peter Gabriel, with his slow smile, penetrating eyes and sometimes languid, sometimes agitated demeanour is, superficially at least, a product of his influences and environment. More relevantly he is a product of his own desires and intelligence, those twin forces which ultimately mould any radical personality.

A public schoolboy from a respectable middle-class background, he is the ultimate rebel; the classless, free-wheeling spirit who wants nothing more than to get up on the table and sing and shout in the face of conformity.

Freedom is the goal, but fun and self expression have always been equally important parts of the Gabriel quest – from childhood to stardom. In his case, the aspirations and dreams of the child are definitely more important to him than the pretensions and ambitions of the rock star. He has always been uneasy with the demands of stardom, while not averse to the benefits, using them to remain operational and to invest in his dreams.

In the early days of Genesis, he knew what it was like to be broke, sometimes even starving as the essentially amateur band tried to establish themselves. After three years of struggle they ended up with massive debts. It was an experience that has always ensured a certain humility among the Genesis school of musicians, no matter how great their success in later years.

Despite the passage of time and the onset of new directions, for many of Gabriel's oldest and deeply loyal fans his most enduring image is not the star of clever videos nor even the passionate, tormented voice of 'Come Talk To Me', 'Love To Be Loved' and 'Blood Of Eden' from the sometimes dark and despairing *Us*. The Peter they admired is the Peter of old, the narrator with laughter in his soul, who gave the world such characters as the bailiff Winkler in 'Get 'Em Out By Friday', 'Harold The Barrel' and the menacing 'Watcher Of The Skies'. They loved the youth in black and adorned with silver, who declaimed, 'Stand up and fight, for we know we are right' in 'The Knife' and regaled them with such quirky tales as 'The Return Of The Giant Hogweed'; the Gabriel who shocked and delighted audiences when he appeared clad in masks, batwings, a flower and even a red dress and fox's head. He well may have been indulging in sensationalism, but he did it with such conviction that it became true theatre.

Today you can see eyes glaze over and looks of disbelief when you mention 'Genesis' to recent converts to the delights of popular music. It is difficult to convey the impact they first made, as scratchy archive videos and poorly mixed vinyl albums cannot now do full justice to the band that was once so young and fresh and – above all – so different.

Yet together with his more subdued colleagues, Gabriel the singer, flute player and part-time bass drummer, helped devise a heady mixture of visual and musical innovation that once proved irresistible. At a time when pop music was teetering between Glam Rock and Heavy Metal, Genesis offered something much deeper. That Peter was later able to build on this early success and create a musical life and worthwhile career beyond Genesis is a great tribute to his innate artistry and sense of purpose. It hasn't always been easy for him – and he sometimes faltered. But he never gave up. Many of his contemporaries, who enjoyed early success in the Seventies, found it almost impossible to re-establish themselves, once their initial brush with fame had subsided. They would spend years wandering in a cultural wilderness, vainly searching for a new direction. Many gave up the struggle and today rely entirely on their past to support a diminishing career on the nostalgia circuit.

But Peter Gabriel embarked on a journey of rediscovery when he left Genesis amidst emotional scenes in May, 1975.

His path was never clearly signposted. He would follow his inclinations, play his own music and still hopefully remain that coveted being – a rock'n'roll star. Was it always foretold and predestined that Peter Brian Gabriel should be a seeker of knowledge and purveyor of musical truths? Certainly his background provided many of the elements that would forge his character and shape his destiny.

Peter Gabriel was born on February 13, 1950 at Woking Hospital, Surrey. The future rock musician came from a gifted family with fascinating origins. His father Ralph was an electrical engineer and inventor, and his mother Irene a concert pianist. Their interests plainly influenced Peter's own passions for technology and music albeit in quite different ways.

The ancestral name Gabriel has Spanish origins and may well go back to the days of the Armada of 1588, when many a shipwrecked sailor from King Philip II's storm-tossed invasion fleet found himself castaway on British soil.

Peter's father Ralph Gabriel was born into a family of timber merchants known as Gabriel, Wade & English, originally based in Cornwall and founded by Christopher Gabriel, in the 17th Century. Another famous ancestor, Sir Thomas Gabriel was once the Lord Mayor of London, who served in the year 1866. The 20th Century Gabriels were no less industrious and ran their own dairy farm at Coxhill in Chobham, Surrey, where Ralph Gabriel grew up in an attractive country house. This was later sold to raise cash and Peter's parents moved into the smaller Deep Pool cottage, which was part of the original property.

Recalls Peter: "My father was born into a family of timber merchants. Most of the family members had safe jobs with the firm. My father was much more of a thinker than the rest of the family." Mr. Gabriel studied at the University of London and became an electrical engineer. He worked on the development of flight simulators and while employed by the British company Rediffusion, designed a revolutionary cable television system called Dial-A-Programme that made early use of fibre optics. Peter remembers that when his inventive father came home from London after a hard day devising radical new innovations, he would get off the train and stand on his head for a few minutes of relaxing yoga. He would doubtless have approved of his own son's later penchant for inhaling helium gas and flying through the air on high wires.

Peter's mother Irene came from a musical family and had four music loving sisters. Her mother used to sing with Sir Henry Wood, noted conductor at the Promenade Concerts, the annual London event fondly known as 'The Proms'. Peter was given piano and dancing lessons and was also taught to ride from the age of three. Says Gabriel: "I had a very happy and free childhood. My father was quite an influence. He had a very creative mind. He was always in his workshop and could build things out of nothing. My mother's family were all musical. They were a real Victorian family with five sisters, all of whom would play different instruments and sing together at musical evenings. At Christmas there was always a collection of aunts gathered round the grand piano. I had to learn piano because everybody in her family did."

However quite early in life he staged a minor rebellion against parental guidance. "I was having so many lessons I had a little revolution and said: 'No more piano lessons, no more riding lessons. I'm going to stop all this and watch TV.' "

He later regretted calling a halt to his formal musical studies, but remains a competent piano player and flautist. He would resume his piano studies after leaving Genesis. Meanwhile he grew up enjoying life on the farm and playing with animals, pets and many girlfriends. "I had a very liberated sex life, from the age of four to seven, which I never really recovered from," he admits. "I found it quite easy to get on with other kids. I wasn't a macho sporty male. I would prefer doctors and nurses with the girls behind the flower beds to cowboys and Indians."

These early experiences at least gave him a safe form of sexual education. However there were times when he was left alone while the rest of the family pursued their various hobbies and pursuits. "Riding and pony clubs didn't really appeal to me so I would find myself wandering around in a world of my own. That's probably when I started my preoccupation with fantasy. My favourite thing on the farm was to build a dam across the river and build a central circle in the middle of the dam in which I'd build a fire. Then I'd sit on the bank and wait until the water was high enough to wash over the fire. I'm sure a psychiatrist would have some meaningful analysis for this."

Peter was sent to a nearby nursery school and then went to a prep school near Woking. "That was where most of the flower bed activities took place," he remembers. Later he went to St. Andrew's Boys School where he stayed as a boarder during the week, before cycling home at weekends. Eventually in September, 1963 he was sent to Charterhouse, one of England's best known public schools, which was inadvertently to become famous as the birthplace of Genesis, although the founders of this staid academic institution would probably not have wished for such notoriety. The school at Godalming, Surrey, was founded in 1611 by a London builder, Thomas Sutton, on the site of a London monastery, and moved to its present site in 1872. While girls have been admitted since the Seventies Peter went there during the Sixties, when the school still had a 'fagging' system and older pupils bossed around the younger boys, requiring them to perform menial tasks such as tidying their rooms, cleaning shoes and delivering bottles of milk. According to Peter it wasn't so far removed from the semi-fictional *Tom Browns' Schooldays* and he wasn't especially happy there. In fact he states quite bluntly: "I hated it. It was terrible. I think I was very sensitive at school. Everything was a huge drama and many nights I would spend awake trying to get to sleep."

He describes the experience as traumatic and from the first night disliked the cold, impersonal dormitories with their lack of privacy. These sleeping quarters were large rooms with cubicles divided by hardboard and at night they would be filled with the sound of muffled conversations and whimpering voices. Recalls Peter: "Everyone seemed to be nervous and unhappy and there were some boys crying when I first went there."

Although this was the Swinging Sixties and The Beatles had shaken up England with its own class levelling social revolution, Charterhouse retained many traditions that seemed to date from the 19th Century. Older boys had privileges such as being able to have their jackets undone, while juniors were expected to keep theirs buttoned. New boys had to learn these customs and school slang by heart and after two weeks they had to pass a so called 'New Hops Test'. Those who failed were made to stand on a table and sing songs while the prefects pelted them with bread rolls; a fairly harmless but nevertheless humiliating experience. Those who flagrantly broke the rules, however, were caned.

There was more aggravation outside the school. Lads from nearby state schools would hide in the bushes, jump out and beat up the Charterhouse boys, then steal their bicycles. Eventually the public schoolboys would gang up themselves and cycle to school in huge groups, like animals herding together for protection. The experience and attitudes among the boys would have a profound effect on Gabriel. He said later: "I hate the class system and I think that the [public] school system is one of the most effective means by which England perpetuates its class divisions."

All through his first year at the school Peter felt miserable and resented and feared the power of the older boys, who even made fags warm their toilet seats. Peter realised the idea was to raise a breed of 'leaders of men' who would be discouraged from mixing with their 'inferiors'. In mitigation the system gave insecure teenagers a degree of self confidence, but he felt it was based on an antiquated and ideologically unsound premise.

Nevertheless, there were some advantages to be had from attending the school. Charterhouse encouraged a keen interest in music and the composer Ralph Vaughan Williams was an 'Old Carthusian'.

Peter's own interests in pop music had begun, naturally enough, with The Beatles. "I can remember exactly where I was when I first heard 'Love Me Do'. I also remember when The Beatles made the first worldwide TV satellite link, singing 'All You Need Is Love'. I felt like, 'We've made it'. Very naïve stuff, but I was very excited. I felt part of that generation. It was a really exciting thing to watch and feel – even if you were just a spectator. I was just a weekend hippie. Later on the first gig I went to see was John Mayall's Bluesbreakers at The Marquee."

As part of his contribution to the social revolution going on outside, Peter would offer a unique service to like-minded pupils. He would dye their shirts in a range of psychedelic colours, which proved popular until it was found the dyes were running in the wash and Matron discovered the boys' white underpants were turning red, green and blue. Another of Peter's enterprises involved producing brightly coloured fashionable hats and much to his delight found they were accepted for sale at some of London's top street markets. Marianne Faithfull bought one and wore it on BBC TV's *Juke Box Jury* show. Recalls fellow pupil Anthony Phillips: "Peter was a clever boy. He had some hats made by Dunns. Everyone used to buy his hats. He also used to dye everybody's T-shirts for them at Charterhouse. Our white shirts became turquoise. A colourful man Peter. He always had a lot of creative ideas."

Among Peter's closest friends at Charterhouse was Tony Banks (born March 27, 1951), a fine classical pianist, who would eventually become keyboard player and a founder member of Genesis. Tony, however, was never completely relaxed and Peter describes him in those early days as being "a bit edgy". Their friendship developed out of a mutual interest in the piano. Said Peter: "There was one piano in this house and as soon as classes finished there was a scramble to occupy it. You could sometimes reserve it but after a while it became a free for all. As soon as the games period finished we would have a fight for access. Sometimes I'd climb through a food hatch to see if I could beat the others."

Tony remembers that they used to play soul numbers by Otis Redding and that Peter would sing them very well while he played the piano.

Says Peter: "Tony and I were a combination of best friends and worst enemies. Like any long-term relationship, as with a married couple, you get to know each other's Achilles' heel and can turn the screw to pulverise the opposition. He was slightly better at it than me largely because he had a better defence mechanism. It was all part of our relationship."

Says Banks: "We were both pretty unhappy at school. Neither of us liked being away from home and the restrictions got us down more than they did most people. You weren't allowed to walk through certain doors or across certain bits of ground or have certain buttons undone. So we both got into people like Otis Redding and into the idea of playing music. Technically we weren't supposed to have our own record players or radios at school either, which was one of the reasons it was so exciting."

Among his other school friends were guitarist Mike Rutherford (born October 2, 1950), a jolly soul, and fellow guitar player Anthony Phillips, a somewhat more explosive personality. Says Peter: "I remember that Tony and I were both lectured about mixing with 'undesirable elements' by the house master."

Apparently the master was referring to Mike Rutherford, but not to 'Ant' Phillips who was a keen cricket player and was therefore acceptable company for impressionable youths. It's hard now to imagine the dignified and well spoken Rutherford as an 'undesirable', but in those days an interest in pop music was construed as 'subversive' and an unwelcome trait. Even at state schools in those days it was possible to receive six strokes of the cane for playing rock'n'roll records on the premises.

Mike recalls that he was officially banned from playing the guitar the whole time he was at Charterhouse. "Pop music was a symbol for the revolution and it was about to over-throw the Establishment and bring the country down." As at all public schools there was a disproportionate emphasis on sport-ing activity, fresh air and exercise, much of it conducted in austere conditions, perhaps in the mistaken belief that such exertions might take the boys' minds off other, less hearty pursuits, such as sex and pop music.

In this somewhat formal and stultified atmosphere, the only place where Gabriel felt any sense of freedom and where he could express his individuality was the school's billiard room. Here the pupils were allowed to play their own records on an old Dansette type record player, a primitive but ubiquitous machine familiar to the generation of British teenagers that bought umpteen million seven inch singles during the Sixties.

Peter: "We had a beaten up Dansette in a wooden cabinet. You could only play it for an hour and a half every day." Gabriel took his favourite Otis Redding singles to school, turned up the volume to sledgehammer proportions and danced wildly until he broke into a sweat. He even climbed on the tables and sang in his best soul voice. "This ritual gave me an immense feeling of relief," he recalls. One of his school friends remembers seeing Peter in the wood panelled school hall, strutting his stuff in a top hat and singing to a crowd of 600 boys.

Says Anthony Phillips: "Peter used to jump on tables and start singing which was quite out of character because he seemed such an ordinary bloke."

Rather than just play records, Gabriel and his friends began to assemble the first two school groups, known as The Garden Wall and The Anon, which came together in May, 1965. The idea was to create some original music inspired by their twin passions for pop and soul, while taking advantage of their burgeoning technical skills. Mike Rutherford played rhythm guitar in The Anon, joined by Anthony Phillips on lead guitar. Their band was completed by Rivers Job (bass), Richard Mac-Phail (vocals) and Rob Tyrell (drums). Peter sometimes lent The Anon his drum kit which was his pride and joy. Anthony Phillips remembers him looking extremely nervous about handing over his drums which he'd been playing in a jazz and soul band, although not with much skill according to Tony Banks. Says Tony: "He always had the idea of the beat, but he didn't quite have the co-ordination."

Tony Banks, Peter Gabriel and drummer Chris Stewart made up rival outfit The Garden Wall. However, when some of the members left school after the summer term, come September the two bands united as The New Anon. They made their first demo tape on a friend's machine, featuring material written mostly by Rutherford and Phillips, with Tony and Peter (who added an extra song), brought in to improve the sound.

Peter had quickly formed the impression that being a pop star was an attractive option as far as future employment went. It would certainly get him attention from the opposite sex. As a self confessed 'fat and spotty teenager' (his first girlfriend thought otherwise), it occurred to him that The Rolling Stones and Beatles never had any trouble getting girls, so he wanted to become a musician too. "No, it wasn't quite that simple . . . I wanted the money too!" he jokes.

He started writing simple pop songs at the age of 12 and his first effort was called 'Sammy The Slug'. Says Peter: "Everyone else was writing about girls and I was writing about slugs, which shows what I was interested in! But I had this dream when I was eleven and I saw a fork in the path where I could either be an entertainer or a farmer. I never thought I would be a singer because I didn't think that I could sing. When I was young they thought that I had a nice choirboy voice, but when I tried to sing rock songs it sounded terrible."

However Peter did think he might have a future as a percussionist and he thoroughly enjoyed playing drums in a variety of groups. He was given his first snare drum by his parents when he was 13 and gradually built up a useful kit. A friend's brother sold him an old Premier tom-tom for £7 and although it didn't have a particularly good sound it enabled him to play as hard as he liked.

"I used to play drums in a dance band called M'Lords and then in a soul group called The Spoken Word. I still wanted to be a drummer at that time, but I also wanted to be able to write songs. Playing in a band was more Mike and Ant's thing. I was just an afterthought. Tony was originally going to play the keyboards and then he used that as a way of getting one or two of our songs onto a tape that was done in Chiswick at a studio owned by a friend called Brian Roberts. Richard MacPhail, who later became our tour manager, was the main singer and he was a better singer and performer than I was at the time. But the others seemed to prefer my voice to Richard's."

Tony Banks encouraged Gabriel and urged the others to accept him in his writing role. At first Peter felt his compositions tended to be over complex. He was trying too hard to cover all possible avenues, but when the band started to write together things improved and the material became tighter and more focused. At least two of the songs that appeared on the first Genesis album were written while they were still at school.

Recalls Gabriel: "Tony Banks and I were beginning to build up a rapport – of sorts. There were definitely things about each other's early musical offerings that we *didn't* like. But there were many elements that we did like and so we concentrated on them. When we started to write songs together, that's when we thought we might get them recorded. Tony and I were thinking of being songwriters, while Mike and Ant were really into playing in a group and doing Stones imitations at parties. I still wanted to play the drums, but not so much with this kind of material."

Peter and Tony shared tastes in pop music and while they were still at school, they used to sneak down to a record shop in Godalming and just hang out, listening to the latest soul records by artists like Otis Redding and James Brown. "It was brave of us because loafing around in cafes and record shops was 'out' and if we were caught we would have been punished," remembers Peter. "But I loved to hear Otis Redding and his strong, soulful passionate ballads were amazing. He was my hero as a singer and a lot of that music was part of what drove me to consider music for myself. I was a teenager, very impressionable and ready to be impressed."

In January 1967 the boys decided to send their effort to bespectacled Jonathan King, an old Carthusian and ex-Cambridge undergraduate who had made waves as a singer, composer and general 'live wire' since enjoying a smash hit with his own composition 'Everyone's Gone To The Moon' back in 1965.

When Jonathan heard the tape he was sufficiently impressed to pay for another demo, and offered them a one year contract with Decca Records, which they duly signed in December 1967 while still 17-year-old schoolboys. He even gave them their bold new name – Genesis. Jonathan King was obviously the best contact in the music business that the impressionable young group could have found.

Says Peter: "We were using the old boy network. And I think at that time King seemed quite happy to use the young boy network. He gave us some money to experiment with and told us to produce a demo. He was interested and I would have to go down to the nearest phone box, struggle with my coins and try and locate this person from the pop business."

However green, the public schoolboys were no suckers and tended to regard everyone involved in the music business with the deepest suspicion, including their new found benefactor. Said Peter: "All the original demos that King heard were with acoustic instruments which he thought gave us quite a novel sound. He was an interesting person and came up with a lot of outrageous ideas for us. We talked about a name for the group with Jonathan. His first suggestion, which the rest of the band have forgotten although I haven't, was Gabriel's Angels, which didn't seem to register with the others."

King suggested Gabriel's Angels again when Decca found there was another band called Genesis in America. Eventually Jonathan produced the band's first studio session, held at Regent Sound in London. King wasn't greatly impressed by their first songs. Then Tony and Peter came up with something written more in the style of The Bee Gees, which they guessed he would prefer, although Jonathan didn't seem to realise it was being done to please him. Called 'The Silent Sun' it was released in February 1968 with 'That's Me' on the B-side. Peter was lead vocalist on both tracks.

Says Peter: "I do remember that we tried to write something

that sounded like a Bee Gees ballad. I tried to sing like Robin Gibb on the second verse. I'm sure we would have denied it at the time, as we have denied other influences at later stages. Anyway it worked and it was put out as a single." It was also included on their début album as was 'A Winter's Tale' their second single released in the following May. Neither got into the charts and the record company began to get cold feet. Peter remembers how they were treated.

"We used to go to Decca, give our name at the desk and the man would phone up and say, 'There's a group called The Janitors here to see you.' " In this atmosphere the band seemed on the verge of breaking up and their drummer Chris Stewart actually quit the group. However he was swiftly replaced by John Silver. King meanwhile remained convinced the band had potential. He pressed on and took the bold step of recording an entire album with the fledgling band during the summer of 1968 called *From Genesis To Revelation* (Decca), which was eventually released in March 1969. As there was still some concern about the oft-rumoured American Genesis, the band's name was excluded from the label copy. The band's line-up on this pioneering record included Peter Gabriel (vocals, flute and percussion), Anthony Phillips (guitar), Michael Rutherford (bass, guitar and vocals), Tony Banks (keyboards, guitar, vocals) and John Silver (drums).

The project was an ambitious attempt to tell the story of the creation of the world and the evolution of Mankind in Biblical terms. Says Peter: "It was terribly pretentious. The history of Man's evolution in ten simple pop songs. I suppose the main thing we were trying to do at that time was break the barrier between folk and rock. *From Genesis To Revelation* was supposed to be the history of the universe." Even Peter admits that, "This was a very duff concept!"

However whenever he has listened to it in retrospect his judgement on their first effort hasn't been so harsh. "Listening to it now, I think there are some things that showed we had melody-writing potential. I think Ant was the best songwriter of us all at that point. Tony did some good melodies, but they were a bit stiff."

The ten songs were written and rehearsed during school holidays at John Silver's home, and recorded in just one day at

Regent Sound and the band, who had barely done any live appearances let alone recording, were clearly nervous. The songs were strong and Gabriel sang well, although he kept taking cold showers to help him hit the high notes! Although Tony Banks' piano work held it all together, the rhythm section lacked punch and Jonathan decided at a later stage to add strings arranged by Arthur Greenslade. The aim was to fill out the sound but the band felt this was unnecessary and indeed the strings took up the whole of one of the stereo channels, consigning the band to the other. Anthony Phillips was particularly disappointed with the sound and stormed out of the studio when he heard the finished version.

Recalls Tony Banks: "We did the whole album in a day. We got into the studio at 9 a.m. and worked right through until midnight the following day with Jonathan producing. We were very young and it was an amateur sort of approach but there were a couple of good songs and I think the album was quite good. It has been endlessly repackaged since but it sold nothing at the time. When we made the album we had never really played 'live'. It was based on piano and acoustic guitar with other things overdubbed. My favourite track was 'In The Wilderness'. Peter's voice sounds really good on it. We were just out of school and it was fun for us. To be given the chance of making an album was amazing. Jonathan selected the tracks but we had a whole stack more. I still have the tapes of all sorts of songs that never made it onto that album. Jonathan was very good for the band in the early days. If it hadn't been for him, we wouldn't have got going."

Certainly Peter sang in a distinctive fashion on such oddities as 'In Hiding' on which he sings, "I have a mind of my own . . . I will take off my clothes that I wear on my face."

When the album was packaged in a hymn book style black and gold cover, shops mistakenly displayed it in their religious record racks and it sold a paltry 650 copies. There were no radio plays and reviews, apart from a burst of praise from hippie bible *The International Times*, lacked enthusiasm. It seemed Genesis were going nowhere – with no revelations in sight. The band parted from Jonathan King, but kept the name he'd suggested. It was time to try their luck on their own.

*   *   *

When the boys left school after their exams Tony Banks went to Sussex University to study physics, philosophy and maths. He was torn between the choice of an academic or musical career. Genesis won. Peter Gabriel, after studying for his 'A' levels, was lined up to go to the London Film School, but he too chose to stick with the band. He recalled some years later: "My parents were disappointed that I didn't go to university and that I didn't go to film school either, which I rejected so I could work with Genesis. Their prime concern was not really that my lifestyle was rebellious, although we had traditional arguments about length of hair, but that I wouldn't be able to get a job later on and make a living. That worried all our parents at that time. John Mayhew, who was the drummer with the band after Charterhouse, left the group because of parental pressure and went off to university in the States."

While Tony and Peter agonised over their future, Ant Phillips and Mike Rutherford were determined that Genesis should survive and prosper and find their own direction, even though they were now cast adrift without Jonathan King's help and guidance. Although Mike had gone to Farnborough Technical College, he took the plunge and became a professional – and severely broke – musician.

The band set to their self-appointed task with renewed enthusiasm. It was as if they now had to prove themselves to a doubting world. They began writing more material and busily rehearsed a 'live' set at Richard MacPhail's cottage near Dorking. They still hadn't played any gigs and were wide-eyed innocents compared to most rock musicians of their age. MacPhail, formerly vocalist with The Anon, now became their road manager and loyal confidant. The cottage which proved so useful actually belonged to his parents. As they were planning to sell the property it lay disused and MacPhail's father gave the band permission to use it rent free. It was a wonderful offer but within the close confines of the cottage rows and arguments frequently developed. It was frustrating for Peter because he had a clear idea of what he wanted to hear in the music they were creating together, but couldn't always easily explain his more abstract concepts of time and space. Where the band were busy putting the notes together, he was thinking about leaving spaces and concentrating on the rhythms, a technique that would only flower properly long after he'd left them.

As Genesis flung themselves into the task of rejuvenating the band they recruited a new drummer to replace John Silver, and John Mayhew joined in July 1969, responding to an advertisement in *Melody Maker*. At last the band could start gigging and they played at various clubs and parties. Peter was always busy on the phone hassling gigs. When it was time to hit the road, the well-heeled boys treated each gig rather like a picnic, preferring to take a hamper of food with them, rather than stop off at a motorway service station for egg, chips and beans.

Their first paid engagement in September 1969 was at a private party. It was very cold, nobody paid much attention but the megastars-in-waiting were paid £25. Many months were spent writing and rehearsing, from November until April. By the spring of 1970 the fledgling band had created some of its most remarkable works including 'The Knife' that would be featured on their next album *Trespass*. Their set would consist of pure Genesis music, with no 'cover' versions of other songs allowed, and there would be no compromises. It certainly required an act of faith on behalf of promoters and party givers to book them.

To drum up custom, they played at a special audition for social secretaries and promoters at a London university, where they played a 19-minute version of 'The Knife'. This led to bookings at Eel Pie Island and Twickenham Technical College. Their first major London show was at Queen Mary College in February 1970. They also made trips to Birmingham and Manchester, travelling in a battered old van. Barely earning fifty pounds a performance, they were so broke they could just afford money for food and guitar strings, and sometimes they had to go without either. None of them had accommodation of their own and they were forced to squat in various parents' houses, while the occupants were away.

Eventually Banks and Gabriel shared a friend's flat in London's Earls Court, which gave them a working base not to mention a social life, as the erstwhile schoolboys and students grew up and became men o' the world. One of Peter's regular girlfriends was Jill Moore, whom he had met at a party way back at Christmas 1965. She was 14 and he was 16. He was the first boy to arrive at the party and thought she was: "The prettiest girl in the room – so it was quite simple." Eventually their lives would become entwined in a relationship and a marriage that would bless them with children but ultimately foundered on the rocks of dissent and misunderstanding – or perhaps as a woman might argue – too much understanding.

For the band all the stress, strain and poverty endured during these early years seemed worthwhile, especially when they received an encouraging response from an audience at Queen Mary College. The students sat and listened attentively to the strange new music instead of quaffing pints of beer and indulging in coarse badinage, as is their wont. The band's mysterious 'sound' was clearly defined by 'The Knife', an imaginative, extended work that became one of their most popular pieces. On this dramatic opus Genesis showed how they understood the value of dynamics in a performance. Unlike most rock bands who played at maximum volume from beginning to end, Genesis learned to hypnotise rather than deafen an audience by building up tension from quiet beginnings. When they finally unleashed roaring chords and yelling vocals, the quasi-symphonic Genesis experience proved both exhilarating and bewitching.

Although they were assiduously playing gigs and rehearsing at the cottage, Peter knew they had to get back into the record industry, which was vital if they were to survive and prosper. Peter tried his hand at hustling for attention, going round to various record companies and agents and often receiving a frosty reception. "I would go in and get palmed off by the telephonist or receptionist. You could spend the whole day there and not see anyone. The others in the band didn't seem to take it that seriously. But if we didn't get a deal, I knew nothing would happen. The band used to think they could just go on making music in the cottage."

Peter would walk into Warner Bros. and demand to see the managing director to hand over the band's latest demo tape. Even if he received a refusal or rejection, he was philosophical: "At least it came from the top."

Sometimes this cold attitude from the music biz was hard to take. Banks and Gabriel went together to see an agent in the hope of getting work and assistance. He told them in no uncertain terms they should give up and go back to their non-existent day jobs. It was a demoralising experience that made them feel as if there was a black shadow of doom hovering over them. But the pair put on a brave face and went straight back to rehearsals. "We played the music that we were convinced could inspire the world," says Peter. There was no chance they would ever go back to their 'day jobs'.

Yet despite this prevailing lack of vision amongst the entrenched old guard of the music business, the Sixties remained a time of liberation. Young people everywhere were experiencing a new kind of freedom, even wilder than the rock'n'roll years of the Fifties. There was no *need* to work in the conventional sense. You could be a self-sufficient hippie, bent on tasting the forbidden fruits of life. With increased leisure time for all, drugs were becoming an important form of recreation. Smoking dope was fun, and there was new alternatives to grass and pills. As a result many came to believe that the gothic sounding music Genesis was creating was entirely the result of experiments with the mind altering LSD. After all – everybody else in the music business seemed to be indulging. Yet Gabriel and his friends were far too sensible – or just too nervous – to get involved in druggie activities. With their overstimulated imaginations, they had no need for hallucinogens.

Peter told *Rolling Stone* many years later: "The only drug I was interested in was acid, but I was too frightened by my dreams in regular hours to contemplate that. I had very vivid dreams and I was fearful of letting go of control."

He did have some teenage experience with hash which made him giggle then become violently sick. As a result he kept away from drugs for years – until one day in the early Eighties when he found an abandoned hash cake in an empty recording studio. As an experiment he tried eating the cake. Typically he planned to tape record his experiences. Nothing much happened, so he ate more of the cake. Suddenly he felt a weird and painful pressure in his head that made him fall over the recording desk and succumb to a panic attack. He became convinced he would die, as people often do when they find themselves lying on the bathroom floor after a night in the pub. He decided to stagger home – if only to say a fond farewell to his wife and children.

It was half a mile across fields to get to his house and he was still carrying a tape recorder when he fell into a dark void.

Peter had begun to experience revelations about the meaning of life. He became convinced that life was organised into five videotapes which were all running out of sync. Later, when he was fully recovered he played back the tape. "Soon after I came upon this profound piece of wisdom, you hear me collapse into a ditch. So there's this funny tape of me thinking that I am going to die."

Safely tucked up in bed he was given some milk with sugar to calm down. He looked so stressed his wife Jill thought he had been in a road accident. But says Peter: "The strange thing was, my kids didn't think there was anything different about me."

Meanwhile, back in the Sixties Genesis would create their own kind of mind altering experiences – without recourse to artificial stimulants – which may explain why they all survived to tell the tale. As for Peter – he was only just beginning to unlock the power of his mind.

II

LOOKING FOR SOMEONE

PETER GABRIEL SOMETIMES gives the impression of being an impractical dreamer. Yet a determination to be independent, get his own way and succeed in the teeth of adversity has always been a crucial part of his make up.

After the initial brush with Jonathan King, Gabriel knew that if they were to survive and prosper Genesis had to find a sympathetic new mentor. He commended himself to the task with a typical mixture of intuition and blind faith. He met with constant rebuffs from disbelieving cynics, but never gave up hope. He was convinced that if the band played regularly in London, at the heart of the music business, the right people would eventually hear them. Soon Peter and the band's faith would be rewarded.

The lads had roamed the country playing support slots to up and coming bands like Barclay James Harvest, Rare Bird and even T. Rex. Then one night in March, 1970 Genesis played at Ronnie Scott's Club, London. The jazz mecca in Soho's Frith Street was normally the haunt of such stars as the Buddy Rich Orchestra, Oscar Peterson or George Melly and his Feet Warmers. But the Scott Club had its eye on rock music as an alternative attraction and a spare upstairs room became a convenient venue to try out new bands and hopefully draw a discerning audience. It was no throwaway gesture either. The long T-shaped room was fitted out with a bar, comfortable sofas, and decorated by rising young artist Roger Dean, who went on to design the distinctive album covers for many rock bands including Genesis' closest rivals Yes.

Dean was trained to design buildings and furniture while studying at Canterbury College of Art and The Royal College of Art in the late Sixties. He was still a 24-year-old student when he was given the Scott project. Says Roger: "In 1968, I was asked to design the discotheque upstairs at Ronnie's. It was where Genesis played in their early days. The idea was to create a landscape in foam. There were murals on the wall and the seats were filled with polystyrene. The fire brigade who inspected the club were very concerned about the amount of foam we had used. Then inevitably there was a fire at the club. The foam furniture wasn't touched, but the murals were burnt off the walls!"

Despite the space age ambience, for some reason it was always difficult to attract people 'Upstairs'. Maybe after a few drinks, the gravitational pull of another secluded bar further downstairs was more powerful. At any rate Peter Frampton, lead guitarist and singer from The Herd, was among those few revellers who chanced upon a decidedly new group playing to themselves in the Upstairs 'disco' one night. Certainly there were more people in the band than there were in the audience. As Ronnie Scott might have said, "The chuckers out were chucking them in". Frampton and a friend (the author) intended to have one drink and then depart to a more happening night-spot. But his musician's ear was caught by the intensity of the band's performance. He stayed, listened and was transfixed.

Frampton would long after recount the tale that he was among the first in London to hear Peter Gabriel in action. He witnessed the strange young singer leaning over a single bass drum, glaring menacingly out into the dim recesses of the empty room. The band played with passion to a tiny audience and yet seemed to be locked into a world of their own. For them it didn't matter if there was anybody there or not. Or perhaps they just couldn't see beyond the foam-filled sofas.

It wasn't all doom, despair and low attendance during those early weeks of 1970. The band were invited to record a show for BBC Radio 1 and they performed six songs for *Night Ride* which was broadcast on April 1, 1970. The numbers aired were 'The Shepherd', 'Let Us Now (Make Love)', 'Pacidy', and 'Stagnation', 'Looking For Someone' and 'Dusk" from the album that would be called *Trespass*. The band's line-up for this breakthrough broadcast was Gabriel, Banks, Rutherford, Phillips and Mayhew. The presenter's report to the BBC's panel of experts was: "I rate this group very highly" and the panel themselves commented on the band's "intriguing tone colours". Coming from the highly esteemed world of wireless telegraphy at Broadcasting House, this was praise indeed.

As the word spread, thanks to the broadcast and yet more gigs, several other music biz folk visited Genesis at the Tuesday night residency. Among them was Tony Stratton-Smith, head of the newly formed independent Charisma label. He had been urgently advised to see the band by his label's A&R director, John Anthony.

Tony, a portly, avuncular, former sports journalist turned pop group manager, was instantly impressed by the band and would soon find himself inextricably involved in their affairs. 'Strat', as he was known, was a much loved and influential member of pop's business fraternity. He brought a touch of humanity and a streak of intelligence to a profession not always noted for either quality. He'd also led a fascinating life and his personality was rounded by a range of diverse experiences. Peter Gabriel in particular found him both sympathetic and encouraging.

Born in Birmingham in 1933, Stratton-Smith was a local newspaper cricket correspondent before joining the RAF. After his wartime service, he went to Fleet Street and was a sports' editor on the *Daily Sketch* and later the *Daily Express*. He just missed travelling on the plane which crashed in Munich in 1958, carrying the Manchester United team. His life was spared when at the last minute he decided to cover another match the same day. Apart from his involvement in sports journalism, he was a novelist and he wrote a book called *The Rebel Nun*, a biography of the martyr Mother Maria Skobtzova. The early rock'n'roll years seemed to pass him by, but he was introduced to the world of music after a chance meeting with the composer Antonio Carlos Jobim on a trip to South America. On his return to London Stratton-Smith decided to investigate the music publishing business and became friendly with Beatles' manager Brian Epstein. Eppy's business success encouraged Strat to try his hand at pop group management. His first act was Paddy, Klaus & Gibson, who later switched allegiance to Epstein's NEMS organisation. Next came his favourite band The Koobas, and he also managed an outfit called Creation, who had a 1966 hit single called 'Painter Man'.

Among this band's more outstanding attributes was the pre-Led Zeppelin use of a violin bow on the guitar strings and the creation of 'action paintings' during a performance. Although Creation seemed to be doing well at venues like London's Flamingo Club, Strat was disappointed by the failure of The Koobas and vowed henceforth to give up management. His resolve cracked when he was impressed by the pleas of progressive group The Nice. During a chance meeting at the Speakeasy club, their keyboard player Keith Emerson convinced Strat to take over the reins and try his hand at management once more. As his own business affairs recovered from a financial crisis and other problems, Strat not only began running bands again, but set up his own independent label, Charisma Records in 1968. It was a bold step. Only Andrew Oldham's Immediate and Chris Blackwell's Island Records had managed to gain a foothold in the face of the 'majors'. The new 'indie' eventually featured a range of highly individual acts, including Rare Bird, Van Der Graaf Generator, Audience, Clifford T. Ward, Lindisfarne and even Monty Python's Flying Circus who made comedy albums for the label.

Charisma was launched with a bang. The first single release by the new label was Rare Bird's 'Sympathy' which was an international hit. However, it was the strange band playing to empty houses at Ronnie Scott's Club who would become the biggest and most important act on the brave new label. Strat understood and appreciated Genesis and especially liked their charismatic young singer. In turn the group found him kindly and helpful, even when they were at their most stressed out and angry. Above all, Strat's gambler's instinct led him to take chances on their behalf. When Phil Collins eventually joined the band, Phil was amused by the sight of his worthy manager, clad in string vest, breakfast cigarette in his mouth, wandering down Wardour Street in search of the nearest betting office, intent on putting a pound each way on some dubious horse. Strat later invested in a string of race horses and became a leading figure in the turf.

Genesis could have been a non runner, but Stratton-Smith believed in them and was determined to make them go the distance. Greatly impressed by their performance at Ronnie's he immediately offered to sign them to Charisma. At the same time he agreed to become their manager. In the process Peter Gabriel had found his mentor. Even though there was an ultimate parting of the ways, Peter never forgot the help and encouragement that Strat gave him during the early years. The immediate result of his arrival on the scene was that the band could begin work on its second album *Trespass* which was duly released in October, 1970 to great critical acclaim. But it didn't happen overnight. There was much hard work and financial input from Charisma. One of Stratton-Smith's assistants, Gail Colson, emphasises that the backing of 'The Boss' was crucial to the success of the band: "I don't think they could have carried on if it hadn't been for Strat. He subsidised them to a ludicrous degree."

Gail Colson would in time become the cornerstone of the Charisma organisation, driving the business into top gear as it developed from label into agency and management company. Early on in her career she had been secretary to Kinks' producer Shel Talmy. After meeting Strat she became his trusted assistant and eventually managing director of Charisma. When Peter left Genesis to become a solo artist, Gail became his personal manager. Having handled such diverse talents as Viv Stanshall and the Bonzo Dog Doo Dah Band, Gail certainly knew how to cope with rock's wilder personalities and did the job with flair, determination and a touch of acerbic wit.

The entire Charisma staff turned up to see Genesis play another gig Upstairs at Ronnie's. Recalls one of the staff men: "Peter Gabriel was playing just a bass drum and flute. The group had previously supported Rare Bird and Dave Fields their keyboard player had recommended Genesis to John Anthony, who was Strat's in-house record producer. He was also a DJ at the Speakeasy at the time. He suggested we all go to see them. Strat just signed them immediately, but there was strong competition from Island and the Moody Blues' label Threshold and also from Polydor. There were four labels after them altogether, but Strat offered them £20 a week each and they jumped at the chance! Obviously they liked him as well because he was a cultured man and in those days, although there were more cultured people about in the record world then, he was head and shoulders above most of the yobs who worked in the industry."

It was plain that the group had to reach a wider public and couldn't go on playing to a dedicated few in a Frith Street disco. Another important figure in their success story stepped forward. As the band began work on the first album for Charisma, they also began playing regularly at the Friars Club, Aylesbury, where the promoter David Stopps encouraged this fresh, inventive band with its quirky lead singer. The newcomers quickly gained a dedicated cult following among students, hippies and anyone who could see their potential. The venue itself became a home from home for the band, offering a virtual guarantee of enthusiastic support which buoyed them up, even during their most despairing moments.

The club was first mooted at a time when the British rock scene was booming. In the wake of The Beatles and Rolling Stones had come a flood of R&B and blues bands who were supported by a thriving gig scene. Fans flocked to hear live groups but by the late Sixties audiences had become sated with the basic 12-bar blues format and were ready for more adventurous music. They proved receptive to the advent of the psychedelic underground spearheaded by innovative outfits like Pink Floyd, Tomorrow and Traffic. Everyone thought their music was far out, until they heard Peter Gabriel and the chaps from Charterhouse.

It was in this heady atmosphere that in April 1969 David Stopps, a local musician, was approached by his friend Robin Pike with a suggestion. "Why don't we start a rock club in Aylesbury." David's first reaction was, "Aylesbury? No, it will never work. High Wycombe maybe."

The pair of music fans lived in Princes Risborough, a town to the north west of London halfway between Aylesbury and High Wycombe in the county of Buckinghamshire. Eventually Pike, Stopps and a group of other friends got together to put on their first promotion, at the New Friarage Hall in Aylesbury. It was the first of many such events that would last well into the Eighties.

For their début they booked a sub-psychedelic band called Mandrake Paddle Steamer, support by folk singer Mike Cooper. They drew 200 people but lost £35. "That was a huge sum in those days," recalls Stopps. "The next week we presented the Pretty Things, the third week Free and things started to pick up."

Friars Aylesbury became a familiar name on the rock circuit, even to people who had never been there, by their bold display advertisements in the *Melody Maker*. These bold black bordered ads announced such attractions as Black Sabbath, Edgar Broughton, Mott The Hoople, Blodwyn Pig, King Crimson, Van Der Graaf Generator and Hawkwind. The fledgling promoters even put on the mighty Pink Floyd at a special gig in Dunstable. Says David: "Pink Floyd made us so much money that it subsidised the 57 weekly Monday gigs in Aylesbury from June 1969 to July 1970 when the first incarnation of Friars was closed down."

David first became aware of the band that would become most closely associated with the venue when he read an *MM* review of their first album *From Genesis To Revelation*. He also began to notice their name cropping up in gig advertisements. Then one day in March 1970 Stopps' mother took a phone call from Richard MacPhail, who was trying to get his boys a booking at the club. "I was out sticking up posters or something and she ended up having a long conversation with Richard about vegetables, cheese-making and honey. When I returned she said: 'This very nice man called Richard phoned from a band called Genesis. I think you should put them on.' "

Although David wasn't entirely convinced about his mother's talent spotting ability he was sufficiently intrigued to call Richard back and set up a date for Genesis. As a result Genesis played their first gig there on Monday April 13, 1970 "for the princely sum of £10".

When the band arrived at the gig David found them a friendly bunch of well mannered hippies. "At the time everyone had very long hair and wore headbands, beads and velvet trousers that were skin-tight at the top and flared at the bottoms." The band began to set up for their first Friars sound check – the triumvirate of Peter, Mike, and Tony with Anthony Phillips on guitar and John Mayhew on drums. As the evening performance began the audience were intrigued by the lead singer who stood menacingly behind the famous single bass drum – all that now remained of his own kit. Peter often explained that the rest of the band had gradually taken it away from him piecemeal – to allow their regular drummer to keep time! Peter would kick the drum at crucial moments as he delivered the intriguing lyrics with a chilling intensity, and told bizarre stories between numbers that delighted and enthralled the crowd. It was extraordinary. Here was a band without a hit, sans press coverage and yet they had won a fanatical underground following that grew larger by the day. It was understandable. Nobody had seen a band like them and Genesis provided a complete listening experience. Undoubtedly they were playing highly sophisticated music, yet they were accorded encores at their very first Friars' appearance.

Recalls David Stopps: "Immediately they started playing you could tell this band was different. The music was very melodic and infectious but the main difference was Peter. He had this bass drum right on the front edge of the stage and would take great delight in belting hell out of it!"

In the days before drum kits were miked up and put through the PA system, Peter's use of the bass drum added to the power generated by Mayhew's kit. But it wasn't just the extra kick that made such an impact. "There were the stories that Peter told the audience between numbers. They were brilliant, dryly witty and very obscure. They were just as entertaining as the songs in some cases."

The stories had really begun as a way of filling in those embarrassing moments when the guitarists were re-tuning their guitars between numbers. Anthony couldn't do any announcing as he was consumed with stage fright. Slowly the witty little spoken fill-ins by Peter became suspense filled sagas, delivered in a dry, almost laconic monotone that enthralled the audience and became an integral part of the show.

Despite Peter's rapport with audiences the rest of the musicians seemed stressed and uncomfortable on stage. The band were still coming to terms with 'live' performance. When they first started they had no idea how amplification worked, or how to set up a PA on stage. If they went out of tune or missed a cue, it was a cause of acute embarrassment leading to tension between Gabriel and the others. There was also the need for each individual to express himself within the band, without making too many compromises. Inevitably there were arguments behind the scenes but the crowd's reaction at Friars gave them the encouragement they needed. They also had a manager to take off some of the pressure.

David: "The band went down a storm that first night at Friars and they played three encores. I remember paying Peter the gig fee of £10 and Peter asked me and our DJ Andy Dunkley if we thought they had done the right thing – coming on again for the third encore."

The DJ opined that they should have stuck to two encores and sent the crowd home wanting more. David supported the band and said they were absolutely correct in playing a third encore. "I remember the discussion getting quite heated with Peter looking on somewhat confused." Stopps would always encourage his bands to play as many encores as possible. "As a result we got longer sets out of bands than anyone else!"

Encores aside, a £10 fee wasn't going to keep the band alive. Often encumbered with the description 'art rock band', Genesis were in truth just as much impoverished rebels as any latter-day punk outfit. Their public school background was no help in this situation. It was talent alone and not image that helped them gain the public's ear. As they became associated with long, complex, sophisticated pieces of music like 'Supper's Ready', they confused critics, especially in America, who could not abide anything longer than a three minute riff. Ironically the band themselves never forgot their pop roots. After all, it was the short, sharp shock of hit singles that ultimately won international success for Genesis, their 'new boy' Phil Collins and Peter Gabriel.

Despite all these apparent contradictions, some crucial factors remained constant. What most endeared Peter and the band to audiences at Friars was the indefinable magic to be found in the themes, characters and concepts that permeated their songs. Something deep and mysterious lay at the core of the vision inspired by their batwinged messenger. Peter, in the eyes of his fans, was the embodiment of the Genesis spirit and there was tremendous excitement generated by the music and ideas unleashed on these first gigs and later enshrined in the classic albums *Trespass, Nursery Cryme* and *Foxtrot*.

Genesis concerts at Friars and elsewhere became eagerly awaited events, lodged in the minds of audiences for years afterward. David Stopps today heads a successful management company, based in New York – and Aylesbury – but has many fond memories of his Genesis days.

The band's second appearance at Friars was on June 15, 1970 and this time they were paid £30. There was a much bigger crowd and the band went down a storm as news of their impact began to spread. The first phase of the club ended in July 1970 when it was closed down by the venue's owners, who objected to the promoters and their bands "making a racket!" It would not re-open until April 1971 at the Borough Assembly Hall in the town centre.

Life was never plain sailing for Genesis. When the group finished their first album *Trespass*, two members immediately left – guitarist Anthony Phillips and drummer John Mayhew. A Charisma record plugger groaned: "Strat had invested all this money into a completely unknown band and then they slapped him in the face."

Although it must have seemed a shock move to the record company, there were understandable reasons for the departures and in the end the result was a much improved band. "Two of them left before the band had even gone out on the road to promote the album. And to put out an album like *Trespass* in those days with five long tracks and no obvious single was a risk. We did put out 'The Knife (Part One & Two)' later as a single and if you can find a copy it's worth £500."

The record was released in January 1971 with a picture sleeve that showed two new replacement band members, but not Ant Phillips or John Mayhew, who actually played on the record.

One of Strat's pluggers was directed to take the singles to Broadcasting House, London, in search of amenable DJs. He took it to the BBC but nobody would play it, so he had to throw them all away in a dustbin. If he still had them now he says, "They'd be worth a hundred grand. And I threw them all away!" In the end he got one play, but only because the producer was an old mate of Strat's.

Trespass was recorded at Trident Studios, London, during June and July 1970 while the band were off the road. In the middle of a session Peter had the onerous task of telling producer John Anthony about the departure of one of their number. John was just relieved it was Ant Phillips and not Tony Banks, Mike Rutherford or Peter. "Thank God!" was the cry.

Finding a new guitarist would not be so difficult, and as for their decision to have a clean sweep and replace the drummer, it was generally agreed that John had trouble keeping up with the band. He had replaced the departed John Silver during the writing sessions for *Trespass* at the MacPhail's cottage. When it was deemed Mayhew too had to go, Peter put an advertisement in *Melody Maker*, in August 1970 asking for a drummer who would be 'sensitive to acoustic music'. Among the applicants whose numbers they scribbled on a pad was Phillip Collins, a chirpy West Londoner and former child actor. He had played the part of The Artful Dodger in the West End production of *Oliver* but more importantly he was a very good drummer.

Phil was born on January 30, 1951 in Hounslow and he came from a showbiz family. As a child he had played enthusiastically on a tin drum from the age of three and was given a home-made kit when he was five. He became involved in acting and modelling and went to the Barbara Speak Stage School, when his grammar school wouldn't give him time off to perform in *Oliver*. He had a part in a Children's Foundation Film called *Calamity The Cow* but when he got uptight with the producer over his role, he was written out of the script. (The film was actually brought out of the archives and shown at cinemas in the early Eighties, when Phil had become an 'overnight' superstar!) The movie wasn't a very happy experience and as he preferred listening to rock music to acting, he turned to the idea of being a full time musician.

He teamed up with a guitarist friend Ronnie Caryl and played in a band called Hickory which evolved into Sixties' group Flaming Youth. They recorded an album called *Ark 11* which wasn't a million miles from *Genesis To Revelation* in concept. But it too was a flop and the group broke up. Phil found himself going to gigs and watching his favourite bands including Yes at the Marquee. When he heard Yes were looking to replace their drummer Bill Bruford, he considered applying for the gig but he bumped into Tony Stratton-Smith at the club. Strat told him about the vacancy with Genesis and urged him to make an application. Then Peter phoned Phil and asked him down to play. Although Phil had lost his chance to play with Yes, by a quirk of fate, some years later he would play alongside Bill Bruford when both drummers worked together in Genesis.

Phil's arrival would have enormous impact on the band. He not only provided a dynamic new force on the drums, but his humour and good-natured banter helped ease the uptight tension inherent within the group. They were less likely to take themselves so seriously with Phil around. Collins would of course remain 'around' as Genesis' drummer and ultimately their lead singer when Peter left, a post he held until his final departure in 1996. Bereft of hang-ups, Phil was able to communicate readily and bring a combination of sound sense and alert response to the band's needs. His drumming was supremely confident and technically adept and his developing style was perfectly suited to the complexities of the music. He could also sing and became heavily involved in writing and arranging.

Phil remembers the day Peter Gabriel called him to audition. He was invited down to Peter's parents house in Chobham which proved to be a mansion complete with swimming pool. Phil was highly impressed and, as an impoverished musician, somewhat intimidated. But he set up his drums on the patio where Peter, Tony and Mike had some equipment including a grand piano. Phil listened to the band's latest album *Trespass* then went for a dip in the pool while he listened to another drummer they were trying out. He heard him play a long warm-up drum solo and then muff his way through the tunes. When it came to Collins' turn he just breezed through such pieces as 'Twilight Alehouse', 'The Knife' and a new one called 'The Musical Box' without any problems. The band auditioned fifteen drummers but both Peter and Tony felt that Phil was their man, musically and personality-wise. Peter phoned Phil and told him he'd got the job and Collins was so excited he gave his mother a hug, feeling both relief and delight.

After a short holiday the band began rehearsing at The Maltings, a disused oast house that belonged to Mike Rutherford's father. As Phil studied the material on *Trespass* he became aware of the tension within the band caused mainly by the departure of Ant Phillips. Sometimes it seemed as if they might break up, as they couldn't find the right replacement. They tried to carry on as a four piece band with Banks playing all the lead lines, using a fuzz box to emulate the guitar lines. Despite the rows that developed between Peter and Tony during this difficult time, gradually new material took shape including 'The Musical Box' which would be featured on their next album *Nursery Cryme*. They had taken on a dep guitarist but still weren't happy.

Then at Christmas 1970 it seemed like the future of Genesis was secured, when Peter spotted another advertisement, in *Melody Maker*. This time it was from a guitarist and songwriter who claimed he was seeking other musicians who were 'determined to strive beyond existing stagnant music forms'. Peter called the number and found guitarist Steve Hackett. The band were due to play at London's Lyceum Ballroom on December 28 and Steve went along to watch them play with their dep guitarist. He was very impressed but felt he could do better than Mick Barnard, the guitar player who had been recommended to Genesis by David Stopps as a replacement for Ant. When Peter had approached David Stopps, asking if he knew any guitarists, Stopps had suggested Barnard, a friend he had managed in a band called Farm (formerly Smokey Rice). Mick played guitar with Genesis during the Autumn of 1970 before Hackett finally took over.

Born on February 12, 1950, Steve Hackett had black hair, a beard, moustache and glasses and appeared very studious. When Peter first met him, he thought he looked like Jonathan King. They had tried out faster, more flashy guitarists, but it turned out that Steve had just the right combination of sounds and styles for Genesis. He would play strange angular solos over their riffs, interject unexpectedly loud squeaks and squeals and yet perform in acoustic mode with perfect taste and discretion. Although the first few gigs with their new guitarist proved nerve-wracking, as the usual equipment failures and feedback sapped nerves and tried their patience, it seemed that once again Peter and Tony had found the perfect team player to join their motley crew. They were no longer 'looking for someone' and with the classic line-up of Gabriel, Rutherford, Banks, Hackett and Collins in place, Genesis could go onwards and upwards.

They continued to receive enormous support from promoter David Stopps who had been putting on shows even while his regular club was closed. One of the best remembered was a gig at the British Legion Hall, Princes Risborough, on October 6, 1970. This was their first with Phil. As usual the equipment broke down and there was a delay of 30 minutes. As the audience sat growing increasingly restless, the trusty Richard MacPhail was frantic with worry. Armed with a screwdriver, fuse wire and torch, he tried to find the offending loose connections.

Says David: "During these 'screwdriver periods' Peter would put a lot of echo on the vocal mike and do this improvised chant which actually sounded quite good. When years later I first heard Peter's song 'Biko' I knew that those screwdriver periods had finally paid off."

Just to add to the band's tensions and nerves, the police were busy outside, booking Mike Rutherford, not for a police charity gig, but for not displaying a current tax disc on the group's van. There were a few more Stopps' promoted appearances at this time, including their fourth gig for him, at his other club in Bedford on October 23, 1970, followed by shows at Aylesbury College and Grammar School.

In October *Trespass* arrived and it represented a huge advance on the hesitant performances on their first album. Even before the arrival of Collins and Hackett Genesis sounded much more confident and sure-footed. The opening song 'Looking For Someone' seemed like a clarion call, re-establishing the band and shaking off all memories of the past. Peter's voice, once so angelic, has a surprisingly rough edge as he sang "Looking for someone . . . I guess I'm doing that. Trying to find a memory in a dark room, dirty man, you looking like a Buddha, I know you well . . . yeah!" There is a touch of Rod Stewart about the throaty, stabbing phrasing that Gabriel uses here, and when he sings of being "lost in a subway", there is even a hint of one of his future works, the controversial *Lamb Lies Down On Broadway*. Lost souls and probings into the dark, inner secrets of mankind, are twin themes that would recur in many of Gabriel's later works.

On 'White Mountain' he sang of foxes and wolves with that subtle use of dramatic narrative which conjures the special mood of a children's radio play, like John Masefield's *The Box Of Delights – Or When The Wolves Were Running*. Recalls Tony Banks: "*Trespass* was totally different from *Revelation*. By this time we had played live quite a bit and every song on the album had been performed on stage. We had a selection of at least twice as many songs as appeared on the album, and the versions changed rapidly."

Apart from subtle and imaginative items like 'Visions Of Angels', 'Stagnation', where Peter proclaims: "I want a drink to wash out the filth" and 'Dusk' the major work on the album was of course 'The Knife'. Peter has described it in simplistic terms: "It was an aggressive number about a revolutionary figure on a power trip." Yet this exciting and dramatic arrangement became a showpiece number on their live shows, when it could last for twenty minutes. When it was released as a two part single in January 1971, it proved nigh on impossible to promote as Charisma's hapless plugger soon discovered. But this was no mere chart fodder. 'The Knife' was an opportunity for the band to show its full potential and for Peter to extract the maximum in dramatic vocal effect. "Now!" he would snarl and chant. "Stand up and fight, for you know we are right!" Just before a wild and frantic climax, there came a quiet passage where Gabriel's flute playing established a sense of order and beauty, before the chaos of war reigned once more. The musicianship and command of dynamics displayed on this ground-breaking number alone firmly established Genesis as a band possessed of remarkable skills and Gabriel as a uniquely gifted performer.

Says Tony Banks: " 'The Knife' started a whole new era of music. We were trying to do something different that nobody else was doing at the time, which was extended pieces. It set us off on a new road. After all, we had decided to go professional between the first two albums. The original drummer John Silver didn't want to do that, so we found John Mayhew, but I can't say we were very pleased with the final results. We were always hypercritical."

Peter has described the origins of 'The Knife' as being partly inspired by the example of The Nice, whom they saw at the Marquee Club. "They were musical and very powerful," says Peter. "I remember sitting down at the piano trying to write something that had the excitement of 'Rondo' by The Nice. I played the first riff to Tony and he was obviously into it because The Nice were a band that we both liked. After that Tony did the second section and then we played 'The Knife'

41

together." The new piece fitted perfectly into the concept of the band. "We would start with soft numbers and work up to aggressive ones. If we kept the power in the back, we could introduce ourselves slowly like a folk band and then gradually we could bring in more and more electric instruments and then we would finish off with this very aggressive number. I knew we had the power to grab an audience. The lyrics for 'The Knife' were partly about me being a public schoolboy rebelling against my background. I'd been heavily influenced by a book on Gandhi at school, and I think that was part of the reason I became a vegetarian as well as coming to believe in non-violence as a form of protest. And I wanted to try and show how violent revolutions inevitably end up with a dictator figure in power."

The public and many critics were stunned by the impact of 'Trespass' and 'The Knife' which became a topic for endless debate and discussion among fans. The group themselves were more concerned with day-to-day problems, like equipment, tuning and standards of play. They wanted everything to improve. They could hear the music in their heads and the way they wanted it to sound. Peter, Tony and Mike later admitted they weren't too pleased with the drumming, despite Mayhew's heroic efforts on 'The Knife'. They also disliked the production because the sound was a trifle murky. However the album cover seemed to please everyone. It was one of the best designs of the early Seventies, which helped establish the concept and flavour of the band. The relatively Spartan but atmospheric artwork by Paul Whitehead showed two Aubrey Beardsley-esque romantic figures peering through a castle window. This peaceful scene was rent in twain. Opening out the gatefold sleeve revealed a bejewelled, serrated knife slicing through the picture.

Trespass eventually sold around 6,000 copies worldwide and although it wasn't earth shattering the band were encouraged. Says Tony Banks, who along with Mike Rutherford remains keeper of the Genesis flame to the present day: "We got quite a response 'live' and we were building up a following all around the country. There were a lot of good things on that album and it started us in the direction we have carried on with ever since."

In January, 1971 Tony Stratton-Smith sent Genesis off on the road on a package tour with two other bands, Van Der Graaf Generator and Lindisfarne. It was a cheap price ticket tour of nine UK cities which helped bring Genesis to the attention of a wider public. It certainly won them more friends in the press and they regularly stole the show. When the tour opened at London's Lyceum on January 24, Michael Watts in *Melody Maker* wrote a glowing review of Genesis adding: "Peter Gabriel, frantic in his tambourine shaking, his voice hoarse and urgent, is a focus for all the band's energy."

In the battle to gain acceptance Peter Gabriel, who lived out the characters and moods of his songs with a passion few singers could emulate, took increasing risks during a performance. His communication with audiences became legendary and dangerous. The fifth time Genesis played at Aylesbury was on June 19, 1971. It was something of a homecoming for band, fans and promoter. By now the club had a capacity of 700 and was running Saturday nights instead of Mondays.

David: "Audiences were suddenly much bigger and yet the old Friars Aylesbury chemistry was still very much alive with multiple encores demanded. This was undoubtedly one of Genesis' best ever performances and the audience was euphoric. On 'The Knife' Peter got so carried away that he went to the back of the stage and started running straight forward. When he neared the edge of the stage he was bound to stop . . . but he didn't! I think a feeling of wanting to be one with the audience overcame him and he leapt off the five foot high stage and straight out into the audience at great speed."

Peter Gabriel was at this moment in effect inventing stage diving, a phenomenon that would not become a regular occurrence until the thrash rock boom of the late Eighties. Meanwhile Peter descended into the midst of the audience. Most of them scrambled aside at the sight of this unguided missile heading their way. Remembers Stopps: "They all parted except for a couple who were still dancing and presumably thought they were hallucinating and that this couldn't possibly be happening. Peter came crashing down, right on top of them."

Stopps and MacPhail helped their errant singer to his feet but unsurprisingly only one of his feet was still working. Peter was carried back to the stage with agony etched on his face.

Somehow he managed to finish the song, literally down on his knees. At the end of the number the rest of the band left the stage, not realising that their resident wild man of pop was badly hurt. Peter was still on his knees, unable to move. His fellow bandsmen returned and carried the singer back to the dressing room. An ambulance was called and Stopps announced to the wondering audience: "The artiste has left the building . . . and gone to the Royal Bucks Hospital."

It transpired that Gabriel had severe fractures and had to have metal pins inserted into his leg, which was bound up in a plaster cast. He had to walk with a crutch for several weeks. Although a foolish act of bravado, the flying leap impressed Stopps: "This experience, although extremely painful, clearly inspired Peter to get into physical contact with audiences. In later years he would stand with his back to the audience on the front of the stage and fall backwards, where he would be carried around the crowd on a sea of hands. This was obviously a safer approach to the one he tried in Aylesbury in June, 1971."

The day after Peter was taken to hospital, Stopps phoned the band's agent to inquire if he would be well enough to perform at the next Friars gig, booked for their Bedford club on July 2. "Yes, they'll do it," was the blunt response from Paul Conroy, then working at Terry King Associates. Many years later Conroy would become head of Virgin Records, the label that took over Charisma and sported such mega acts as Peter Gabriel, Phil Collins and Genesis.

Peter's flying leap inadvertently led to the use of a new stage prop, although one with a practical purpose. Says Stopps: "For some bizarre reason Peter left his crutch behind when he arrived at the Kempston venue in Bedford. The venue was right in the middle of a park and the only thing we could find to double as a crutch was a broom. I remember the rest of the band disappeared and went off to the pub in the early part of the evening, leaving Peter looking rather forlorn on his own with his plaster leg and his broom. We had a stall selling posters and magazines and I suggested he might like to sit behind the stall and help. It was a great success with lots of plaster leg signing. The broom supported performance was also brilliant – under the circumstances."

After another short holiday the band began rehearsing again

at The Maltings. New material took shape including 'The Musical Box'. With Hackett and Collins in place, Genesis were ready to prog rock! Peter was content, perhaps for the first time since the band had been formed.

"There was a definite change when Phil came into the band. The way Phil sat at the kit – I knew he was good before he'd played a note. He was a real drummer – something I was never that convinced of with Chris Stewart or John Mayhew. Up until then, we were a group of fairly ramshackle musicians, trying hard to communicate through our music. Phil was not really a writer at that point but he changed our attitude and brought us closer together."

III

NURSERY CRYMES
AND FOXTROTS

LIFE IN A male dominated rock band can seem like being in the army to a sensitive young musician. There may be companionship and shared aims, but there is also tension, stress and perhaps even a degree of bullying. What the artist needs most is a sympathetic and understanding partner. Love now blossomed in Peter Gabriel's life to the point where marriage beckoned. He had been going out with his steady girlfriend Jill Moore for some years, but even though much of his time was taken up with the band, soon he would be more concerned with matrimony.

Peter and Jill were engaged in December, 1970. Then on March 17, 1971 the couple were married in a service at the royal chapel of St. James' Palace. Jill's father was Sir Philip Moore, the Queen's assistant private secretary, which entitled her to a marriage in royal surroundings. After a reception at the palace, the couple honeymooned in Tunisia, where unfortunately Peter suffered from a bout of food poisoning. On return to London they moved into a basement flat in Wandsworth.

Despite the couple's royal connections, money was still tight and accommodation frequently grim. A year later they moved to another flat at Camden Hill Road, Notting Hill Gate, with a hole in the bathroom roof which the landlord refused to fix. It was perhaps unsurprising that Peter later launched an attack on landlords in the Genesis classic 'Get 'Em Out By Friday' from their fourth album *Foxtrot*.

Although a happy couple and very much in love, no little strain was placed on the marriage by the pressure of band work. Peter was constantly on the road, out recording, doing interviews or attending meetings. Quite often he came home very late at night, exhausted after a gig and Jill was plagued with worries about where he was and what was happening to him. In fact her worst fears were confirmed one night when he failed to come home at all. She panicked and stood waiting outside their home in the early hours of the morning, increasingly convinced that he had been killed in an accident. In the end Mike Rutherford appeared in a car and comforted her with the news that Peter was sitting safely in the back. But he had been injured and had broken his ankle. It was, of course, the night he had jumped off the stage at Friars Aylesbury.

At least while the band was still poor and fighting for fame, the role of a musician's wife was clearly defined. She could be relied upon to provide support and comfort. But when the band later became more successful and Peter was elevated to stardom, it became harder for Jill to cope with the pressures placed on her by Peter's schedule. As she later admitted, she became jealous and resentful. During the early years she could at least try to understand the importance Peter placed on his musical ambitions and the needs of his burgeoning career.

Gabriel would make many fine recordings with Genesis, but undoubtedly many of his most sublime moments were to be found on their third album *Nursery Cryme*, unveiled to the world in November, 1971. Here were the songs Gabriel fans grew to love and remember with affection, as he poured his heart and soul into 'The Musical Box', 'The Return Of The Giant Hogweed' and 'Harold The Barrel'.

Technically the album was a reasonable improvement on *Trespass*. It was produced once more by John Anthony, but this time he had assistance from engineer David Hentschel, who went on to become Genesis' regular producer. This was the first of their albums to feature Steve Hackett and Phil Collins, and their presence had an immediate impact both on the writing and the sound of the band. Phil in particular brought new strength to the rhythm section and he sang well too when he was featured on the brief but haunting 'For Absent Friends'.

The album had another superb Paul Whitehead cover and was undoubtedly one of the best designs produced during the heyday of Seventies' album art. It was inspired by the opening track 'The Musical Box' which tells the tale of Henry Hamilton-Smythe minor (8) whose head is knocked off by young Cynthia Jane De Blaise-Williams (9) during a violent game of croquet on the lawn. The subtly detailed Victorian scene depicted by Whitehead resembles something out of *Alice In Wonderland* and shows a sallow, yellow lawn stretching into infinity, with a dark eyed Cynthia wielding her croquet hammer surrounded by severed heads. Apparently Henry wasn't her only victim. Careful study of the cracked antique style painting reveals many hidden delights, including Harold the Barrel himself, standing on a ledge and surveying the gory scene. According to Peter's darkly surreal story, after Cynthia beheads Henry, she discovers his treasured musical box in his nursery. She opens it and as 'Old King Cole' begins to play, Henry's wraithlike spirit appears. Explains Peter: "Henry had returned, but not for long."

Here was a definitive example of Gabriel's capacity for irrational thought. He envisions Henry's body ageing rapidly after a lifetime of pent-up carnal lust and desire surges through him. Just as he is about to seduce Cynthia, a nurse arrives to investigate the noise. "Instinctively Nanny hurls the musical box at the bearded child, destroying both."

It's a bizarre but wonderful tale that is full of suppressed sexuality and violence. Peter toys with the lyrics with a furtive, tiptoeing fascination. Even the most simple lines about 'Old King Cole' are made to sound chilling and he is at his most sensual when intoning the word "flesh" before shouting the grand finale, "Why don't you touch me, now!"

Steve Hackett and Mike Rutherford's haunting guitar lines set the scene and avid listeners can hear Phil providing background vocals ('Bvs' as they are known in the trade), helping Peter deliver a wonderful piece of musical theatre. Peter has explained that his grandfather's house at Cox Hill was the inspiration for 'Musical Box'. He recalls its formal garden with a croquet lawn, goldfish pond, rose garden, squash court and a greenhouse, surrounded by vines and fig trees. "There were lots of privet hedges and places to get lost. However I felt that beneath the formalised structure of all this Victoriana, there was an underlying violence, which I tried to get across in the song."

'The Musical Box' grew in stature and power on 'live' performances over the years. Many of the subtleties lost on the original vinyl version can now be heard with greater clarity on the remastered CD version, although sadly the impact of the original LP artwork is reduced on the minuscule CD booklet.

Work on *Nursery Cryme* began with rehearsals at Luxford House, a 16th Century Tudor house at Crowborough near Tunbridge Wells, owned by Tony Stratton-Smith. Any number of great artists had worked there, enjoying the seclusion of the peaceful Kentish countryside, including Neil Diamond, Leonard Cohen and Charisma's very own Van Der Graaf Generator. Genesis also found it the perfect place to relax, get to know the new members and work out a routine for future 'live' shows. However they had an album to write to a deadline.

Tony Banks found it strange working with a new guitarist after the departure of his old friend Ant Phillips and he later expressed the opinion that *Nursery Cryme* wasn't such a big improvement on *Trespass*. Said Tony: "Even with two new members, the album was surprisingly similar to the previous one."

What does stand out is the way Peter Gabriel's dark humour comes to the fore, notably on 'Harold The Barrel', the album's fifth track. This tells the tale of a 'well known Bognor restaurant owner' who disappears after cutting off his toes and serving them to his customers for tea. He tells the story in the cursory manner of a local newspaper report. Says an eye-witness: "Father of three, it's disgusting, such a horrible thing to do. He can't go far, he hasn't got a leg to stand on." The police, the Mayor and the great British Public all scold the fugitive until he is eventually located on a window ledge threatening to jump. Warns his mother: "You can't just jump. Your shirt's all dirty and there's a man here from the BBC." But even a policeman's kindly appeal of "We can help you" is greeted by a defiant cry of "You must be joking, take a running jump." Peter and Phil share the vocals and roles on a song rich in comic characters and observation.

Fans were captivated by the tale and word also quickly spread about 'The Return Of The Giant Hogweed', another delightfully dotty and dramatic tale. It was inspired by contemporary news reports about a weed that had spread through the gardens and waterways of Southern England. The opening riff, strident, defiant and insistent became one of the most familiar to

Genesis audiences over the coming months and its jazzy instrumental sequence was interspersed with a flowing Tony Banks piano solo. This was Genesis working as a team and producing a structured but ever changing piece, full of surprises and contrast.

Sang Peter: "Turn and run, nothing can stop them, around every river and canal their power is growing." He fantasised about the Hogweed seeking its revenge on humankind and indulging in a triumphal dance. "Mighty Hogweed is avenged. Human bodies soon will know anger. Kill them with your Hogweed hairs . . . Giant Hogweed lives."

Of the remaining tracks 'Harlequin' was attractive if unmemorable, while the concluding item, 'The Fountain Of Salmacis', was another stab at a seven minute extended work that had orchestral overtones – and overtures.

Despite the flow of new ideas, balanced by the retention of traditional Genesis values, the album was not greeted with delight by Tony Stratton-Smith, who found it disappointing. The record company failed to promote the new record and sales were slow, until the band suddenly had news from the Continent. *Trespass* their previous album had gone to number one in Belgium! This had been the result of a TV appearance there and a show they had performed in Brussels in January, 1972. Even more exciting was the news that *Nursery Cryme* had been embraced by fans in Italy, who loved the dramatic flourishes and operatic tone of much of their work. The record went to Number 4 in the Italian charts. Hastily Genesis flew to Europe, crossed the Alps and went to Italy in April for their first ever tour, where they were greeted with hysterical scenes. The reception by the Italians proved the band's salvation.

They may have been treated with distant reserve and a slow response from the majority of British audiences (Friars Aylesbury excluded), but on the Continent – ah ha! Genesis were greeted as heroes. They played to crowds of 6,000 or more who cheered the songs and applauded at every opportunity. It was the boost the band sorely needed, especially after their own manager had seemed in danger of losing interest. The Italian experience also won them the support of influential journalist and photographer Armando Gallo, who became the band's chronicler and a major authority on their work.

There is a wonderful video clip of Genesis being interviewed for Italian TV where Peter is being asked about the inspiration for his fantasy songs. "It sort of comes out here," he explains, taking off his shoe and holding it to his ear, while a stoned-looking Phil Collins lies back, grins and giggles and a stony-faced Tony Banks looks decidedly unamused.

It was during a trip to Naples that the band first devised one of their most famous works – the magnificent 'Watcher Of The Skies'. The music was written during a sound check before a show at the Palasport in Reggio on April 12, and the lyrics were written by Tony Banks and Mike Rutherford a week later. They were inspired by the spectacle of an afternoon landscape devoid of people. The song was about the Earth suddenly becoming depopulated, much to the consternation of a visiting alien. The piece also provided Peter Gabriel with one of his most spectacular visual performances, although it was premiered in England in the most unpromising of circumstances.

'Watcher Of The Skies' was first performed at the Lincoln Rock Festival on May 28, 1972. As often happened when Genesis tried to play in the open air, it poured with rain. In fact there had been three days of rain by the time Genesis came out to play to a cold, wet, miserable crowd on a Sunday afternoon. They desperately wanted some rock'n'roll to warm them up, and not even the dramatic power of 'Watcher' with its doomy Mellotron introduction by Tony Banks, nor even a full blown 'Musical Box', could really move them. Previously converted fans, however, felt that Genesis had given a fine performance in the circumstances and even hardened music business reps suffering in the mud now began to realise they were a major new force. Despite the fact they appeared in daylight, were on a bill with the Average White Band and The Beach Boys and they were playing largely unfamiliar material, Peter was determined to make a strong impact.

He chose this otherwise grim and forbidding event to showcase his most theatrical appearance thus far. He had shaved a strip of hair from his forehead (a forerunner of today's popular undershaves), and his eyes were lined with heavy black make-up. Dressed all in black he wore a jewelled necklace and amulets that made him look like a young Egyptian prince. A month later Genesis repeated the show in the more congenial surroundings of the Olympia, Paris, on June 26, where this time 'Watcher Of The Skies' went down a storm with French fans. Then two days later, came the opportunity to play a really worthwhile show at home in England.

David Stopps was still carrying a torch for the band and decided to help them out by putting on a special concert at Watford Town Hall. First they played for him at Friars Club at Bedford Corn Exchange on June 16. Then came the Watford show on June 28, when they were supported by Flash, a new band led by ex-Yes guitarist Peter Banks. David Stopps advertised the event in *Melody Maker* and proudly proclaimed: "Genesis are the finest and most original band to come out of Britain for years."

Recalls David: "1972 had seemed a strange period for Genesis. It was a year where they seemed to be making little progress, but at Friars they were always megastars. I remember talking to the band at this time and there was a certain amount of despondency in the air. They didn't seem to be making any progress nationally or internationally and I had the distinct feeling that they were thinking of breaking up. There also seemed to be some financial problems."

The band had discovered that after all their work and struggle they were heavily in debt to their record company. Giving up at this point seemed like a sensible, if defeatist, course of action.

Shaken by this "appalling thought" and stirred into action, Stopps suggested that they make a concerted effort to win them stronger media support. He wanted to help them get the 'big break' that had so far eluded them. He came up with the idea of a special Genesis Convention. "We had to pick a large venue, so we chose Watford Town Hall where we had previously presented Elton John, The Faces and The Kinks."

David began a heavy advertising campaign in the *MM*, adding for good measure 'Listen to their albums *Trespass* and *Nursery Cryme* and collapse with approval.' Another said 'Home Counties Genesis Freaks Unite – Your time has come to shine.' Peter Gabriel had a thousand rosettes made saying 'Genesis '72' which he would throw out into the audience. The show drew a big crowd and was highly successful, if not from Flash's point of view. Recalls Peter Banks: "It was a dreadful gig."

Was it the sound? "No, it was Watford. The problem for us was our bass player Ray Bennett broke a string on the first number – and bass players normally never break strings. Everything ground to a halt." Flash had a huge new PA system for this début gig, which they lent to Genesis, through a kind of roadies' barter system. "At this time Phil Collins had his first jamming band called Zox & The Radar Boys in which I sometimes played lead guitar. It was this group that later evolved into Brand X."

Despite PA problems *Melody Maker* reported that Genesis received an ovation from the crowd who leapt from their seats to cheer a stunning barrage of dynamic material including 'Watcher Of The Skies' and 'The Knife'. "The music and attitude have changed, improved and progressed until they have reached that most exciting time for all groups, when they have not quite cracked the publicity barrier, but are enjoying the much more worthwhile and rewarding acclaim of genuinely appreciative audiences. The feeling of excitement of a band that is happening musically and knows it is only rarely experienced. That feeling is happening now, with Genesis."

David Stopps: "Unfortunately the performance itself was again beset with technical problems. But despite this the band gave it everything and so did the audience who were determined to make it a success."

As ever, Peter Gabriel could see the funny side of all this yearning for success. He decided to play a little game with the adoring Friars fans. The next gig at their club was held on September 2, 1972. "And it was extraordinary," says the promoter. "Peter greeted the audience when the band came on stage by announcing 'We will judge your appreciation of tonight's performance by the amount you boo or hiss . . . any clapping or cheering will indicate your disapproval.' So after the first song there was this massive deluge of booing and hissing and so it went on right through the set. By this time they were playing most of *Foxtrot* which would be released a month later. One chap arrived late, missing the announcement and came up to me totally confused. 'They're brilliant, so why is everyone booing?' "

In an interview later that month Peter told me: "We had a great night at Aylesbury when we asked the audience to boo instead of cheer. Then last night we played at Greenford and it was easy to recognise the Aylesbury contingent – they were really abusive. They really are a great audience! They like the concept of our music and we like people to like us – it's very simple."

It was the first time I'd met Peter and found him not only charming but helplessly vulnerable, strangely mysterious and at times possessed by an oddly eerie presence. I felt he was quite capable of using the power of his mind over people, as he fixed them with a penetrating look and a smile that seemed to hint at an intuitive knowledge of dark forces. Then he'd release the spell with a creaky laugh and the mood he could conjure at ease would dissipate into the ether.

The shaven-headed one sat at one of the battered tables of a Fleet Street pub where the locals were fortunately used to seeing a procession of strangely clad pop stars on their visits to nearby newspaper offices. Jim the Irish barman had served both Marc Bolan and David Bowie in all their finery without batting an eyelid. The sight of a shaven headed Gabriel, while impressive, did not impede the flow of jokes, real ale and packets of cheese and onion flavoured crisps.

As Peter sipped his beer, he explained that his latest gimmick might have been part of a subconscious desire to join the Hare Krishna movement – or else it was just "the result of a nasty shaving accident!" The growth of Genesis' support over the previous months had been encouraging. Explained Gabriel: "Originally we tried to do folk type numbers and it's all worked up to a crescendo. Now we've got an act we're starting to take control of the audiences. In the past we bodged our way through things. I suppose it started for us at the legendary Friars Aylesbury. That's when people first got to know us. It's all built up mostly through gigs, rather than through publicity. People seem to know our numbers and those who dislike our music the first time pick up on us later. I don't consciously think about it all as an act. A lot of it is based on fantasies without them taking over from the music. There is a lot of freedom in the music and nobody has to compromise too much. In our writing we are trying to do something that hasn't been done before and that is to write a combination of sections that match. 'The Musical Box' was composed in that way. It's quite a complicated story about a spirit that returns to bodily form and meets a Victorian girl. He has the appearance of an old man and the relations with the young lady are somewhat perverted, so he gets bumped off."

Peter denied that he was in any way the 'leader' of the group. "No! We just squabble. We have a democratic system. There are five in the group and three represents a majority. When we are on stage we really feel the energy coming off – man! The energy flows in and we push it out. We need success to get the band into the next stage. And anyway the band is £14,000 in the red at the moment."

By now the band were busy writing and rehearsing songs for the next album. They had already completed work on 'Watcher Of The Skies' as well as 'Can-Utility And The Coastliners' and 'Get 'Em Out By Friday'. These would take pride of place on the next album *Foxtrot*. But they also had various bits of uncompleted songs. Tony Banks had a piece called 'The Guaranteed Eternal Sanctuary Man' he'd written some years earlier at university. Peter had a newer song called 'Willow Farm'. Other fragments and ideas came together until gradually they were amalgamated into one huge arrangement that would last for nearly 23 minutes and take up most of the album. This major new work was called 'Supper's Ready'.

In years to come, it would be hailed as the band's most glorious achievement. By the time it appeared on *Foxtrot* their manager was finally convinced. This was the album that would make them rock giants.

Released in October 1972 *Foxtrot* was produced by David Hitchcock and recorded at Island Studios, London. Says Tony Banks: "This was a major leap forward, but it was such a sweat to make this album. The first producer we had was called Bob Potter who Charisma had brought in. He was with us for a few days and really didn't like what we did at all. He particularly didn't like the opening to 'Watcher Of The Skies'.

"He said: 'We don't need this, it's awful.' It was uphill stuff so we got rid of him. We got in David Hitchcock. He wasn't really right either and didn't know what was going on. We had to work around him all the time. He was a nice enough guy but in terms of sound we disagreed very strongly. Despite all that the album produced some of the best things of all. We had just done the first bits of 'Supper's Ready' with the original engineer, then we did the last half with John Burns as engineer. Suddenly there was power and excitement and I came out of the studio for the first time wanting to listen to something over and over again. 'Supper's Ready' was vastly better than anything we had done before. 'Watcher Of The Skies' became a classic 'live' song even before we recorded it. The Mellotron introduction became our trademark. I thought all the songs on the album were good. It was kind of similar to the previous two albums but a lot better and I really thought we had got something down on record that sounded like what we were trying to do. The group was really working together as a unit."

Even so there were disagreements behind the scenes at the studio and frequent rows between Tony and Peter. Gabriel even tried to keep the band out of the room while he sang his lines to 'Supper's Ready', knowing that he might offend Banks by singing over part of his keyboard solo. Says Peter: " 'Supper's Ready' was a gamble. There was some resistance in the band over the length of it and people were very nervous. We were taking risks with stuff that we knew was likely to be uncommercial, which wasn't guaranteed to get radio play and which was probably going to get knocked in reviews."

He needn't have worried. The album received great reviews. Heard today it seems extraordinary their first engineer couldn't understand the relevance of the Mellotron chords that usher in 'Watcher Of The Skies'. Never before or since within the parameters of rock has there been such a doom laden, menacing and dramatic introduction.

It was a mood setting masterstroke and as the drums and bass began to pound and paved the way for Peter's vocal entrance, the effect was as exciting as any barrage of 'thrash'. Influenced in part by Gustav Holst's 'Mars' from *The Planets*, the piece has similar warlike overtones, but the arrangement is pure Genesis. Amidst the snapping, snarling drums, Steve Hackett unzips a series of extraordinary guitar whoops. Banks and the rhythm section exchange fearsome riffs, soft then loud, a device which made hairs stand up on the backs of the audience's collective neck.

Returning to the opening theme, Phil Collins rounded the whole thing off with a mighty roar of tom toms. Truly an inspired piece of work which has never lost its appeal.

'Watcher Of The Skies' also encouraged Peter to introduce one of his most striking stage accoutrements, a pair of batwings worn over his shoulders. It caused a sensation among fans at the band's headlining concerts. The whole album was packed with good songs, sustained by their most professional production thus far. It remains effective when heard on CD, and is thankfully free of the muddy mixes which marred their earlier recordings.

Peter displayed tender feelings for poetic, romantic imagery on 'Time Table', an attractive melody which offered solace after the album's thunderous opening. 'Get 'Em Out By Friday' by contrast was angular and aggressive, its jazzy rhythm set by Phil at his most fluid and inventive on the drums. The Hammond organ stomped furiously behind Peter's vocals as employing almost Dickensian diction, he told the tale of eviction and repossession. For those unfamiliar with this particular Gabriel saga it features 'The Winkler' a bailiff employed by Styx Enterprises property developers. He attempts to evict Mrs. Barrow and her family on the orders of one John Pebble.

The plan is to get people out of houses and into more economic blocks of flats – 'in the interests of humanity'. Even when the family agree to leave their home for a flat in Harlow New Town, they discover their rent is raised. In a science fantasy twist it is revealed that by the year 2012, genetic engineers will order that all humans must be restricted to four feet in height, so more people can be packed into tower blocks. Anyone over this height is thrown out! Chants Peter: "Get 'em out by Friday! You don't get paid until the last one's well on his way."

Phil Collins played the role of Genetic Controller with a suitably robotic voice in a TV news flash put out on 'All Dial-A-Program Services' – a sly reference to Mr. Gabriel Snr's early cable TV invention that passed unnoticed by all but the most clued-up Genesis fans. "This is an announcement from Genetic Control. It is my sad duty to inform you of a 4ft restriction on humanoid height." There is more skulduggery from the cast of characters before this inspired ditty reaches a dramatic climax.

While 'Can-Utility And The Coastliners' and the brief Steve Hackett guitar interlude 'Horizons' have their place on the album, 'Supper's Ready' at 22.58 minutes drew the most heated debate and attention. In America there was a feeling among critics – used to their rock'n'roll in short three minute chunks – that this was all too overblown. The damning phrase 'pretentious' that a furious Pete Townshend once said should be erected in large letters and then burnt in flames was muttered in dark corners.

In fact 'Supper's Ready' was a collection of songs, moods and ideas, linked by one particularly haunting theme into one absorbing and rewarding entertainment. Peter's famed introduction "Walking across the sitting room, I turn the television off, sitting beside you, I look into your eyes . . ." is a clever ruse, as if the listener has arrived late in the theatre and is only just in time for a scene-setting introduction. The steady pulse of an acoustic guitar melody interspersed with a background choir and floating piano interjections, help build the air of mystery and suspense even as Peter's presence comes and goes like a will o' the wisp.

'Supper's Ready' was divided into seven sections comprising 'Lover's Leap', 'The Guaranteed Eternal Sanctuary Man', 'Ikhnaton And Itsacon And Their Band Of Merry Men', 'How Dare I Be So Beautiful?', 'Willow Farm', 'Apocalypse In 9/8 (Co-starring The Delicious Talents Of Gabble Ratchet)' and 'As Sure As Eggs Is Eggs (Aching Men's Feet)'. The pieces were allowed to unfold with great poise and skill as if part of some major orchestral work. Phil Collins' drums were held in check and unleashed only during the battle scenes depicted in 'Ikhnaton' but these violent explosions eventually faded away to the musings of 'How Dare I Be So Beautiful' which contains one of Peter's most chilling lines: "He's been stamped 'Human Bacon' by some butchery tool (He is you)."

The comical prancing of the Beatle influenced 'Willow Farm' which follows, gave Peter the opportunity to wear another of his best remembered stage costumes – a huge flower's head. Peter's flute and Steve and Mike's acoustic guitars added to the poignancy of the piece until it transmuted into the violence of 'Apocalypse In 9/8'.

Phil launched the piece singing, "With the guards of Magog swarming around." The rumbling riff built over this odd time signature pushed towards a magnificent climax that frequently engulfed concert audiences in a trance-like state of fevered anticipation. Here was true dark metal heaviness that few bands could match. In the light of today's digital recording technology the album does now seem lacking in impact. But even so, as the church bells chime and Collins holds a press roll behind Peter's final soulful exclamations: "Hey baby don't you know our love is true," the magic of 'Supper's Ready' transcends the analogue fog.

The piece somehow encapsulated both Genesis' musical ambitions and Peter Gabriel's own strong sense of imagery. From the band's point of view it represented the culmination of years of writing together, and even though it fell together, almost as Mike Rutherford says, "By accident", it brought together the strands of romanticism, humour and surrealism. For Peter the lyrics meant an exploration of the forces of good pitted against evil. He once told me a story while sitting in a grace and favour apartment near Kensington Palace which he shared with Jill, that the room we were sitting in was haunted in some way. It seems he and Jill were badly affected by tales of spiritualism told to them one night by producer John Anthony. It reached the point where they felt an evil presence in the room that caused a window to blow open and Jill to go into a trance. Writing 'Supper's Ready' was a kind of exorcism. It was a strange suggestion – whether you believed in such things or not.

As soon as *Foxtrot* appeared on October 14, 1972 it entered the UK charts at 25 then trotted up to Number 12 and was swiftly hailed as a milestone (not a millstone) in the band's career by an enthusiastic music press. "Genesis have reached a creative peak with this collection of songs," praised the *Melody Maker*.

The album was helped on its way by another distinctive cover design by Paul Whitehead on a gatefold sleeve. As detailed, if not quite as immediately striking as 'Nursery Cryme' it showed a group of mounted huntsmen on a sea shore, stymied in the chase after their prey, in this case a woman in a red dress with a fox's head, (or a fox with a woman's body), standing on a small ice floe. There is much fun to be had in studying the details of the painting, which reveal a nuclear submarine and references to the previous cover, including a floating mallet, a piece of Hogweed and even a distant view of Cynthia, still on her croquet lawn. The red-coated horsemen were originally chosen by the artist as a statement against the upper (and lower) class sport of fox hunting.

When he heard 'Supper's Ready' being recorded and was able to discuss the music with Peter, Whitehead realised he could make a more relevant connection particularly with 'Apocalypse In 9/8'. As a result the fox hunters became the four horsemen of the Apocalypse (in this case seven). The division between land and sea represented life and death, although the sea itself was full of life, including a large shark. Busily cycling towards the shoreline from a nearby Holiday Inn was the tiny figure of Peter Gabriel, who Whitehead knew spent a lot of time pedalling rather inexpertly around London. He still is keen on cycling as an alternative means of transport.

There was no doubt Genesis and Gabriel were at a peak of creativity. Yet they still faced enormous economic problems. Recalls their song plugger: "Even by this third album the band still hadn't sold more than 15,000 copies which wasn't making anybody any money. When *Foxtrot* was finished Peter Gabriel came in and asked what could they do to improve things."

Many have wondered how Peter came to adopt his role as theatrical rock icon. Some thought perhaps he had been inspired by the great surrealist painters, or suggested the costumes he wore were the result of some acid inspired vision. There is a more prosaic view.

His plugger claims he sat him down and said: "You've gotta do something outrageous. Everybody else who is making it these days is either throwing mics around, smashing up drums or head butting TV sets – like The Who. It's all to get publicity." The widely held belief is that was when Peter decided to wear costumes on stage. "He'd written the album and said: 'Why isn't anybody interested in us?' I said it was because they were just nice blokes and they weren't exciting on stage. He went away and put all the costumes on, which all the band hated. They were embarrassed and thought he was mad. They thought people would laugh at him because he put a red dress on for *Foxtrot*. It was well over the top by anybody's standards – even today. But after Peter did that the band completely stole the show everywhere they went."

The group had been due to go on a major tour from September to October, 1972 and there's no doubt Peter had been worried about the lack of attention from the public at large. Before the tour began he took a bicycle ride from Notting Hill Gate to the Charisma Records office in Soho, where he met booking agent Paul Conroy.

The advice offered was that if he seriously wanted to get into the music papers, he had to do something "outrageous". Conroy suggested they get someone to dress up as the fox from the LP sleeve to promote the album. Peter instantly realised that if anybody was going to dress up as a fox it would have to be him – and on stage to boot.

Before the UK tour was due to start the band were booked to play a one-off concert at the National Boxing Stadium in Dublin, a shed-like building with rows of high bench seats that ringed the stage. In 1969 the Bonzo Dog Doo Dah Band had performed there with The Nice and Yes on another Charisma sponsored tour. The Bonzo's lead singer Vivian Stanshall had alarmed the locals by shouting loudly with cupped hands: "There's a pig loose in the theatre!" Keith Emerson of The Nice had followed this performance by stabbing his organ with a dagger. It seemed the visiting Charisma acts made a habit of causing shock and outrage among Dubliners. On this occasion Peter Gabriel was about to cause even greater mayhem.

He had taken up Conroy's suggestions with a vengeance. The gig was going well in fairly normal fashion, until it came to the time to play 'The Musical Box'. As the band tore into this final number, Peter went off stage, then returned to astound the audience with his transformed appearance. He was wearing a long red woman's dress and a fox's head.

There was something so strange and surreal about this combination of sly ambiguity and sexuality that the crowd were stunned. The band were amazed too, as Peter had kept his plans a secret and they knew nothing about the costume change.

He had borrowed the dress, an expensive Ossie Clark number, from his wife Jill. The terrifying thing was the dress seemed to fit Peter perfectly and it suited him. After the show some members of the band questioned the wisdom of pulling such a stunt which might detract from the music. But some, notably Steve Hackett, stood by Peter and felt that as the band were singularly static on stage most of the time, sitting at their instruments like a string quartet, then anything the singer did to liven things up was worthwhile. It would certainly do the trick, for within weeks of the outfit being seen back in Britain, the band found themselves on the front pages of the music press.

Recalls Gabriel: "The first night of the tour was the boxing ring in Dublin which was not the usual place you'd go into to perform in a red dress. I remember when I walked out wearing this costume there was a sense of shock and horror in the audience. I thought – 'great, I'll have a bit more of this.' "

The *Foxtrot* costume made a great picture, but the band had earned their celebrity status after years of hard work. The front cover of *Melody Maker* not only won them more fans but increased the fees they could command, overnight. From being paid a paltry £300 a night, they could now expect at least £600 a show. And by now they had a show that everyone was talking about. With Peter at the helm, spinning the funny stories that had begun life as mere fillers, together with the costumes and a gradually improved and more reliable PA, Genesis were rapidly becoming one of the most sought after acts in the highly competitive rock world. This was at a time when Led Zeppelin, Deep Purple, The Who, The Faces with Rod Stewart and Paul McCartney and Wings were barnstorming around the country. Rock was serious business and the opportunities were enormous, particularly in America, whence Genesis and Charisma were now at last turning their attention.

Yet despite all this optimism and the opportunities sparked by Peter's bold moves, the longed for 'big time' eluded them. The band's financial affairs remained dire. Says their erstwhile plugger: "By now they owed Charisma a quarter of a million pounds, which was an enormous amount of money in those days. Strat had lots of advice to dump the band. People said they'd never make it. I remember him taking a journalist down to the Greyhound, Croydon to see the band. I bought him dinner and he assured me: 'They'll always be a college band.' But Strat had tremendous faith in them. He took them to America to headline a concert which he paid for. It was the annual WNEW charity concert in New York. He invested £25,000 in flying them over there but they were a hit and it helped them to break America. They didn't think the New York show was very good, but that was only by their own high standards. By anybody else's standards it was fabulous. They had a tremendous stage act and they had great faith in themselves. It wasn't a blind belief but a really intelligent belief in what they were doing and Peter had real faith."

When things went wrong the ever present inner tension mounted and disagreements about music, style, fashion and policy raged away from prying eyes. "Peter was never difficult, he was just adamant that what they were doing was right. He is braver than any artist I've seen. He is timid and shy and yet he is also the bravest. I saw him once at the old Green's Playhouse in Glasgow, which was the roughest gig in Britain. Genesis were on the same bill as Lindisfarne and a couple of other groups. Peter was booed just for walking on stage. He stood there with his hands crossed until they stopped booing. They were throwing things and the band were saying, 'Well shall we start?' and he said, 'No, not until they stop.' It went on for some minutes until they gradually stopped booing and then they went into 'Watcher Of The Skies'. At first they hated him and it seemed like they were going to eat him alive, but in the end they loved him. Even blockheads like drama and there were a few blockheads in that night!"

Everywhere it seems people were suddenly turning on to the new star now being hailed as a successor to Bowie and Bolan in the Glam Rock stakes. This was not quite what the studious musicians who helped create 'Supper's Ready' had in mind. Slowly seeds of resentment began to germinate. At the same time, some of their oldest fans began to feel left behind, taken aback by the sudden lurch into the big time.

Says David Stopps: "With the release of *Foxtrot* Genesis' career took off in a very big way in the UK and Europe. This was very rewarding to see but it was a double-edged sword. On the one hand they had the breakthrough they so richly deserved. But horror of horrors, this also meant they were now too big to play Friars Aylesbury anymore."

Stopps did put them on once more with Peter Gabriel at the helm, at Dunstable Civic Hall on February 26, 1973, during the *Foxtrot* tour. "It was a wonderful performance but I remember Peter coming up to me and saying, 'It's not the same as Aylesbury.' "

Peter expressed his fondness for the old club in June 1973 when Friars Aylesbury celebrated its birthday. He offered to write something for their special magazine and Stopps was delighted with the following article.

"Many times we have seen the effect of a human being fed music and beer simultaneously. It can cause aggression, bubbles in the stomach and a powerful form of audio-nasal communication. When we first arrived at the old Friarage Hall we discovered a species capable of enjoying both at once. Perhaps they had been sent from Mars or Jupiter or even High Wycombe. We were welcomed, warmed, digested and liked. This was a most pleasurable experience. 'Take us to your leader' we said afterwards to a wandering Friar and we were led to a locked chamber in which a dark-haired man by the name of Stoppo was leaping with himself, and consistently making merry. He excited us with his terrific wit, imagination and money. He seemed completely unaffected by the usual club runners problem of the diminishing member. Since that day we have been overcome by the number of friendly Friars members.

"Some bands have the habit of expressing their fondness for an audience in the back of a van. This is a very quick relationship. I was given two screws at a Friars gig that will be with me until I'm in my grave. They are metal, about eight inches off the ground and in my right leg. Such is love.

"Thank you for letting the Hogweed grow in your fertile back gardens. We know where home is. HAPPY BIRTHDAY. Love. Peter Gabriel for all of Genesis.

"PS FRIARS LANTERN: a flame like phosphorescent flitting over marshy ground (due to the spontaneous combustion of gases from decaying vegetable matter). According to Russian folklore, these wandering lost Friars are lost spirits not unlike Gabble Ratchet."

The club made a huge cardboard birthday cake and at the crucial moment, out popped Peter Gabriel to loud cheers. It seemed like the Genesis party was just beginning . . . but it was a party that would end in tears.

IV

SELLING ENGLAND BY THE POUND

AMERICA, FAME AND fortune beckoned as Peter Gabriel led Genesis towards rock's promised land. In the process he bemused his fans with a carnival parade of costumes. Here a fox's head, there a giant flower, batwings, a geometrically shaped red box and an old man's mask. Intriguing and innovative to be sure, but who was the man behind these masks? Was this venture into spectacle just an exercise in showbiz excess? In truth his motives were entirely laudable. It may have been true that he was encouraged by his advisors to go over the top in the battle for recognition. But what the singer wanted most was to involve his audiences, to provide them with startling ideas and images. He wanted to shock and amuse, but he also wanted to make them think, as he illustrated the stories in his songs. He saw music in cinematic terms and was in a way inventing promo videos – without the video tape. When people came to a Genesis concert they were guaranteed an increasingly elaborate show – but it was all done in a meaningful way, as befitted their constantly evolving music. Even so, there was a danger of Genesis becoming forever associated with phantasmagoria and the theatre of the absurd. There came a growing need within the band to express themselves in more concise form. They knew they had hit singles inside them. Peter Gabriel and Phil Collins were equally capable of writing chart toppers – they just hadn't done it yet!

But hey – this was the early Seventies . . . and with *Foxtrot* still winning new listeners, there was much work to do within their existing framework. There was no need yet to start looking over their shoulders and worry about accusations of excess.

Just as Britain was waking up to Genesis and their flowery lead singer, so America was being tantalised with the possibilities. However it would not be easy to convince States-side audiences. The US had grown used to a stream of British wannabes knocking on their door, from The Beatles to Herman's Hermits. By 1973 a UK accent was no longer a passport to acceptance. If a band wanted to make it in the States, they had to be special and they had to work hard. Genesis were certainly brilliant in their field, but nobody had heard music like this before. 'Supper's Ready?' 'Watcher Of The Skies'? This ain't workin' – this ain't even rock'n'roll.

In December 1972 Genesis took the plunge and headed for America to play their special charity concert in New York. It was bitterly cold but brilliantly sunny as the nervous Englishmen arrived in a city getting ready for Christmas. The streets of Manhattan were lousy with jolly fat guys going, "Ho, ho, ho". Actually they weren't lousy, but very friendly and welcoming. It was the first time any of the band had been to the States and the culture shock left them speechless. Yellow cabs, skyscrapers, hamburgers, hot dogs and multi channel TV – it all seemed like a big movie set. The noise and bustle of New York was invigorating and particularly exciting, as so many aspects of the American way of life had still to make their appearance in England.

Mike Rutherford remembers going to a soul food restaurant where a cheerful Mama dished out hot spicy meals. She had to carefully explain to Mike the highlights of her exotic menu, but he still looked bewildered by some of the items. "Tell me, what exactly *are* black-eyed peas?" Conversations with cab drivers, too, were classic examples of Charterhouse v. The Bronx which usually resulted in complete bafflement all round. But Peter Gabriel was entranced by the city, its restless energy and polyglot population. As he embarked on long walks around Manhattan the steam billowing up from vent pipes in the streets seemed to hint at a whole underground world seething below his aching feet. The seeds of an idea were sown in New York that would eventually flower into a major new Gabriel concept. Meanwhile – there was music to be performed.

As far as the press corps invited to accompany the band on their first American trip were concerned, the band was due to make its début in New York's Philharmonic Hall. It transpired later that there was a secret warm up gig the night before in Boston, Massachusetts. Genesis played at Brandeis University, apparently to a handful of students. The gig was plagued by equipment problems and the all important Hammond organ, being set to a different voltage, was out of tune. Matters would not improve in New York and the result was a concert that teetered on disaster – at least as far as the band were concerned.

Tony Stratton-Smith had set the wheels in motion for the trip. Charisma had signed a distribution deal with Buddah Records for the States and although *Nursery Cryme* had been a difficult album to sell, they felt more confident about *Foxtrot*. The plan was to put on a special show that would give the boys a chance to do their best in front of an audience of DJs and press from all over the States and Europe. If Genesis were put on as a support act on a package tour, their long set pieces and even the costumes and effects would seem pointless and out of place. A headlining début was a gamble but Strat was determined to take a chance. After all, if America liked what they saw – then Genesis would be well on the way to becoming financially viable – at last. Even though *Foxtrot* was in the Top Twenty back home, the sales potential of the American market could transform their fortunes and ensure they had a solid future.

The charity show was sponsored by the WNEW radio station, whose DJ Scott Moony had loyally supported the band on air. With everything hinging on a successful night, the band's tour manager Richard MacPhail was in a state of nervous tension. He arrived in the States a couple of days before the band to try to check out the equipment but he already knew they were lumbered with a PA system that was prone to failure. He had a taste of the problems that lay ahead in Boston.

Tony Banks told me despondently just hours before the New York show: "Yesterday was terrible. We were two hours late and we had only ten minutes sound check. Nobody seemed interested in the music."

On the day of the New York concert it was discovered that the Philharmonic Orchestra conducted by Leonard Bernstein intended to rehearse all afternoon in the hall that bore their name. Richard and his charges fumed, fretted and waited.

In the end Genesis and their equipment were allowed in for their desperately needed sound check at 4 p.m. Support band String Driven Thing was due to start at 7 p.m. It was a close run thing. Earlier in the day the band assembled at the offices of Buddah Records which was suitably plastered in advertising slogans, posters, balloons and cardboard cut outs of the group.

Peter Gabriel took one look and chuckled: "My whole life changed when I started using Genesis." Everybody else in the office paused in their frantic promo work and they chuckled too. Gabriel's laugh – like a rusty bedspring – was infectious. That night the laughing mood deserted Peter as he came off stage, his face dark with anger, demanding an immediate return flight to London. Only a slight frown that flickered across the normally beaming countenance of Tony Stratton-Smith prevented Peter from hailing a cab to JFK airport. It would be some hours before he could be convinced that the concert had been anything less than a failure.

Yet during the show Peter had grabbed a new and untried Genesis audience with a stunning performance filled with wit and menace and the band had played perfectly. Only they knew it could have been so much better. For them an out of tune guitar was mortifying, a blown speaker a criminal occurrence.

For most of the entourage accompanying the band the afternoon began at the 'Office Pub' just across from the record company, where much Tequila Sunrise was consumed. Peter declined to take part in these somewhat predictable festivities and instead planned a trip to the Museum Of Modern Art. Eventually a London Transport double decker bus appeared to drive the guests from the Hotel Americana on to the Philharmonic Hall. Guests sitting on the top deck, unaccustomed to such a mode of transport, yelped in fear as the bus approached a low bridge, quite convinced they were about to be decapitated. Fortunately the bus arrived with its passengers unscathed to find a mob of fans milling about, many wearing Davy Crockett hats and clutching bottles of Tennessee sippin' whiskey. Maybe they thought Genesis were a Ted Nugent style heavy rock band. They were in for a surprise. Roll out 'Harold The Barrel' and bring on the 'Watcher Of The Skies'.

The British contingent, press and musicians alike, were quite unused to a full blooded teenage New York audience in action.

At home in the early Seventies a British audience would still remain dutifully seated, politely applauding each number and only waiting until the encores to express anything approaching a cheer. New York audiences in contrast yelled comments at the artists, paced up and down the aisles, leapt about in their seats, stood up, and hurled paper darts. It was a cross between a scene from *The Blackboard Jungle* and The Last Night At The Proms.

Even the local celebs didn't quite know how to handle their exuberance. Alison Steele the 'night bird' DJ from WNEW wandered on stage and began a rather floaty address to her public. "I feel very strongly tonight you are all reincarnations . . ." she began.

"Rock'n'Roll!" yelled back the crowd. The British contingent, seated in the midst of this mayhem, felt their hearts sink. How would these lusty, vociferous New Yorkers react to an unknown band playing intricate arrangements, all in a style noted for its marked absence of rock or any kind of roll? Well String Driven Thing did their thing and escaped unscathed, then after a suitable wait for roadies to finish putting chewing gum on the fusewire, the first long note from Tony Banks' mighty Mellotron filled the air and the lights dimmed. Peter Gabriel stood impressive and impassive, his arms folded, face painted white and hair shaved over the forehead, the Egyptian prince once more come to weave his magic. Clad all in black with the silver necklace encircling his throat, he began to sing and then talk as his character transformed. All who knew Peter well and even Jill his wife, noted that once on stage Peter ceased to be the person they thought they knew. He became a staring, grimacing succubus, a warlock possessed of the ability to frighten his best friends – or entrance them with a strangely sensuous sex appeal. The effect was hypnotic as the soft, husky voice changed into a strident verbal assault that tolerated no heckling and brooked no interruptions.

After the unstoppable thunder of 'Watcher Of The Skies' the previously boisterous youths sat with jaws sagging as Peter told his strange tales of women unzipping themselves on subway trains and falling into halves. When he disappeared and then dashed on stage wearing a long red dress and his huge fox's head, there was a gasp of stunned surprise. Two blinding explosions and clouds of smoke further pinned the audience back into their seats, Davy Crockett hats now lay abandoned and the whiskey bottles were forgotten.

Everything was going beautifully until Mike Rutherford's bass pedals broke down, and a blast of feedback threatened to destroy the mood the band had so painstakingly built up. In the midst of the crisis, Peter held on to the audience, talking to them in disarming fashion and even taking Polaroid pictures, asking the front rows to "say cheese". Once the electrics had been kicked back into life, the band began to play and Peter returned to the stage in a dazzling white satin outfit to deliver the ultimate knockout blow 'Supper's Ready'.

A storm of applause greeted this magnificent climax. I made my way back to the dressing room – past a youth bleeding from a knife wound – only to find the door barred. Everyone was advised to keep clear of the band for at least the next half hour. A glum and depressed group were eventually located backstage. Peter was furiously angry with the sound system and much to everyone's surprise seemed to think it had been a poor performance. Even the normally unflappable Mike Rutherford had slammed his guitar down on the floor when he came off stage. Angry words had passed and Peter had made his threat to fly straight back to London.

The next day I had a chance to talk to Peter and he had calmed down sufficiently to say: "I felt very angry at first that we didn't have a sound check and although I don't feel as suicidal as I did at first, I wouldn't like to do another gig in those circumstances." After that he set off in a yellow cab intent on feeding the squirrels in Central Park. As he headed towards the cab a small child, strangely clad in a bright yellow suit and pointed hat, walked past and gave Gabriel a menacing stare.

"Ah ha, the Phantom Squirrel Hunter Of New York," smiled Peter. I was hoping the encounter would inspire a new character for a song. One did eventually appear, but clad in a leather jacket rather than a pointed hat.

In February 1973 Genesis began a series of headlining British dates and in March they returned to America for their first US tour. It was to be a year of hard and heavy work and British fans began to fear they might lose their favourite band to America. But the group played a show at home that was not just one of the finest in their career, but one of the most memorable rock events of the time. The Genesis show at London's Rainbow Theatre on February 9, 1973 was not so much a concert, more a kind of sustained magical experience. The music transcended the normal confines of a 'gig' to the point where it took over the band, mesmerised the audience and became a kind out of body experience.

Those who saw the show still talk about it in some awe. Even the band seemed pleased. The venue was perfect for rock music. Once The Astoria, the converted cinema had been home to many important pop concerts during the Sixties. The Beatles had played there and in 1967 there came the famous occasion when Jimi Hendrix first set fire to his guitar (with the aid of a drop of lighter fuel). Frank Zappa was pushed off the stage by a fan when it became The Rainbow, and Eric Clapton staged his comeback show there. Fortunately nobody set fire to Peter Gabriel or pushed him off the stage on the night of the Genesis concert, but he could have walked on water as far as the fans were concerned.

The musicians appeared seated at their instruments, except that most of the equipment was hidden behind a white gauze curtain lit with UV rays which also provided a ghostly effect. On this occasion everything worked perfectly. Steve Hackett played his bizarre squeaks and squeals between more delicate guitar work, Tony Banks went ballistic on his Mellotron and Hammond, while Mike Rutherford sat operating his row of bass pedals, strumming acoustic and bass guitars. Phil Collins sang and swung those drums, while Peter edged to the front of the stage, a dark wraithlike figure intent on casting a spell over the black mass of audience beyond the blinding footlights.

Once again Gabriel showed how he could transform himself into some supernatural being in which the normal bawdy bluster of rock's reality could be suspended – if only for a few tantalising moments. During 'Watcher Of The Skies' he wore his famous batwings and glowing eyes. For 'Musical Box' he put on the fox head and during 'Supper's Ready' he wore the daisy headdress, enlivening the 'Willow Farm' interlude with a silly dance. He put on a strangely disturbing red geometrically shaped red box for 'Apocalypse In 9/8'. Amidst a flash of light, Peter took off a black cloak to reveal his shining silvery white outfit – representing the triumph of good over evil.

71

It was also a triumph of Genesis over apathy, criticism and neglect. By now no one could ignore the band which was regularly making the front pages of a music press mostly fulsome in their praise. Rave reviews of the Rainbow concert encouraged new fans to flock to the rest of the UK shows.

Two shows at the Free Trade Hall, Manchester and at De Montfort Hall, Leicester were recorded in February for the *King Biscuit Hour*, a long established US radio show. The tapes were later used by Charisma for a 'Genesis Live' album released in August. The tapes were mixed at Island Studios and the album was produced by John Burns. Although the band weren't too keen on a 'live' album the quality was excellent and captured the classic Genesis line-up at a peak of their playing powers and when their best numbers were still fresh.

The album featured definitive versions of 'Watcher Of The Skies', 'Get 'Em Out By Friday', 'The Return Of The Giant Hogweed', 'Musical Box' and 'The Knife' and was dedicated to Richard MacPhail who had left the band in April 1973. The cover showed the band bathed in blue and white light, with Peter wearing his red box. The sleeve notes featured his story of the 'young lady in a green trouser suit' undressing and unzipping her body on the tube train. If only it had been a double album with a 'live' version of 'Supper's Ready'.

Said Tony Banks: "This was never intended to be a 'live' album and we said we really didn't want one out, as it was too soon. Then the record company said they wanted to put it out in Germany and we agreed, being pretty naïve. So then they said they had to put it out in England or there would be trouble with imported copies. Then we had to put it out everywhere."

The King Biscuit Hour was broadcast in America in March, which helped to pave the way for the band's US return. However despite the warmth of their reception in New York the previous Christmas, by the time the band came back, they found they still had a mountain to climb. Vast numbers of American concert goers and record buyers had never heard of them. Nevertheless the group persisted with their policy of headlining shows and gradually built up a following as they travelled the country, mainly along the East Coast in a convoy of vans and cars. When they got to Canada they were jeered by Lou Reed fans when Reed's band and Genesis shared a bill.

Peter didn't mind this display of polarisation – any reaction was better than being ignored! It was a case of getting their heads down and forgetting they were heroes back home. Sometimes the tension caused them to snap and once again Mike Rutherford was at the forefront of un-Charterhouse behaviour – throwing a vase of flowers across a hotel reception after being refused a room for the night. It turned out to be a plastic vase but at least the hotel relented and gave them a room.

The grind of touring the States in uncomfortable conditions over, the band could return home with time to think about a follow-up to *Foxtrot*. Their fifth studio album *Selling England By The Pound* proved to be quite a radical departure. I was privileged to hear this album for the first time on Phil Collins' car stereo player, with most of the band squashed inside his tiny Austin Mini.

Written during the summer, this album was markedly different from its predecessors. There was emphasis on shorter material, like 'I Know What I Like (In Your Wardrobe)' which gave the band its first chart hit. Phil Collins had a stronger vocal presence, notably on 'More Fool Me', and the overall sound was vastly improved.

This was evident on the opening piece 'Dancing With The Moonlit Knight' on which Peter's vocals were sharply defined and the instruments better balanced. Phil's drum sound was brought into the mid-Seventies with a new clarity and power. There was also a new style on the cover art. The Paul Whitehead era was over and the sleeve sported a cover painting by Betty Swanwick. And yet despite these innovations, the technical superiority and the introduction of new extended works like 'The Battle Of Epping Forest', and 'Cinema Show' the feeling was that *Selling England By The Pound* lacked the mystery and magic of *Foxtrot*.

That wasn't the sort of mood that could be turned on like a tap. *Selling England* represented a more mature and seasoned Genesis, a band that had come a long way from Watford Town Hall – via the M1 and the North Circular. The album got to Number 3 in the UK, while 'I Know What I Like (In Your Wardrobe)' with its clever mix of pop simplicity and Genesis style, got to Number 21 in the singles' chart. Genesis fans were stunned to hear their favourites actually being played on the radio. Peter enjoyed himself on a song which began: "It's one o'clock and time for lunch." An African drum added to the battery of unusual sounds that helped the loping rhythm of a piece that concluded with another surreal line from Peter: "Me – I'm just a lawn mower. You can tell me by the way I walks." Peter sang this 'live' wearing a farmer's hat with a straw stuck between his teeth. However despite this success in England, it would not be until 1978 that a Collins fronted Genesis finally got a hit single in America when 'Follow You Follow Me' reached Number 23.

Tony Banks remembers that the band wrote the whole album in one six week stint before going into the studio. "It was quite a difficult session. It was hard to get things going. 'I Know What I Like' was good and the second half of 'Cinema Show' worked well." There were some arguments about the inclusion of 'After The Ordeal', a piece written by Steve Hackett to conclude the rather wordy and overblown 'Battle Of Epping Forest' which was based on a news story Peter had read about a battle between East End gangsters. Said Peter: "I felt I had a responsibility to try and steer us towards being more accessible. I really got carried away with the lyrics for 'Battle Of Epping Forest'. I enjoyed writing them but they didn't fit the music and by that point it was too late in the day. What happened was I insisted on doing most of the words as I thought I could do them better than the others – which I think was true. The problem was that I was incredibly slow, so that often by the time they saw the lyrics, they would have done their parts. The backing tracks would be complete but there were no melodies and no words."

This eleven minute marathon was matched by a more successful performance 'The Cinema Show' which became a good live number, spurred by Phil's sophisticated drumming. 'Firth Of Fifth' with its superb piano and flute theme by Tony and Peter would also become a stage favourite. Whatever their feelings about *Selling England* it produced a hit single and changed the band's status. Says Tony: "We had found our feet . . . four years after we had started and a lot of groups had come and gone by then! This did well for us in England but we weren't doing anything in the States. And nothing much changed for us with the next album."

*   *   *

Towards the end of the year an important change came within the Genesis organisation, when they asked promoter Tony Smith to take over management duties from Tony Stratton-Smith. The new Tony in their lives had inaugurated rock shows at London's Lyceum Ballroom with his father. John Smith had promoted The Beatles in their early days and son Tony had helped him out before becoming a successful promoter in his own right. He went on to promote tours by The Who and Led Zeppelin and put on The Who's 1968 *Tommy* tour, which included an appearance at the London Coliseum. This incidentally was attended by a keen young Who fan – Phil Collins. Tony Smith later set up various Charisma package tours, which included Genesis. When called upon to promote the 1973 UK Genesis tour Smith was alarmed to find the band in disarray. Glasgow was the first date of their *Selling England By The Pound* outing but they had to cancel the gig because their equipment was in a dangerous condition. The wiring leaked high voltages from the lighting rig to the PA and the musicians risked electrocution if they went on stage. It seemed to symbolise the chaos that surrounded their operations. A huge and escalating debt to the record company was also cause for alarm.

Tony Stratton-Smith appreciated there was a conflict of interest in his roles as both manager and record company boss. It seemed more sensible if the group worked with a day-to-day administrator, while they remained signed to Charisma Records. The band took legal advice, and renegotiated their deal with the record company on better terms. Tony Smith gave the group some much needed professional advice and then finally agreed to become their manager. It was a role he had avoided while busy as a promoter, but he would now handle Genesis with considerable aplomb for the next three decades. He would find himself dealing with upheavals along the way, but he presided over the band's most commercially successful years with a calm professionalism, as he put their affairs in order. Backstage chaos receded, but he then found himself confronted by a major crisis involving Peter and the rest of the band.

Selling England By The Pound had produced a hit single but Peter planned to do something much more adventurous on the next album and he would insist on writing all the lyrics wedded to a single unifying concept. The result would be *The Lamb Lies Down On Broadway*. Hailed by fans as the best of all Genesis' works, this ambitious, imaginative project inspired the band's biggest ever stage show.

Meanwhile in December, 1973 the band were still on the road. They had played their first US shows on the West Coast where they performed six nights at The Roxy in Los Angeles. By now Peter's costumes had become even more elaborate. He dressed as Britannia, complete with a trident, during his performance of 'Dancing With The Moonlit Knight', a Procol Harum-ish number which contained the poignant line "Old Father Thames – it seems he's drowned; selling England by the pound." He also wore a balaclava helmet to act out 'The Battle Of Epping Forest'. It all helped to promote a promising album which became their first US chart entry.

In January the band returned to London for some superb concerts, hailed by the home audience and critics as some of their best ever shows. The band played five sold out nights at the Drury Lane Theatre and a highlight (literally) of the show came when Peter flew on a high wire across the stage at the climax of 'Supper's Ready'.

It was a device used by actors playing Peter Pan in panto-mimes, but it hadn't been used in rock presentation before and it caused quite a stir. There was also a wince of sympathetic pain felt amongst the audience at the sight of Peter being winched up in a harness that threatened to split his difference. It was later revealed that when he tried the same stunt in New York the 'flying' wire caught around his neck and he only just escaped being hung – which might have upstaged Alice Cooper but wouldn't have been the most dignified last exit.

Using a stereo Sony cassette-corder, the author taped a complete show at Drury Lane from a seat in the front rows. The sound was superb and captured the full band with Gabriel and Collins at their dynamic best. This recording, which would now be worth many millions of dollars, was subsequently erased to make use of the tape for an interview I did with a man who wrote TV jingles. Of course, I could have bought a new C60 – but why bother when you could see Genesis any night of the week? I was also well aware of the fact that illegal tape record-ing seriously harms the music industry and was not something I could indulge in without risk of heavy fines and imprisonment. In fact a fragment of 'Watcher Of The Skies' remains and it sounds – like a million dollars.

During the summer of '74 the band's 1971 effort *Nursery Cryme* made its first appearance in the charts as new fans discovered the group's back catalogue and *From Genesis To Revelation* was released in the States in a typical record company move to capitalise on the band's new-found success. Even so it still wasn't much of a success in terms of sales. *Selling England* only got to Number 70 in the US charts while *Genesis Live* hovered at 105. The band needed to pull off a blockbuster to really crack the American market.

Work on the new project began at Headley Grange, a Hampshire location previously used by Led Zeppelin. Some believed the house was haunted, a fact which further unsettled Peter who was always susceptible to influences from the spirit world. Back in the material world the band agreed they should go for a 'concept' album and various ideas were discussed. Eventually Peter's idea for *The Lamb* was accepted and he was given the go-ahead to write all the lyrics.

Unfortunately this onerous task came at a time when Peter was undergoing considerable personal pressure. His wife Jill was eight months pregnant with their first child and the couple had moved into a new home, a cottage near Bath. The move represented the paradox in Peter's life at this time – an increasing desire to escape from the pressures of the music business and constant touring while balancing the need to maintain his lifestyle and income.

At the same time an exciting career move beckoned that seemed to hold out the promise of an altogether different future. When the band played at The Roxy in Hollywood, a top film director had come down to see them play and had been mightily impressed, particularly by Peter's macabre spoken interludes. He was no less than William Friedkin, director of *The French Connection* and *The Exorcist*. Friedkin had read Peter's story of the woman unzipping herself on a train on the back of the *Genesis Live* album. Having now seen Gabriel in action, the intrigued Friedkin was convinced the singer's ideas were well suited to the motion picture industry. With a new film project in mind he sent Peter a telegram, asking him to a meeting. It seemed there was a chance that Peter might be able to collaborate on a script. It was very flattering and exciting. How could Peter turn the offer down? After all he had once considered a film career after leaving school. But when Tony Banks heard about the idea he was against Peter becoming involved, stating flatly that the group should come first.

Gabriel appreciated this, but was now torn between loyalty to the band and the opportunity just waiting to be seized. He decided to give Hollywood a try. The problem was Friedkin hadn't got the go-ahead for his project from the film company and he couldn't offer Peter anything as substantial as a contract. It was a terrible dilemma and Friedkin didn't want to feel he would be responsible for actions that might break up a successful group. The singer suffered many sleepless nights, waiting for a decision to be made. During Peter's absence, Genesis carried on rehearsing and recording the material they were still busy writing for the new album. Although nothing was said in public, Peter had to all intents and purposes quit the band.

In the end, after some diplomatic efforts by management, including both Tony Smith and Tony Stratton-Smith, Peter went back to the group, but was greeted somewhat frostily. It seemed they were already getting used to the idea of working without him. The next problem was the mass of writing that needed to be done. With Peter driving back and forth to be with his wife, and still desperately trying to put together the strands of a complex album concept, it was no wonder he began to feel like quitting.

The Lamb remains perhaps Genesis' most controversial album. Gabriel made a conscious decision to get away from the more airy fairy nature of the topics he had covered on *Trespass, Nursery Cryme* and *Foxtrot* albums which in the pace of the early Seventies, already seemed like relics from a past era. The story was in part influenced by Peter's brush with New York City and he chose as his main character Rael, a young Puerto Rican punk, clad in a leather jacket. The name itself didn't sound especially Spanish but it had a kind of Esperanto-like international flavour. He certainly wasn't Harold the Barrel. Oddly enough The Who's Pete Townshend had written a complex song entitled 'Rael' which appeared on *The Who Sell Out*, and the same musical theme reoccurred under a different name on *Tommy*, but Gabriel was apparently unaware of this.

As Peter developed his story, so the tale seemed to reflect his own situation, a somewhat tormented schizoid figure undergoing a transformation. Peter once patiently explained the whole story to me, but it was still hard going for the uninitiated.

The album itself was patchy. It contained moments of brilliance, but there were areas when it could have benefited from tighter editing. The whole project seemed unwieldy, especially translated into a stage show. Despite the flaws which could all have been corrected given more time, *The Lamb* was a monumental effort and was in many ways the last gasp of the great progressive rock movement. This era saw bands like Yes produce such massive and contentious works as *Tales From Topographic Oceans* which caused similar dissent within the ranks. In fact Genesis disliked being compared to Yes or ELP. Certainly their approach was quite different even though all the musicians involved came from the same roots. In retrospect it now seems as if Peter was deliberately trying to offer the last word in overkill with *The Lamb*, before retiring gracefully from the battlefield to seek pastures new.

While the outside world were still buzzing about the growing success and recognition now accorded Genesis, as is often the case, the band were actually a year or more ahead of both public and industry. The average fan might see the band perform once or twice a year. The record shops stocked the occasional Genesis album and single. For the members of the band it was a seven day a week grind, involving month after month of touring and recording. In between they had to keep the vital spark alive. The spontaneous joy of making music was often subverted by the peripheral activities of the music business. They *had* to keep working to make money to keep themselves and their families and employees afloat. What had started out as a musical challenge amongst friends had become an organisation that needed constant nurturing. In the midst of all this they had to please the critics, their manager and their record company with a shrink wrapped new work of genius.

Peter was involved not only writing all the lyrics but in composing some of the music and he contributed such pieces as 'Counting Out Time' and 'Chamber Of 32 Doors'. He found the task of writing a huge mass of material very daunting and time consuming. Writing to order has never come easy for him, and even in recent years, while working on his solo albums, he has found it difficult. On one occasion he was even locked in his own studio by a frustrated producer, insisting Peter finish some lyrics.

In the end Mike Rutherford and Tony Banks helped out with *The Lamb* lyrics and co-wrote the words to 'The Light Lies Down On Broadway' which appeared on the fourth side of the original vinyl double LP. The album was recorded at Glosspant, Wales with the Island Mobile studio during the summer of '74. There were some 23 tracks on the completed record set.

Says Peter: "Once the story idea had been accepted we had all these heavy arguments about the lyrics. My argument was that there aren't many novels which are written by a committee. I wrote indirectly about lots of my emotional experiences in *The Lamb* so I didn't want other people colouring it. In fact there are parts of it which are almost indecipherable and very difficult, which I don't think are very successful."

By the time it was all recorded the band were already pretty much tired of the whole thing. Only now they had to take it out on tour and sell Genesis by the pound. Peter came up with some of his most elaborate and hideous costumes to act out the parts of the various characters.

The lumpen Slippermen for example were particularly gruesome while the Lamia was positively weird. Three large screens were employed to project images to illustrate the story while Peter acted out the role of Rael wearing heavy facial make-up. (This apparently did not endear him to real Puerto Ricans when the show came to New York.) One clever ruse was to employ two Raels on stage. One was Peter but the other was an identical dummy and from a distance it was impossible to tell them apart. Impossible that is until the road crew decided to play some tricks on the hapless singer. One night the dummy was adorned with a banana protruding from his trousers, while on another occasion a completely naked roadie took the place of the replica Rael. Such escapades did not show a great deal of respect for the composer in residence, but by now there were rumblings from the band as well. Phil Collins was beginning to find the whole thing decidedly silly and was annoyed when Peter's vocals couldn't be heard through all the costumes. Sitting at the back and trying to keep time, not to mention inject some life into the proceedings, was more like playing in a pit band for a Broadway show than getting it on with a rock band. No wonder he began to jam away from Genesis with his jazz-fusion band Brand X. Even Steve Hackett felt *The Lamb* was too self-indulgent and admitted he couldn't really commit himself to the project either musically or in spirit. Mike Rutherford was more charitable. He felt that it had some great moments and that the critics hadn't listened to it properly.

Tony Banks was philosophical but frank about the fate of the album and its ramifications. "Being a double album it was much more difficult for people to promote and it was the only album to sell less than its predecessor. It didn't do so well in England as *Selling England*, and it didn't sell in America." The record company tried to release various singles off the album but they all suffered from acute lack of radio play.

Said Tony: "I thought 'Carpet Crawlers' had a good chance. Making the album started off great but it turned into hell by the end. And by the time we had finished we were fed up with it, because it took so long to do – about five months. But the result was one of the strongest we had ever done. I think it has so many strong moments although it's flawed and has lots of things wrong with it. I'm not too crazy about the story myself. It was just something to hang songs on, although the individual lyrics are great. The album spawned a very important live show and we went to town with all the effects. It's funny, people look back on that album now and say it was a classic, but it got unanimously bad reviews at the time. Nobody liked it and it went down badly. Peter wrote the story and all the lyrics. This was a bone of contention. We had internal problems within the group, so it wasn't the happiest time for us."

The band set off on a North American tour that would move on to Europe. They had 102 concerts to perform and for an hour and a half they were expected to win over audiences with entirely new music before they could encore with a few Genesis favourites. It was hard graft. Genesis were still engaged in winning over American audiences and Phil Collins felt it was a mistake to hit them with such heavy stuff. And yet – the shows invariably went down well. There is after all no crime in a band introducing new material to its audience. The greater crime surely is to go on recycling greatest hits for years. All that was needed was a more balanced programme. Whatever the challenge Peter was up front – taking the brunt of all the flak.

The group had only just arrived in Cleveland, early into the US tour dates, when Gabriel took his manager aside and told Tony Smith that he wanted to leave. It was a body blow to Smith who had only just begun to see the band turn round and get itself on a commercial footing. He must have felt like Tony Stratton-Smith, who having signed Genesis to Charisma way back in 1970, saw two members quit even before a tour was booked. This time, however, it was the star of the show who wanted out. And that was the reason. Peter didn't want to *be* the star of the show – not any more – not if it caused so much resentment. The rest of the guys had begun to feel that with all the attention on the special effects and costumes, nobody was noticing their presence or contribution. And there were other reasons. Gabriel felt that he'd said and done everything he could within the framework of Genesis. It was time to move on. Even worse he had grown to hate the rock scene, the music business and his role within the group.

"I was beginning to dislike myself for doing what I was doing," he revealed. "The group didn't like what I was becoming and I began to feel my hands were tied. I went into Tony Smith's room and told him I was leaving and he tried to talk me out of it saying, 'Hold on a couple of days.' I said it was final. The rest of the band were told a few days later in Canada. Their position was that we had worked eight years to get this far and now finally we were about to make it and I was pulling the carpet out from underneath them. I felt terrible but I knew that I'd made up my mind and I can be really obstinate. I wanted a career where I had the opportunity to take on other projects but the band had this army-like attitude. There was no room to be flexible. You were in or you were out."

Tony Banks couldn't get Peter to change his mind, but it was agreed that Peter would say nothing to the press about his impending departure until the tour was over. It would have been too much of a bombshell for the band to have their singer quit mid-tour, before they had even found a replacement.

Peter Gabriel's shock departure from the group would be a

bitter blow to all concerned. It seemed tragic that Peter should contemplate leaving Genesis, just as they were about to reap their biggest rewards and greatest success, after so many years of hard work. Some thought it the ultimate folly, without understanding the background to his decision, or knowing anything about the behind the scenes build-up of tension. In the end, the rift freed Gabriel to launch his own career. It gave Genesis a push into a new direction and allowed Phil Collins to become a superstar. But none of these events could be predicted when Peter's departure was first announced. For many it was simply the worst news since The Beatles split. With Gabriel, Collins and Hackett still in the ranks, the original Genesis could have carried on for several more years and created who knows what brilliance?

Meanwhile, before the news became public it was crucial to present a united front. Peter became his own spin doctor, still doing interviews and not giving anything away except the odd guarded remark that would only make sense in the light of later developments.

Did he feel resentful about the pressures on him? "Bastards," growled Peter when I tackled him on the subject after his official departure. This uncharacteristic show of aggression was a rare glimpse of that darker side which Gabriel himself would later acknowledge and examine in the maturity of middle age.

Quite apart from the pressures of stardom there were more important matters closer to home. It was during the recording of *The Lamb* that Peter's daughter Anna was born. His beloved first daughter arrived on July 26, 1974 at St. Mary's Hospital, Paddington. It had been a difficult birth and Anna had to be induced. She had caught an infection while still in the womb and her umbilical cord was wrapped around her neck after the doctors had turned her twice. When she was delivered her lungs were full of fluid and she was starved of oxygen. She was so weak there were fears for her survival and the doctors feared she might die. They wouldn't let her mother see her for a week. Although Anna recovered after six months of worry, Peter had realised, with the onset of fatherhood, that there were more important things in life than rock'n'roll.

Peter recalled in a *Rolling Stone* interview (1987): "That was a major drama for me. My wife remembers that before the birth I was away with the band at the time. The band remembers that I was away with my wife all the time. I think I was the cause of bad feelings, because I was the first one of the group to have children and until you have kids you have no real understanding of that emotional experience."

Even though the band had been sticky about Peter's attempts to carve a career writing film scripts and had been miffed about his handling of *The Lamb*, when push came to shove, they didn't really want him to go. Tony Banks continued his attempts to get his old friend to stay on. But Peter's mind was made up.

Says Tony: "The birth changed him quite a lot and it was difficult for us to accommodate that, because at that stage in the group's career, we still wanted to do as much touring as we could. And after he wrote ninety nine per cent of the lyrics to *The Lamb* I think he felt he would never get that chance again, and that we wouldn't let him do it. I tried very hard to persuade him not to quit the band but he's not quite as taciturn when it comes to people he knows well. He gets a certain set look and he is obstinate. So he left."

The departure date was set. He would leave in May, 1975. Now deep down his main emotion was relief. Once he had left Genesis, he could rest, recuperate, live with his family and come back to face the world – in his own time and on his own terms.

V

Behind The Mask

WHILE *THE LAMB LIES DOWN ON BROADWAY* was trundling around America, Genesis fans at home were blissfully unaware of the rising tension within the group. They knew nothing about the impending departure of the singer who had become an idol and was widely seen as the embodiment of the group.

Aficionados would remember the moment and the place where they heard that Peter was leaving Genesis with the same clarity they would later profess to remembering some cataclysmic world event. In my case it was in April, 1975, while sitting in the audience watching Genesis play a major London concert. Gail Colson of Charisma told me the news. Many of those in the know backstage were apparently in tears. After all, this wasn't just any old band, this was family – a group whose supporters at the record company and even in the media regarded with a fondness normally shown towards precious offspring. Surely the band couldn't be breaking up – not *now*? But of course the band wasn't breaking up. They fully intended carrying on – but without Peter.

The previous month I went to Paris to see Genesis perform *The Lamb Lies Down On Broadway* in its entirety. The show was a great success and the Parisians went wild. The next day I interviewed Peter at the Paris Hilton, still unaware of his decision to quit. He had been suffering in silence, yet I found him eager to communicate. There was no hint of impending doom. He talked enthusiastically and was at great pains to explain the story of *The Lamb* – sensing that I had a comprehension problem.

At 9 a.m. I was still sleeping off the previous night's revels when there came a knock at my bedroom door. I thought it was a maid with her feather duster at the ready. I was about to say

"Can't you read that Do Not Disturb sign?" when the familiar figure of Peter Gabriel appeared. "You ordered some words sir?" This was an unexpected form of room service. At this stage Genesis had been on the road since Christmas. Peter's nightly portrayal of the character Rael had been exhausting but the show had helped to win over the mainstream rock audience and this, I thought, had given Peter greater confidence.

"The leather jacket and jeans I wear as Rael has given us a much more raunchy appearance and we can sense a change in the audiences," said Peter as we discussed the previous night's show. The fans had enjoyed the spectacle and were particularly intrigued by the 'double image' featuring Peter and his lifelike dummy. "Which is which?" – was the cry from the crowd. The trick required split second timing to achieve. "I have to make a blind jump in the darkness from the rostrum to get back before the lights go up. If the spotlight goes on too soon the audience see me sprawling on the floor!" he smiled. Peter had a life mask made for the dummy which was in itself a gruelling experience, one of many he would put himself through in the name of art.

"I had pipes up my nostrils to breathe and was totally encased in plaster. A lot of people hallucinate in that state. It got a bit scary having my face encased. It feels like you are trapped and I had a strong urge to breathe through my mouth. It was very claustrophobic. The plaster got very hot." More unexpected problems ensued. Gabriel had to take the dummy with him to a hairdresser to match their hair. "It caused a few scenes in San Francisco when I took the top of the torso into an elevator. A lady screamed in fear when she saw the legs were missing."

Peter revealed that the group had to employ security guards to protect the masks and costumes after they had several guitars stolen during their trip to New York. The show was tiring for the band and caused Peter much anxiety. "It was hard to get complete darkness in the halls to ensure people couldn't see me moving around during the changes."

Despite narration and back projection many still found *The Lamb* with all its costume changes, allusions and imagery, quite mystifying. But then it was supposed to be mystical. Peter's explanation gives an interesting insight into his creative processes and the way his characters can relate to himself. "The story begins with a dose of reality, establishing an earthy character which develops into more fantastic things. Rael is half Puerto Rican and lives in New York and he'd be the last person to like Genesis! I've yet to talk to the genuine article but that's not important. *He's alienated in an aggressive situation.* The Lamb arrives on Broadway and acts like a catalyst. A very oppressive sky descends over the city and solidifies. It becomes a screen like a TV with the camera behind it. Real life is projected on the screen and starts to break up. It's rather like the Victorian's reaction to early photography. The screen that Rael sees is sucking him in. When he regains consciousness he is in another underworld."

Rael's adventures include being wrapped in a cocoon inside a cave filled with a network of cages and then finding himself confronted by 'The Grand Parade Of Lifeless Packaging' a Gabriel-esque parody of the record industry. Rael also endures a bizarre form of open heart surgery. His journey takes him up a spiral staircase to a hemisphere filled with 32 doors, of which only one leads to the exit. A blind woman guides him out through a tunnel into a cave where he is trapped once more until he meets Death – the Supernatural Anaesthetist. Eventually he finds a pool filled with snake-like creatures with the head and breasts of beautiful women. These are The Lamia. In Greek classical mythology they are one of a class of female monsters with the bodies of snakes. Like vampires the Lamia drink Rael's blood and meet a grisly fate.

Said Peter: "The Lamia enter his body and they die. He finds a more feminine side of his personality which is totally foreign to him, and yet he has fallen in love with a delectable Lamia creature and becomes so engrossed in its attractiveness and the newer side to his personality he never believed existed, that he doesn't notice a strange blue light which causes him to sweat. The Lamia nibble at his buttocks and are killed, a moral for buttock nibblers everywhere."

He attempts to leave this strange scene, only to enter 'a freak's ghetto'. The grotesque, lumpen inhabitants are the Slippermen, all old hands at being seduced by The Lamia. As Rael takes on their loathsome appearance he finds the only way to salvation is to visit Doktor Dyper and undergo yet more surgery. The story becomes ever more convoluted.

"The Slippermen are grotesque and totally sensual beings

whose entire day is spent gratifying every orifice, including nose, mouth and ear. The only way out of this situation is castration. A bird comes down and carries off a tube containing the offending member. He can go through a window to get back where he was in New York."

Going back to the sanctuary of Broadway, he attempts to save his brother John from drowning, but when he looks into his eyes, he sees only himself. "His brother turns out to be another illusion. Eventually he is absorbed into a substance called IT, a purple haze."

There was much more, but it is a saga best absorbed as a theatrical costume drama with music – as Peter intended – and not read as script synopsis. "It's quite a barrage of words," admitted the author. "There should be an award for people who go through it! But I'm a great believer in mumble-jumble sense. I prefer things to give an air of meaning, rather than meaning itself. You can't look for meaning in some of the lyrics, they just present an atmosphere." Peter later claimed he would not feel fulfilled until *The Lamb* was made into a film. "Every instinct I have tells me that the images are incredibly potent. It was the first attempt by a rock artist to do a multi-media thing."

The double album was released in December 1974 and got to Number 10 in the UK charts and by the following month was at 41 in *Billboard*. Despite my great admiration for the band and wish to trumpet their cause to the world, I had to admit I was not greatly enamoured of a work that seemed to lack the charm and mystery of *Nursery Cryme* or *Foxtrot* and didn't rock as hard as *Genesis Live*. There were some fine moments, however, and after 25 years I have grown to like it more and understand it better. The opening theme contained some vintage Mozart inspired piano work from Tony Banks and there were some good pop tunes like 'Counting Out Time' and 'The Carpet Crawlers' which failed to make an impression on the chart. My *Melody Maker* review of the album at the time was born out of frustration and disappointment. "I wish that rock musicians would learn the importance of self-editing. A few golden miraculous notes and some choice pithy words are worth all the clutter and verbiage in the world. Perhaps we must be patient and wait for *The Lamb* to grow on us, but I have the feeling it is a white elephant."

When the band came to London the Empire Pool, Wembley, was packed and audiences were subjected to a barrage of sound they had not endured at more intimate gigs like Friars Aylesbury or even the Rainbow Theatre. Even those used to heavy volume thought Genesis now seemed unbearably loud in this echoing, cavernous venue. In my review I wrote: "Like the hammers of hell their PA system bore into my brain inducing spasms of giddiness."

The band seemed strangely nervous for the first part of *The Lamb Lies Down On Broadway* and were not as relaxed as they had been in Paris the previous month. Peter's verbal delivery had lost some of its bite. Apportioning praise for the various members I added: "Those who claim that Genesis is all Peter obviously don't listen." I was subconsciously hoping such diplomacy might ease the tensions within the group that I had by now begun to appreciate.

But it was already too late.

After *The Lamb* the group played 'Musical Box' and 'Watcher Of The Skies'. This was the last time English audiences would view Gabriel in his full regalia of costumes and guises. He made a splendid entrance in the batwings and glowing eyes, which were full of his old menace. "The most startling apparitions were Peter clad in body stocking inside a whirling cage of snakes; emerging from a long inflated plastic tunnel as the warty monster and the famous 'double image'." It was a great show but in many ways it had begun to represent what Pete had grown to dislike about the rock business. Where once the band had been subtle and dynamic, this was loud, overblown and alienating.

Meanwhile Genesis had already begun work on *A Trick Of The Tail*, their first post-Gabriel album, commenced long before the public and press had become aware of the impending change.

Tony Banks was not exactly grief stricken about the shake-up: "Peter decided to leave and we had great fun writing and recording the next album. There was a lightening of the load and we needed to streamline the band. Obviously we were very sad to see Pete go because he was a very close friend, but something had to give somewhere. It was proved to be good for Peter and good for the band for him to leave at that point. It gave us all a bit more room. The press didn't know he was going to leave but we all did. The atmosphere wasn't as good in the band as it had been in the early days."

Tony insists they didn't want him to leave but they had to make the best of it. "It presented an interesting challenge. The publicity for the band had been very wrapped up in Peter, which slightly tended to over-emphasise his contribution. He was obviously important, but he wasn't The Band as some people saw it. We had the confidence to produce a good album, but we found it difficult to get people to take us seriously, until they had heard it."

Gabriel's final Genesis appearance was at St. Etienne in France, in May, 1975. He was to have said farewell at Toulouse the next day, but the show was cancelled due to poor ticket sales – English lamb of any description not being terribly popular in France. And so Peter's last day with Genesis was something of an anticlimax. According to Phil he played 'The Last Post' on his oboe but nobody in the audience knew why.

Auditions were held to find another singer after Peter's departure, but the first candidate found their material too difficult. In the end Phil Collins volunteered to sing one of their new songs called 'Squonk' which he delivered with such power that everyone realised they need search no further. To help Phil out when the group eventually went back on the road, they brought in a second drummer, Bill Bruford of Yes and King Crimson fame, who was subsequently replaced by Chester Thompson.

When *A Trick Of The Tail* was released in February, 1976 it sold more than any of their previous albums, reaching Number 31 in the US *Billboard* album chart. Said Tony Banks: "The new album was the first to make any kind of sense in America. The music was more immediate and had more striking riffs like 'Dance On A Volcano', while 'Squonk' had a very heavy drum sound. This was the start of a much happier period for us. *The Lamb* had killed us to play on stage and some of the songs didn't work well 'live' but this album produced a whole lot of instant stage hits."

So – Gabriel had gone. And the band didn't miss him. But who were the losers? Said their old manager Tony Stratton-Smith: "In the long term the only thing Genesis lost was Peter's mind, but I believe that was a very substantial loss."

Peter had his own view on the band's future: "They were definitely nervous about carrying on without me. Yet they proved they could because the band became a lot bigger than when I was in it. In reality, they shouldn't have been worried. I think I had more confidence in their ability to manage without me than they did. I knew that in the long run, songwriting was what really mattered, and they are good songwriters."

While Genesis seemed to be positively revelling in their new found independence, what of their charismatic, wayward ex-singer? Was he sitting idly in the countryside growing cabbages, as some proclaimed? Was he weeping bitter tears at the sudden halt to his progress and rejection by his old band, who seemed to be doing obscenely well without him? Eventually Peter took it upon himself to issue a statement to deny some of the wilder rumours circulating and to set his fans' minds at rest.

His open letter to the music press was a mixture of whimsy and sound sense, tinged with regret. Wrote Peter: "I had a dream, eye's dream. Then I had another dream with the body and soul of a rock star. When it didn't feel good I packed it in. Looking back for the musical and non-musical reasons, this is what I came up with. The vehicle we built as a co-op to serve our songwriting became our master and had cooped us up inside the success we had wanted. It affected the attitudes and the spirit of the whole band. The music had not dried up and I still respect the other musicians but our roles had set in hard. To get an idea through 'Genesis the Big' meant shifting a lot more concrete than before. For any band transferring the heart from idealistic enthusiasm to professionalism is a difficult operation."

Peter went on to explain that as an artist he needed to absorb a wide variety of experiences. He wanted to live in a different situation and pick up new ideas from outside music. "Even the hidden delights of vegetable growing and community living are beginning to reveal their secrets," he said. "I could not expect the band to have tied in their schedules with my bondage to cabbages. The increase in money and power if I had stayed would have anchored me to the spotlights. It was important to me to give space to my family which I wanted to hold together and to liberate the daddy in me."

Peter talked about the way fame had altered his perception during the previous seven years and how he began to think in music business terms and felt alienated from his audience. "When performing there were less shivers up and down the spine." He had fulfilled his ambition of being "Gabriel, archetypal rock star". However, he hinted that he was not entirely averse to the idea of future fame – should it come his way. He joked about ego-gratification and the need to attract young ladies, "perhaps the result of frequent rejection as 'Gabriel acne-struck public schoolboy'. However I can still get off playing the star game once in a while." (*Sighs of relief at the record company.*)

As for his post-Genesis plans he hinted in rather sombre tones: "My future within music, if it exists, will be in as many situations as possible . . . there is no animosity between myself and the band or management. The decision had been made some time ago and we have talked about our new direction. The reason why my leaving was not announced earlier was because I had been asked to delay until they had found a replacement to plug up the hole. It is not impossible that some of them might work with me on other projects."

Finally Peter listed a string of denials that he had left Genesis: "To work in theatre" – "To make more money as a solo artist" – "To do a Bowie or a Ferry or furry boa and hang myself with it, or to go senile in the sticks."

When I saw Peter a few months later in December, 1975 he elaborated about his feelings toward Genesis in their final days together: "For me some of the fire had gone. In a musical sense I was proud of my involvement in Genesis and in terms of taking it on the road. But when things get to such a scale, it does tend to drain the humanity out of it."

He added later without mincing his words: "We were beginning to get into the era of the big, fat supergroups of the Seventies and I thought: 'I don't want to go down with this Titanic'."

It was Peter's first interview since leaving the band and he told me he had been spending the previous few months songwriting with a new partner, Martin Hall. He was already thinking about recording, but had absolutely no plans to form a new group at this point. In fact he wanted to concentrate on writing for other artists. "I don't want to get into a band situation again," he said. "That would defeat the object of my leaving.

Everything I do will be worked around my writing." Perhaps more interesting than his songwriting was the revelation that Peter had become increasingly interested in the paranormal, psychic power and communal living. Dwelling near Glastonbury amidst the mysterious Somerset countryside with its ley lines and ancient sites, he was certainly in the right place, although in fact we met for our interview in London. As usual with Peter, it was at an unusual time in an odd place. We had breakfast early one Saturday morning at his grace and favour apartment in Knightsbridge. The flat was small, Spartan, with a Governmental air of cleanliness and order, with a framed photograph of Her Majesty The Queen on the mantelpiece. There was something oddly quiet and intense about the room where we sat, although I may have just been susceptible to Peter's pronouncement that he had previously detected a strong 'presence' there. As far as I was concerned the only strong presence that morning was emanating from the erstwhile lead singer of a famous rock group.

Peter had, as widely reported, indeed been spending some time "in the sticks". He been enjoying village life and settling down to raise a family and grow vegetables in his garden. It was the era of self sufficiency, when many an exhausted rocker (including many in the media), dreamt of a quiet life away from the Speakeasy. Under Gabriel's influence I too raised cabbages and grew 52 – one for each week of the year. Unfortunately I quickly grew sick of the taste of cabbage. But Peter had greater need for peace and space. Just the silence, after having a band blasting in his ears, must have been wonderful. Eventually, of course, he began to think about getting back into music. It was time for lunch and time to pack his hoe and park the lawn mower. But his first tentative proposals had met with rejection. There was little enthusiasm for his idea to record a grand rock opera called *Mozo*.

It became clear that Peter didn't have any great master plan for his future at this stage. It was a time for learning, coming up with new ideas and then seeing what would happen. Yet despite accusations of vagueness, Peter was more likely to take control of his destiny than the average hedonistic rock star reacting solely to circumstances and reaching for the valium. Gabriel had been way ahead of the public when Genesis first began to evolve its music and he had been way ahead of the band when he conceived *The Lamb*. Because Peter did not see himself as a journeyman rocker, he could apply his intelligence to the whole way rock music was made and question some of its works, practices and restrictions.

He had already seen that the supergroup syndrome was alienating audiences and his character 'Rael', with its punk overtones, was a move towards street cred, even if Rael was involved in the most unreal situations thus far devised. Now, in the mid-Seventies, Peter could envision rock becoming more structured, more based on the liberating yet disciplined rhythm machine. He was in effect, anticipating the technological advances of the Eighties. He was excited about the prospects opened up by video cameras, which were emerging from the Sony factory in Tokyo. Even the buzz phrase 'multi-media' was something he had latched onto early in his career. He knew he had to play the record company game and knuckle down to work at some stage, but he wasn't going to take the easy option or the simple route. The ideas buzzing around in his head as he contemplated the world from his eyrie in rural England would eventually see his return to the studio and the stage. He would become a star – as big as any of his contemporaries. But it would take longer than many thought and the way would be strewn with problems and disasters alongside the joys and triumphs.

When I met Peter on that Saturday morning long ago, it soon became clear he had not been moping around or wasting time in the months after the split. For starters he had been involved in all kinds of research and study. He had been taking piano lessons and had even attempted levitation and telepathy. On a more personal level he seemed torn between a desire to reveal all his feelings about Genesis and remain diplomatically quiet. Perhaps having a senior diplomat in the family helped. He even suggested we do an interview in which there would be two answers to each question.

There would be "The true love, positive response and the negative true hate response." But there was no need to stir up a hornet's nest. I asked him if he really had been in hiding, growing cabbages in the country?

"I had actually been growing cabbages at the time I wrote my letter to the press. It was a symptom of a time when I had the opportunity to do a lot of things I'd not been able to do before." Back in the studio and away from the cabbage patch he had been equally busy, investigating more esoteric approaches to sound. "Different harmonies have different biological effects on people," he explained. "I've also been trolling around seeing different people in various communities." It was very ironic but one of the groups of people he had met rejoiced under the name of Genesis. It had been a shock when he found out. "Yeah, I can't get away from them. Let me out!" The idea of communal living was quite high minded however.

"It's not your drug ridden sex orgies, but a group of people working together in a lot of areas. A lot of things which interest me are coming to the surface like ESP, telepathy, UFOs, astrology, Tarot, the rise in mysticism, the prospect of religious wars in the 1990s (. . . *now how did he know that?* . . .), it's all very exciting." Peter felt that the ideas which burgeoned among the hippies in the Sixties (pollution, the environment, the global village etc), were now coming into practical use. At the same time he was fascinated by the mysteries of the unseen world including ghosts and apparitions. "I believe all people have experiences which they can't easily relate into their own terms, whether it is seeing ghosts or having premonitions of an accident. I have been working on various techniques which have produced some amazing results – like picking up experiences recorded in rooms. The exciting thing is anyone can do it. We restrict the powers of the mind very much and it's amazing what you can do if you try."

Peter agreed that such experiments, while fascinating, could also be dangerous and disturbing to the delicate balance of the mind (as I have found myself on numerous occasions – eating cheese on toast before retiring to bed being only one example). Peter took all this rather more seriously. "You aren't given any more power than you can handle. I don't mean power in a black magic sense, but the internal experiences that are going on inside you." He intimated he had tried sensory deprivation in the so-called 'black tank' and found that the night time was his most productive period, which incidentally was when radio activity on the short wave was at its most intense.

I wondered at the time if these concepts might have affected his writing style and that Gabriel fans could expect a series of albums devoted to the black arts. "No – I haven't gone all cosmic. Some of the stuff I'm writing is fantasy and some is simple pop song, which I've been writing with Martin Hall. I've been writing the music and he has been writing the words." (In the event the only collaboration with Martin Hall to appear on the first solo album was the song 'Excuse Me'.) "Some of my ideas are ten minute video fantasies and I hope to be able to get those made for TV here and abroad. I've got no immediate plans for going on the road as such. In many ways that is why I left the band ... if I got back into a full-time road situation again it would be self defeating. Essentially I see this as a learning period. I'm sure the fact that I've made a change and had time to think will benefit what I want to do."

Peter saw himself responding to outside stimuli and impulses as they struck him and then introducing an element of self-discipline in order to get things constructively organised. "Left to my own devices I can go a little haywire at times," he admitted. His plan in late 1975 was to get an album out the following year although he had only cut a few demos and it would be 1977 before a full album saw the light of day.

There was still plenty of preparatory work to be done and in a way Peter felt he was going back to school to catch up on his further education. "I've been having piano lessons. I've now got a better understanding of music and I'm trying to develop my playing."

Peter was not interested in hooking up with local musos in a rough and ready band situation again. He knew the pitfalls of working with classmates and preferred a more business-like set up with professionals, amongst whom he would hope-fully be accepted as the dominant force. It was a sensible philosophy. So many British groups from The Beatles to the Small Faces had been built up in the traditional way, often with brilliant first results but then falling into chaos and anarchy. He was determined to avoid that and to organise a new working environment.

"If I'm going to be working with session people it's going to be very useful if I can write out the music. I feel positive about everything at the moment," he added. It seemed that in leaving the old band a weight had been lifted from his shoulders. He

Peter at Charterhouse, summer 1965.

Genesis in 1974: back row, Mike Rutherford, Tony Banks and Steve Hackett; front: Peter and Phil Collins. (Harry Goodwin).

The foxhead and red dress caused a sensation when Peter unveiled his most striking stage outfit with Genesis in 1972. (LFI)

Levitation! Peter conquers gravity with the aid of a flying wire on stage with Genesis at the Theatre Royal Drury, London, 1974. (LFI)

"Excuse me." Peter at the piano during his debut solo tour, 1977. (LFI)

Peter's 'Shock the Monkey" mask, Los Angeles, 1983. (Pictorial Press)

Peter with Jill Moore, whom he married on March 17, 1971, and (right) with
Rosanna Arquette, Hollywood, California, 1989. (LFI)

Peter at the control board in Real Word Studios near Bath. (Retna)

The Amnesty International line up, 1988: Bruce Springsteen, Tracy Chapman, Yousou N'Dour, Sting and Peter. (LFI)

The Secret World Tour, 1993. (Pictorial)

A shaven-headed Peter at the launch of his CD ROM *Explorer 1*, 1997. (Retna)

The ultimate transformation - Peter hits the 'Big Time'. (LFI)

agreed. "I felt in many ways it was tying me down to one particular role and it was beginning to take out some of my creative instincts. In a musical sense I was proud of my involvement with Genesis, but when things get to such a scale it does tend to drain the humanity out of it. For example I didn't like the Empire Pool gig at Wembley. Personally I wouldn't like to play there again. The size of the audiences was enabling us to put on a big presentation, but it became self-defeating. It was time for a change for me, internally and externally with the band. What's coming out of me now has changed. I've always written the pop songs type things, some of which were allowed to come through in the band. Now I can fiddle about with more poppy things."

How would Gabriel buffs from Watford to Ontario come to terms with the new Peter? "I think they'll be interested in what I come out with. There are people who liked what I put into Genesis. For seven years I put most of myself into Genesis. There was one hundred per cent commitment. And now some of the songs that come from inside me, I hope will get through in the same way. I'd like to make albums important to me and those who buy them, however many it is, and also have some fun with singles."

One of Peter's first forays into songwriting was so odd it baffled his fans. He wrote a piece for the English comedian and singer Charlie Drake, who it has to be said had once enjoyed a parallel career as a hit maker. As far back as 1958 his version of the Bobby Darin hit 'Splish Splash' had graced the Top Ten and 'My Boomerang Won't Come Back' had got to Number 14 in 1961. But it seemed an odd idea.

"I just wanted to do a thing with Charlie Drake and wrote an entertaining song. Nothing particularly arty – it was just fun doing it." Martin and Gabriel had written a song that seemed suitable for animation and they wanted a certain character – Charlie seemed their man. They played him the song and he recorded it. This was all very well, but when would the public see their rock hero again? Did Peter miss performing? "Oh when I've been to see other people I feel like being up there again, but I don't miss it from day to day. I'm really excited about the prospect of video and would enjoy performing in a controlled situation like that."

Gabriel had found working in a competitive band, full of diverse personalities each with his own agenda, creatively restricting not to mention physically exhausting. And the final days with the band had, in truth, not been very enjoyable. Making videos and working with session men seemed much the best way to the promised land.

"I found some gigs with Genesis very depressing," admitted Gabriel. "They didn't want me to say anything until a replacement had been found. But I was getting very emotional with audiences at times. I'd come away wet eyed. On the last tour it did feel an important chapter of my life was about to change. It was highly charged with emotion."

It seemed like it would be a testing time for both Gabriel and Genesis in the coming months. Naturally the press and public were keen to see who would survive and prosper. It was this suggestion that drew the most animated response from Peter: "I'm a bit non-competitive in my attitude at the moment . . ." he began somewhat aloofly. "But in some ways I want to get something out as quickly as possible, before those miserable bastards!"

Gabriel might have given the impression of drift, but there were already signs that he knew exactly which way he was heading. "I don't particularly want a Peter Gabriel solo career as such. I'd like to develop the writing and the video side with a view to going back to recording when the circumstances are right. I wouldn't go back unless I was doing something (a) very strong and (b) totally original. It would have to be different from what I'd done before and from what anyone else was doing. There will be a percentage of people who won't like what I will do, but maybe some will, who didn't like what Genesis were into. I don't know. I know there are still things inside of me that I've tried to communicate before. I don't intend to be that critical of the group, but there are certain areas which weren't flexible. And for me, some of the fire had gone. In fact my absence has given them new found energy. This democratic thing – it didn't really work like that. In fact there was a lot of playing politics. One would pretend that certain things were someone else's ideas to get them through. That sort of thing – which got a bit silly."

Peter agreed that politics operated to some degree in all

bands, but he thought it especially odd that writing royalties in Genesis were shared out five ways, when generally only three people in the band were responsible for writing the words. "That seems to have changed since I left," he noted. He described how the various members of the band began to interact with each other on the road. "You begin to build up roles and ways of acting towards people, intending to side step certain challenges. And in a living situation it is particularly intense. You're stuck with them in the hotel as well! Mostly we were a happy band and you learn to live with and suppress dissatisfactions. All bands are compromises to a certain extent. We used to have arguments, but not so much later on."

Looking towards the future of Genesis Peter thought they could be a whole, strong band without him. He thought with *A Trick Of The Tail* they had achieved a great deal.

"I felt a little strange towards their first album without me. But I haven't felt sad about it." Many wondered why Peter hadn't just done a solo album, like guitarist Steve Hackett who successfully launched *The Voyage Of The Acolyte* and stayed on with Genesis. It was, after all, an option. "Oh, I see. Well not really," said Peter uneasily. "A lot of solo albums are diversion from the central direction, you can spread yourself too thin. I don't think I could have put my heart wholly into Genesis and get into a solo album."

Peter had by then written some 20 songs with his new partner Martin. One of these epics was called 'The Box' and another called 'People In Glass Houses'. Yet you couldn't help get the feeling that Gabriel was more interested in exploring the strange world of the unexplained than strumming the chords of yet another pop song. I wondered if he had ever used his psychic powers in a performance situation? He thought about this for several tense moments before he replied, which made his response all the more unsettling.

"Yes. Actually I'm sure there will be a mystically orientated rock star who will emerge in the next ten years. I'm not sure if it will be a particularly good thing because I'm not sure if rock music brings out the best in people. But it would be interesting. There are certain things I have felt during some performances resulting in the old shivers down the spine, when things were really happening. It could be the result of controllable energy flows. At times strange things seem to happen within me."

The Genesis experience, innocently embarked on while he was still a schoolboy and now abandoned while married and with children, had undoubtedly changed Peter. To outsiders he seemed more confident, more serious, less vague. But these were only surface impressions. His own self-analysis ran deeper.

"In some ways I've been a self-orientated, ambitious person and I'm trying to make myself more sensitive to other people's feelings – with what success I don't know. I feel more real now, although I'm still a dreamer in many ways."

Whatever was he going to do with all his old Genesis costumes – the headdresses and masks? "I'm going to go down to the village and frighten all the children," he grinned. "Or busk the queues outside the next Genesis gig!"

VI

EXPECT THE UNEXPECTED

DRASTIC UPHEAVAL ACCOMPANIED the agonised birth pangs of punk rock in 1976. Yet despite the mighty tumult about such heavily publicised bands as The Sex Pistols, in its own parallel universe, rock music continued to evolve, satisfying the special needs of a large and hungry audience. While the media speculated about the importance of such issues as spitting and safety pins, the public at large were still consuming music with more than superficial appeal, particularly in America, where Gabriel began his long awaited return to 'live' performance.

During the fag end of the Seventies, Gabriel deliberately steered himself away from the trappings of stardom. He was more determined than ever to be accepted as a serious artist with something useful and important to say. The world might be changing around him; the mood and climate might even seem to swing against him, as it did to so many other artists who had only just reached maturity. However Gabriel was one of those artists who himself created change, in a form that had lasting value.

Although never a prolific artist he set about recording the first of four solo albums with encouraging diligence. Each one was called simply *Peter Gabriel*. He had his reasons. The old 'same title' ploy was based on Peter's notion that instead of using entirely different LP covers each time, he would stick to a single brand image. Said Peter: "My idea was that it should be like a magazine that appears once in a while. I thought too often groups would try and present their latest work as 'new' and 'startlingly different' a bit like marketing soap powder, which more often than not, is exactly the same as the other brand. So I thought I would make them look very similar."

This was relevant in the age of the 12 inch LP whose covers acted as a selling point and often became a classic piece of popular art. The advent of the CD in a plastic jewel box has since regretfully reduced the importance of album art. But a good cover can still help trumpet an artists' intentions as well as any advertising campaign.

The new man who emerged from the vegetable patch with shorn and shaven head was now determined to do things his own way. No longer would fellow musos snap at his heels and snarl: "No, you can't write a rock opera; no you can't write a film script – no you can't fly from a high wire." He would have musicians about him who were sympathetic to his aims and he would get the results he craved. Gabriel would also be the ultimate DIY man about rock. If anything went seriously wrong, he would only have himself to blame. He was in the same situation as several other singers from famous bands confronted by the need to establish 'a brand new me'. It happened to Roger Daltrey during The Who's periods of inactivity and to Robert Plant when Led Zeppelin broke up.

Gabriel fashioned himself a much more convincing solo career than his peers. And he was quick to establish himself as his own man – with principles that weren't about to be compromised. It was clear that he wouldn't offer the world a Genesis Mk II with batwings and fox heads, however much people yearned for the good old days. (And they did yearn. At the first Genesis concert without Peter, a man appeared in the audience wearing a set of his own carefully constructed batwings, and stood glaring at the band throughout the performance.) The new Gabriel would be a songwriter, a creative, more serious artist, whose lyrics would reflect his inner feelings in a more cohesive form. There would be powerful concepts . . . but no more whirling snakes.

Said Peter: "I was very aware after I left Genesis that my reputation as an artist was more as a wearer of flowers than as a musician. So I decided to spend some years in the wilderness to get the musical foundation sorted out."

Peter was not alone in his wilderness. He had Jill and Anna and life in the country was pleasant. Yet Jill too had been affected by the tumult of events that surrounded Gabriel and the band over the previous five years, climaxing with Peter's abrupt departure. Peter's references to being "more sensitive to other people's feelings" doubtless related as much to Jill as to Genesis.

Peter and Jill came from similar backgrounds and education but this did not mean they were conventional people, nor instantly compatible. Both were rebels in their own quiet ways, and both would find marriage a difficult discipline. Jill was the daughter of Sir Phillip Moore, Deputy High Commissioner of Singapore. He and his family lived in the Far East for seven years, enjoying the privileged lifestyle accorded those of high rank who worked for Government. On their return to England in the mid-Sixties, the Moores took up residence in Surrey where Mr. Moore began working for the Ministry Of Defence. He later became elevated to the post of the Queen's assistant private secretary. Jill was sent to St. Catherine's girls public school which was quite near Charterhouse in Guildford. It was while attending a party that she first met the hippie boy from Charterhouse. Peter Gabriel was then just 16 and Jill was 15. Peter was self-conscious, still convinced he was overweight and spotty. Jill thought he looked just fine and when he asked her to dance their romance blossomed.

A keen sports player who did well academically at school, Jill was eventually lured into the world of pop music through her association with the strange young public schoolboy. She found herself moving inexorably away from an energetic, jolly hockey stick lifestyle into a world of idleness, sloth and hangovers. Not that Jill was necessarily a slothful, idle person herself, but beat musicians were undoubtedly a breed apart. They thought nothing of drinking brown ale from bottles, smoking hand rolled cigarettes and staying up all night. It was all rather coarse but terribly tempting. Peter was already singing in groups. He was fun to be around. But Jill would quickly learn what it meant to be for ever waiting for the artist to come off stage.

She found the youth with piercing eyes fascinating, but it was difficult for them to meet on a regular basis. Peter was still under the strict regime at Charterhouse and in any case her parents did not approve of such liaisons. As a result dating took place in secret but later, when Peter left school and moved to London, Jill was able to travel up to town to visit him. During the early days of Genesis they remained just good friends. Jill went to the Guildhall School of Music and she too left home to find a flat in town. Her parents, meanwhile, moved to London and took up residence in the grace and favour home near Kensington Palace – the apartment Peter believed was haunted and where we once met for breakfast.

As a couple on the periphery of the royal family they were sometimes invited to special occasions. Jill was invited to a ball at Balmoral where she danced with Prince Charles and Peter danced with Princess Anne. After a lengthy courtship the couple decided to get engaged, causing both their respective parents some concern. The fears were mainly grounded in the fact that Peter – a trainee pop singer – was extremely broke. Nevertheless they got over the shock and Peter was welcomed into the fold.

The wedding took place at St. James' Chapel on March 17, 1971 followed by a reception at St. James' Palace. Guests representing the upper class establishment wore top hats and tails while rock musicians and record company executives sported hippie clothes. The sight of a burly Tony Stratton-Smith in top hat and long hair was a cause for considerable mirth. Peter had not been keen on the idea of a wedding at the Chapel but gave way to Jill's father's wishes. At first the couple lived in a flat in Wandsworth, before moving to Campden Hill Road, Notting Hill Gate. For a while Jill got a job teaching at the Barbara Speake Stage School where Phil Collins had been a pupil. It gave her a life outside the sphere of Peter's activities as an itinerant musician.

Teaching other people's children encouraged her to think of starting a family of her own and by the time Peter was on tour of America during *Selling England By The Pound*, Jill was pregnant. She decided to join him on the tour and found it was just as difficult as she had been warned. While she wanted to be with her husband, he was busy either performing, writing, being interviewed, courted and fawned upon by fans. She reacted in a way that seemed more a cry for help than an act of rebellion. While travelling with the band she developed a relationship with one of the band's roadies. She found it difficult being in the shadow of a rock star and this perhaps was her way of gaining attention.

It was all very painful. She found herself resenting Peter's fame and dreamt about being a star herself. As the roadie involved happened to be one of Peter's friends, it was a cause of anguish all round. Despite these pressures Jill carried on travelling with the band until she was into her seventh month of pregnancy. She then left Peter to carry on working while she returned to England to live on her own at their new home near Bath. There was little chance for the couple to get together and settle their problems. Even when Peter came back from the States, he had to go to Headley Grange where the band were working, to help write *The Lamb Lies Down On Broadway*.

While all this was going on, he was still debating whether to leave Genesis and try his hand at writing a screenplay with William Friedkin. It was no wonder their marriage was under strain. Peter was assailed by doubts and torments. When Anna was born Peter decided to take her and Jill with him on tour to the States for *The Lamb* shows, even though their daughter was just three months old. Friends cooed over the baby who they thought had Peter's eyes. It was a less than ideal situation, taking a small baby on the road with a rock band, but it was Peter's way of spelling out to Jill the kind of pressure and conditions he had to endure at work.

After this bout of rushing to gigs, hanging out in hotels and catching flights, and only catching a glimpse of Peter when he was on stage or being interviewed, Jill's greatest wish was to get away from the whole situation. She went on holiday on her own for a couple of weeks. It seemed they were on the verge of separating. She had married a rock star who many idolised, but felt she couldn't find a way through to him. Eventually she came back to rejoin Peter and Anna at the cottage in Bath. In a final attempt to express her own individuality she cut off her beautiful full length hair. Peter's swift reaction was to shave his own head. And so it was that Peter Gabriel, who had yearned for stardom since childhood, now found fame no defence against a form of rejection by both his band and his wife. It seemed all this was being caused by a celebrity status that others found hard to handle. It would put a strain on anybody. His urgent need to seek refuge in anonymity became easier to understand. In the end Peter and Jill stayed together and had another child, Melanie, born in August, 1976.

His personal life now apparently back on course, he began

work on his crucial first album. The first album to be titled simply *Peter Gabriel* was recorded at Soundstage Studios in Toronto, Canada, in the autumn of 1976 under the auspices of producer Bob Ezrin who had previously worked with Alice Cooper and Kiss. He seemed like an unlikely choice but Ezrin was good at keeping discipline in the studio, even if his upfront attitude sometimes upset the artists. He was introduced to Peter by Neil Bogart of Casablanca Records. Said Peter in 1977: "Bob Ezrin wasn't particularly in love with Genesis' music or me, but of all the people I'd met, his ideas seemed to be the most in keeping with what I wanted from the album – to keep it simple, direct and personal. The main thing was trying to get it to sound different from Genesis. I wanted to select songs that would be different in approach and go for a much simpler thing than we had done in Genesis. I wanted the songs to stand up so that if you heard them with just one instrument and the voice, they would still be good."

Peter assembled a cast of first class musicians including synthesiser player Larry Fast, his hero Robert Fripp (guitar), Tony Levin (bass) and Alan Schwartzberg (drums). Dick Wagner played guitar on some of the tracks and the London Symphony Orchestra was used to flesh out the sound during further sessions at Morgan Studios, London. The album, released in February, 1977, proved to be a complete vindication of Gabriel's decision to alter course and go solo. There was huge interest in what he had come up with after the highly publicised split and few were disappointed with the results.

No doubt he had some anxious moments, particularly about working with mainly American musicians who hadn't really heard much about his past work with Genesis. But this was no bad thing. Peter could introduce those fresh ideas, which he had been mulling over since quitting Genesis. He had new things to say about the use of sound, the way drums were played and the use of instruments like the synthesizer. And of course he also had a lot of excellent new songs just waiting to be made into flesh.

The first to be unveiled was 'Moribund The Bürgermeister' which began with a strong drum machine type rhythm, an important feature of much of Peter's future work. The song, about the phenomena of St. Vitus Dance, had just enough storytelling to placate his older fans.

His *sotto voce* warning cry as the Burgermeister – 'I WILL find out' – was vintage Gabriel. The song had been inspired by a book about medieval ailments and epidemics. St. Vitus Dance is a nervous disorder which attacks mainly young children causing them to develop strange jerking motions. Some 500 years ago there was an epidemic of crazed dancing throughout Europe (a form of Gothic rave culture) and the victims went to the chapels of St. Vitus, a saint who could hopefully cure the affliction and where dancers could buy goatskins of water for ten groats each.

The second track was the hauntingly melodic 'Solsbury Hill' which became an instant hit. It remains one of Gabriel's most popular and appealing songs. Peter had at a stroke erased memories of the contortions of *The Lamb* and rocketed forward into a new era of tightly written, miniature masterpieces. Many thought the line "I was feeling part of the scenery – I walked right out of the machinery" was a direct reference to his departure from Genesis. The hill in question was about half a mile from Peter's home where he often went walking to ponder on the meaning of life. Feelings about the loss of childhood innocence permeate the song, which can best be interpreted as an allegory for his traumatic exit from the band and the life he had given up in the quest for new experiences.

'Solsbury Hill' went to Number 13 in the UK charts. Astonishingly it wasn't a chart item in America and Peter wouldn't have a hit there until 'Shock The Monkey' charted in 1982.

Hard on the heels of 'Solsbury Hill' was the equally compelling 'Modern Love', a real rocker complete with battering drums and yelling vocals which includes the line "I twisted my penis – love can be a strain." 'Excuse Me' was a quirky little barber shop vocal interlude which develops into a jolly two beat rhythm in best Randy Newman style, on which Peter proclaims: "I'm not the man I used to be – someone else crept in . . . I wanna be alone." 'Humdrum' was a fine, moving ballad with Peter singing at his mature best while 'Slowburn' was slightly more frantic, disjointed and full of mood swings. The remaining gems on this impressive début were the bluesy 'Waiting For The Big One', a stomping 'Down The Dolce Vita' (complete with expensive orchestral flourishes) and the superb 'Here Comes The Flood'. Both these pieces were linked to themes about the aborted 'Mozo' project, Mozo being described as a stranger "who tends to leave tumult in his wake".

Peter was obviously enjoying his freedom and said of this first batch of songs: "A lot of my solo stuff is very emotional. Genesis wasn't a platform for personal songs; you couldn't have a good dose of self-pity!" Peter experienced surprise that 'Solsbury Hill' became such a hit. "At one point it wasn't even going to be on the album. On 'Here Comes The Flood' I was referring to a mental flood – a release, a wash over the mind, not necessarily the land. A downhill course which leads to disaster."

Peter imagined a telepathic society where people could read each other's mind and the problems this would cause. "Of course in such a situation there would be no real change for people who have been honest and open with whatever is in their minds, but those who have been rather two-faced and who have kept their thoughts hidden would find it very difficult."

The album got to Number 7 in the UK charts and in March, 1977 Peter began his first solo tour of North America under the banner 'Expect The Unexpected'. The second major phase in his career was now well underway. There were 20 dates to play, on which Peter was backed by the musicians featured on the album.

At a memorable concert at New York's Palladium Theatre, Peter was supported by the rising stars Television, who were given a surprisingly hard time by their home town audience. Gabriel was the main attraction as far as fans were concerned. He put on a blockbuster show. Stripping away the trappings of Genesis he projected himself as a passionate new entity who won over a noisy audience simply with the power of his singing and the breadth of his material. During the show Peter suddenly disappeared from the stage only to reappear lying like a Cheshire cat on one of the balconies, singing through a radio microphone. He then pranced out into the audience, pursued by security guards, still singing and sometimes disappearing under a sea of clutching hands.

It seemed clear that Peter stood on the brink of tremendous success in America. The reaction of the fans was heartwarming as they cheered 'Solsbury Hill' to the rafters. He was busy converting audiences who had either never heard of him before or had simply resisted the overtures of his previous band. Among the other songs performed at that breakthrough concert were 'Moribund The Bürgermeister' and a soulful 'cover' of Marvin Gaye's 'Ain't That Peculiar'. He made only one concession to faithful Genesis followers by appearing in a leather jacket to sing 'Back In New York City' from *The Lamb Lies Down On Broadway*.

His album leapt to Number 38 in the US charts but 'Solsbury Hill' only scraped in at Number 68 – a disappointing hiccup. Worse was to come when 'Modern Love' failed to chart at all in the UK. In April Gabriel made his début London appearance with a band including Robert Fripp on guitar, who preferred to remain discreetly hidden in the background. He adopted the pseudonym Dusty Roads and skulked behind the speakers to avoid detection. It seemed he had been unhappy with Bob Ezrin's style of production on the album and wanted to distance himself from the guitar solos he'd played. In contrast to Fripp's anonymity it was during this period that Peter first began his very physical contact with audiences. It was a brave step but he was usually accompanied by a minder on his more dangerous forays. Even this was no guarantee of safety. Recalls Peter: "The first night I went running out into the audience our roadie Chip was sent to look after me and make sure I got back onto the stage. One of the house security men saw this guy following me and thought he was trouble. They bopped him. There was our security man being beaten up by the house security man while I was poncing away totally unaware of what was going on. Some nights I didn't think I'd get back on stage and I've since doubled my life insurance. At some places the audiences were very polite, stayed in their seats and shook my hand. At other places they mobbed me. But I think if you stay on stage and seem to be above the audience, that invites much more aggressive tendencies. If you walk around being vulnerable, then people are very friendly. I'm not putting over any big superstar thing so there's nothing to hit out at. At least that's what I tell myself as I go in wearing my bullet-proof vest."

In the autumn of 1977 at the height of a 'punk rock' boom, Peter offered the public his own alternative brand of music, touring the UK to a rapturous reception. By October Gabriel and the band had completed a full European tour. It looked like a successful launch, but closer inspection of the books showed Gabriel's organisation had made a loss of £100,000. Undeterred he vowed to press on and record a second album, this time with his friend Bob Fripp producing, rather than Bob Ezrin.

Work began in the spring of 1978 at Relight Studios, Hilvarenbeek, Holland, and at The Hit Factory in New York. The personnel included Peter on vocals, organ, piano and synthesizer, Roy Bittan (keyboards), Jerry Marotta (drums), Tony Levin (bass), Sid McGinnis and Robert Fripp (guitars), Larry Fast (synths), Timmy Capello (sax) and George Marge (recorders).

Gabriel had been a fan of Fripp's since the days of King Crimson and their album *In The Court Of The Crimson King*. He was anxious to work with the mastermind and utilise his more minimalist studio techniques. This resulted in a much looser product than Ezrin's album but Atlantic Records executives were displeased with *Peter Gabriel (2)*. To them it lacked obvious hits like 'Solsbury Hill' even though there was no shortage of imaginative songs and Gabriel was not averse to cutting a rug when required. A stomping 'On The Air' had a striking new wave style vocal and 'DIY' was equally up beat, although the drum sound was rather 'Seventies studio rock' – a bit muddy and tacky. It was the very sound Gabriel would set about replacing on his next album.

'DIY' was intended to have a touch of punk simplicity. More importantly the lyrics were a battle cry for people to try to exert their independence and not rely on others. "Don't tell me what I'll do, 'cos I won't" sang Peter, "Don't tell me to believe in you, 'cos I don't." This was very typical of a personality Phil Collins understood well. Opined Phil: "Peter has always been a man of principles and sometimes he's too much that way for his own good and will stick to his principles dogmatically and be really stubborn with it."

Another of Peter's musician friends, guitarist David Rhodes expresses the same opinion: "He can be stubborn but it's never in a very noisy way. He always gets what he wants. He holds out for things."

'Mother Of Violence' was a beautiful and very restrained performance, originally conceived by Peter and Jill as a children's Christmas carol. 'Indigo' the first track on side two of the vinyl

LP attempted to convey the mood of a dying father coming to terms with death. Peter says that he was partly inspired here by the classic 'Old Man River', a ponderous tune invariably played to audiences on their way out from Gabriel concerts.

'A Wonderful Day In A One-Way World' proved rather gimmicky and featured some unfortunate slide guitar. Despite all the grumbles about Ezrin, the second album was technically inferior and generally lacked the focus of the first.

Its best moments were to be found on 'White Shadow' and the lively 'Animal Magic', a song about the politics of both bedroom and battlefield which contains the ironic line "I'm joining The Professionals – I wanna be a man", 'The Professionals' being a familiar Seventies' advertising slogan for the British Army. Among the remaining songs 'Exposure', 'Flotsam And Jetsam', 'Perspective' and 'Home Sweet Home' were less satisfactory, at least to those seeking the quick thrills of rock'n'roll. This was heavy stuff and not to everyone's taste.

'Exposure' was one of the 'Mozo' songs essentially about the struggle for salvation and this stark piece was co-written with Robert Fripp, who later named his 1979 album 'Exposure'. This album also contained another alternative version of 'Here Comes The Flood' sung by Peter with a mixture of restraint and passion.

Released in June 1978 the new Gabriel album was not greeted with universal enthusiasm. The single 'DIY' failed to chart even when it was re-mixed. Producer Fripp thought Peter had been trying to be too sophisticated in his approach to the album and said he was unable to make up his mind decisively in the studio. But it had a brilliant cover. The first *Peter Gabriel* album featured an effective two-tone picture of Peter sitting inside a rain-spattered car, droplets coalescing attractively on the polished surface. The new album showed Peter's outstretched fingers apparently ripping through the surface of his own photograph.

Gabriel was quite defensive when countering criticism. "I refuse to see it as anything other than a pop album. That's what I went in to make and that's what it is. It's more spontaneous. There are some rough edges and some mistakes but leaving them in makes it more alive. There is more synthesizer on the second album but it's used in a different way. It's used less like a string section. On the next one I want to try a couple of things built up entirely from synthesizers."

It was typical of Peter that he saw his albums as a series of canvases on which he could experiment, using different colours from his musical palette. However his record company didn't see matters in quite the same light. After a discreet elapse of time Peter re-evaluated his work with Fripp and said: "Robert Fripp is probably still my favourite guitar player – he has a menace and he'll cast his shadow over what he's doing and give it an edge that I like very much. But as a producer I don't think it worked too well. Neither he nor I ended up that satisfied with the second album."

In September Peter supported Frank Zappa and The Tubes at Knebworth, Hertfordshire (scene of many an historic concert). Peter was now sporting his shaven head style which many thought made him look ugly and aggressive. It was certainly a jump from the long-haired lover from Charterhouse but the new image was more in keeping with the bad-tempered times. Punk was still lacerating the music industry and Peter was induced to perform a show with The Stranglers at Battersea Park. He went down very well with crowds grown used to new wave bands who seemed surprised that music could still contain strands of quality and threads of intelligence.

Said Peter: "I wanted to play before The Stranglers because they were considered to be a 'punk band', you know, dangerous and anti-establishment. I was interested in playing to a punk audience and seeing how I'd go down with them. In the end it was fine. I went down really well and enjoyed it."

Soon after these shows he returned to America under new management. After negotiations at Charisma, their label manager Gail Colson took Peter under her wing and would prove a trusty ally even if she was sceptical about some of his wilder fancies. He came back to England at Christmas to play seven dates at the Odeon Hammersmith. One of the shows featured Tom Robinson, rising star and gay activist who had scored a Top 5 UK hit with '2-4-6-8 Motorway' in October, 1977. Promoter Harvey Goldsmith had accidentally double booked both artists for Christmas Eve and they agreed to split the date between them. Tom sang 'Solsbury Hill' and Peter sang 'Hold Out' as they tried out each other's musical clothes. The all-star backing band included Elton John on piano, Phil Collins on drums, with Paul Jones on harmonica. A real super group! It was a real Christmas treat and showed a Gabriel more relaxed than at any time in years.

A childhood reading dodgy public school stories like *The Fifth Form At St. Dominic's* seemed to have prepared me for this moment. In my review I wrote: "Tom, the brotherly fifth-form prefect, took Peter, the Owl Of The Remove, under his wing and between them they presented a bold front to the school bullies in the audience. The piano player, an oik from the senior school called Elton John, gave his keyboard a severe thrashing, his percussive power adding to an already impressive rhythm team under the tutelage of the old master Phil Collins. The whole evening was just full of surprises. It was intriguing to hear Rob and Gab (as they were billed) swap songs, although Tom had a struggle singing Peter's tricky 'Solsbury Hill'."

After the success of the 'Rob And Gab Xmas 78' show Peter started planning his third album. He acquired the lease to a manor farm near Bath in 1979 which meant he could work at home, using a mobile studio. A band called Random Hold had grabbed Gabriels' attention and he contacted their singer, songwriter and guitarist David Rhodes. It was the start of a long relationship. He came to rehearse with Peter at Bath and eventually David Rhodes played guitar on the new album alongside Dusty Roads, aka Robert Fripp. Jerry Marotta and Phil Collins contributed to Peter's latest epic which proved to be the most ground breaking thus far and included such important new works as 'Intruder', 'I Don't Remember', 'Games Without Frontiers' and 'Biko'.

The use of two drummers was necessitated when Marotta went back to the States and Phil offered to help out. He soon found himself facing a challenge. Peter wanted to take all the cymbals away when sessions began. It was the first time they'd recorded together since *The Lamb* and Gabriel's ideas about percussion seemed outlandish but soon began to make sense. He simply wanted to utilise the ambient power of the 'live' drum kit and give it extra studio punch. With the tyranny of the crash and ride cymbals cluttering up the sound, the pure rhythm of the drums creating clearly defined patterns would cut through. Cue the next twenty years of studio drum sounds.

Something had to be done to break the stranglehold of sound engineers who had consistently muffled drum kits with gaffa tape and old blankets in the mistaken belief this was the only way to deal with uncontrollable frequencies. John Bonham had shown the way with his power house performance on 'When The Levee Breaks' with Led Zeppelin. Now Peter and Phil would introduce a whole new drum sound. When Phil began fooling around on his kit in the studio, producer Steve Lilly-white and engineer Hugh Padgham discovered a remarkable new effect being created by a device called a gate compressor unit. The sound coming through the headphones and over the speakers was 'gated reverb' which cut off the natural reverberation of the drums. Peter spotted the sound and insisted they record a whole chunk of it. He was inspired to write a piece using the sound which resulted in 'Intruder' the powerful opening salvo on *Peter Gabriel (3)*.

Although it doesn't sound quite so revolutionary today, compared to the sound on *(2)* it was a revelation. The drums locked into a heavy groove, without so much as a splash cymbal to disturb the pulse. It was the dawn of a new era, confirmed by Phil Collins' use of the sound on his hit single 'In The Air Tonight'. Recalled Phil later: "I thought it was a very brave idea not to have cymbals. It made you think!"

The dark, angular and secretive sounding 'Intruder' seemed like mindboggling stuff, especially to nervous record company promotions men. The uncompromising material unveiled on the new album, particularly tracks like 'No Self Control' and 'Biko' resulted in a crisis.

Recalls Peter: "The album was supposed to come out in February. The problem was Atlantic heard it and didn't like it." A&R director John Kalodner, still entrenched in Doobie Brothers style rock'n'roll called it "commercial suicide" and the company decided to drop Peter from their label. The chief executives, including Atlantic boss Ahmet Ertegun, were particularly displeased with 'Biko' and couldn't understand how the record buying public could possibly be interested in Steve Biko, a murdered South African political activist. Another important piece of work on the album, 'Family Snapshot', about an assassin and his victim, was inspired by the man who had shot Governor George Wallace of Alabama. It didn't go down too well with Atlantic either. The label passed on the album – a decision they later regretted.

It was a bitter blow to Peter and his management, but after some hasty negotiations the offending record was eventually released in the UK on Charisma in June, 1980 and on Mercury in the States. Despite the controversy, the third album was to prove a turning point and went on to sell double the amount of the second album and helped establish Peter as a major international artist. It contained not only his most powerful performances like 'I Don't Remember' but featured some of the tightest and most satisfying playing by his fellow musicians, whose style and approach had taken a quantum leap forward. 'I Don't Remember' heard 18 years later still sounds fresh and vibrant. 'Biko' with its strong political theme became one of Peter's most important musical statements. Peter explained that he could identify with Steve Biko because he seemed a very able, articulate and intelligent leader of youth. "I was really shocked when I heard that he had been killed. I am not a political person but this was just something that I wanted to write about. When I started getting into these sort of African rhythms it seemed appropriate. Then I did a lot of research on him and the song was completed."

The news of Biko's death led to Peter embarking on a commitment to the cause of human rights for which he has since campaigned assiduously. A performance of the song 'Biko' was aired during Gabriel's appearance on the 1979 Reading Rock Festival. Peter had a rather unenviable slot, appearing on a Sunday afternoon amidst a host of heavy rockers like Molly Hatchett, Whitesnake and The Ramones. He also came on during daylight and his arrival on stage, hidden inside a large box did not exactly blow the minds of a rather restless crowd. "Come out Peter, we know you are in there," yelled a fan somewhat derisively.

Yet as the festival programme notes stated: "We have come to expect the unexpected from Peter Gabriel." Peter himself offered some thoughts about his aims and intentions: "*In my own head I've always been a pop songwriter with ambitions to extend. For me one of the most important things was to try and get some credibility as a writer, because in the old days of Genesis, people often assumed I wrote everything because I was the front man. Then when I left and the group sounded more or less the same they began to question my contribution."*

Ultimately Peter went down well at Reading and was backed by Phil Collins who sang on selections from *The Lamb* for old times' sake. But during the keynote performance of 'Biko' with its somnolent, African rhythms heavy with foreboding, you couldn't help but get the sneaking feeling that the boozy festival crowd would have been happier with a dose of good ole rock'n'roll. It transpired that Peter hadn't actually completed the lyrics to the song and was largely making it up as he went along, which perhaps explained why the broad masses found it hard to understand.

The slow and mournful 'Biko' was ultimately perceived as a powerful piece, but Peter would score his first Top Ten hit as a solo artist with the more accessible 'Games Without Frontiers', a wryly humorous song culled from the album that got to Number 4 in the UK charts in April 1980. Peter was backed by Kate Bush, one of a number of distinguished guests who included Paul Weller of The Jam and one of Britain's finest jazz saxophonists, Dick Morrissey. The song was noted for its whistling chorus, provided by Gabriel, Lillywhite and Padgham.

Said Peter: " 'Games Without Frontiers' was about *It's A Knockout* (the popular European TV game show). I was pointing out the almost childish activities of those adults behaving in such a way, by trying to be the best nation in the competition. Aggressive, somewhat childish behaviour in adult costume and some territorial battles take place not merely on that TV programme but in other situations as well."

Peter had approached the third album in quite a different way from his previous works. He had begun many of the tracks by writing the rhythm first. "Normally I approach them with chords and melody and perhaps lyrics, but on this album I had a small electronic drum machine on which I used to set up rhythms. I would keep a consistent flowing pattern then the song was written around it and then the lyrics were developing from the sort of insistent almost manic qualities that drum machines have."

Arrangements were built up in layers but after hours of studio work he might scrap many of the superfluous instrumental tracks. "On 'Lead A Normal Life' there were about 15 tracks going on and we wiped most of them, leaving two or three tracks at a time. Paul Weller was working in the next studio and there was one track on which we couldn't get the right guitar feel. Paul was able to go straight to it. The way he plays that rhythm stuff is amazing. I was lucky with this album to get the best musicians around."

Peter believed that words were as important as music in creating an atmosphere. "That was really what I think this album was about. It was about moods and atmospheres, less than specific meanings and melodies. There were certain things I was trying to do on the second album in terms of sound that I didn't get a chance to try until the third. Some of that is experimentation and involves fiddling around using a five quid amp, which we put a lot of the sounds through."

The album which Atlantic had turned down and later tried to buy back (without success) was top of the UK charts for two weeks in June 1980 and a month later got to Number 22 in the US charts, selling some 250,000 copies.

As a man at the forefront of new ideas, he had now suffered rejection from a less than sympathetic record company, but at least he had the last laugh. What he had not experienced was the kind of cruel abuse often meted out by hostile audiences. Peter Gabriel had mainly played to sympathetic fans and appreciative crowds since the earliest days of Genesis. But in 1980, just when his third album was finally released and doing well, he came up against the ugly face of intolerance while supporting Frank Zappa at a concert in Berlin.

It had seemed like a sensible matching of talents. Zappa, after all, was a pioneer of experimental ideas and should have brought along an open-minded audience. But it turned into a traumatic experience for Gabriel, more painful and probing perhaps than a whole course in self-awareness. Sections of the audience clearly didn't like Peter Gabriel or his music and were about to let him know it.

Gabriel: "People were throwing stuff at me and wanted to punch me. There was a guy yelling, 'English pig, go home!' I crawled up on stage and started to do 'Here Comes The Flood' which was literally the quietest number I had at that point, and that didn't work either. I walked off. It was my worst night ever as a performer. Up until then I'd always been afraid of it happening. Now it had happened. Once the hurt and the shock wore off I began to adopt a different frame of mind."

The next show was in Bremen, again with Frank Zappa, and even though it didn't go particularly well Peter felt relaxed and reasonably safe. "I began laughing and feeling at home and the crowd responded. In the end we did much better – it still wasn't fantastic – but I'd overcome my fear of being challenged, of being rejected by an audience."

After this burst of activity Peter seemed to fade from public view during 1981, perhaps to lick his wounds, but it was only the prelude to a storm of activity that would delight and some-times baffle both his closest followers and interested spectators from the outside world. Whatever happened during the Eighties, Gabriel would always be taking risks, coming up with new ideas and setting trends that would have immense impact on the record industry.

During 1981 Peter was engaging in plots and plans rather than performing. He had been hoping to make a film version of *The Lamb Lies Down On Broadway*, starring himself as Rael the Puerto Rican punk. He had already written a screenplay, and even asked Genesis to help re-record the music for a soundtrack but they demurred. He had invited the much admired film director Alajandro Jodorowsky (who had made *El Topo*) to work with him on the film. They had begun scriptwriting back in 1979 and it was hoped that Tony Stratton-Smith's Charisma Films would produce the *Lamb* movie. But problems with Atlantic Records in 1980 meant that it was difficult to raise the finance. Peter had hoped to film *The Lamb* during 1981 but lack of co-operation from Genesis and worse – lack of funds – effectively ended the project. However Peter's film aspirations were not entirely thwarted. He was asked by Hollywood director Martin Scorsese to contribute to the soundtrack of his proposed film *The Last Temptation Of Christ*. After rejection by major movie studios and all important distributors, it was eventually made in 1987 and opened in London and New York in August 1988. The soundtrack became the basis of one of Peter's most experimental albums *Passion* with a rich selection of musicians and singers, integrating many different styles of music.

Another top director Alan Parker also asked Peter to write the soundtrack for his movie *Birdy*. The pair had met in 1984 and

Parker, who had directed such films as *Midnight Express* and *Fame* turned out to be a Gabriel fan. Peter worked on the project with the assistance of Canadian producer Daniel Lanois who had worked on the U2 album *The Unforgettable Fire*. The soundtrack album was eventually released in March, 1985.

Back in July 1982 Peter had switched his attention from film back to music and set up WOMAD – The World Of Music Arts And Dance which held its first festival at Shepton Mallet, near Bath, Somerset. The bold idea was to bring to the attention of pop and rock audiences a plethora of talented artists from around the globe. It was the first public recognition of World Music, a movement which later became culturally important. Peter had the necessary courage to bring these artists to England, but it would cost him dear in terms of personal stress and financial worry. The festival would become a great success in later years, but the first event lost money, leaving Gabriel and the organisers in dire straits.

Peter had first come up with the idea two years earlier when he became excited by the ethnic sounds he'd been hearing and wanted to share them with others. He first realised the potential of such music when he heard an African band playing on a Dutch radio station he tuned into while he was searching for BBC's Radio 4.

He noted that such music had also been exploited in a clever way by bands like Talking Heads. Peter teamed up with like-minded souls, including Thomas Brooman who ran a music magazine in Bristol. They helped him organise the festival and locate the artists. Among the acts they most wanted were the Master Drummers Of Burundi but as more were added to the 'wish list' it was clear an ambitious outdoor event was needed, to be spread over six rather than just one day. The show was delayed until 1982 to allow the organisers time to negotiate with the artists and raise the necessary finance.

The untried team of enthusiasts soon found they had taken on a daunting task. Major companies refused to sponsor the event and no regular promoter would touch it. Even Peter's manager Gail Colson advised him against the project. But WEA Records agreed to offer an advance on royalties for a double album featuring Gabriel, Talking Heads and other participants. Eventually the six day festival was trimmed down to a three day event held between July 16 and 18 at Shepton Mallet and funded to the tune of £70,000. Even though it was cut down, the festival still remained a major attraction, involving the use of four stages and exhibitions featuring 300 artists from 21 countries. There were workshops, lectures, a fairground, art exhibitions and lots of fine food.

Nothing had been tried on this scale before, nothing that is that hadn't been sponsored by an entire Government or the United Nations. Although there were some big name acts on the bill including Peter Gabriel and Echo And The Bunnymen, local authority restrictions limited the pop groups to small indoor venues. This meant that despite selling all the tickets for these shows, the cash flow was limited. Only the more obscure acts from Indonesia and Egypt could play on the big stages outdoors. The show was to have been filmed by the BBC but they pulled out just a couple of weeks before showtime. This was the first of a series of problems to hit the show. The album was late, there was insufficient publicity and finally the expected crowds failed to materialise. Said Peter: "We had been fired up by our own imagination and enthusiasm and thought everybody else would be."

There were worried faces backstage as the full scale of the disaster sank in. They had to pay all the contractors, the artists and their airfares and there just wasn't enough income to pay for it all. Although Peter had put some of his own money into the project, it wasn't enough to fend off creditors who were owed nearly £200,000. "We ran into big debts that were beyond my resources."

Although much of the blame for the debacle lay at the door of the inexperienced organisers, Peter felt responsible and he was on the receiving end of much anger and even threats from those who felt they had been ripped off. "There was some very dodgy stuff going," recalls Peter. "The liquidators simply studied the list of those involved and I looked like the only target worth squeezing. It was quite an unpleasant experience. I suppose if you are living off other people's dying businesses, it's a strange business to be in anyway. When the shit hit the fan people identified me as the only fat cat worth jumping on so I got the aggro, a lot of flak and nasty calls. Jill actually got a death threat aimed at me, an anonymous caller saying, 'I'm going to kill you afterwards', and all that stuff. Very nasty. Not the sort of thing I want to live through again."

It was certainly a shock to the system and Peter realised he had been naïve in not appreciating the business risk, even though he fully believed in the concept. "The experience made me a little more worldly-wise and more cautious. I've not been involved in the management of WOMAD since then, except as an external advisor."

Despite the problems he remained proud of the first festival. "It was a wonderful turning point for me, despite the dark side. There was a sense of a pivotal event which was fantastic for the people who were there. We were naïve in that we were in a missionary state of extreme excitement. When you get swept away like that you're prone to being overambitious. But it was a bold experiment. In truth all the gut instincts were correct, we were just a little ahead of our time."

In the end Genesis came to the rescue. A band meeting was called and it was decided to help Peter out by staging a special reunion show at Milton Keynes Bowl later in the year. It was part of a Genesis tour and Peter would be invited to take part in a one-off fundraising show, back in his old role as the lead singer. It would be an historic event and an emotional occasion. Rehearsals took place in London and although Peter had never expected to be reunited with his old band, under the circumstances, it was the wisest course to take. Quite apart from getting out of a financial jam, it was a signal of reconciliation and Peter was touched that his old colleagues would want to help. The fact that the money raised was going to WOMAD made it all the more acceptable.

"That was wonderful and it kept the whole thing going," said Peter. It was decided to perform some old classics like 'The Knife' and 'Musical Box' and nearly 50,000 people came from all over the world to see the show held on October 2, 1982. Sadly it rained all day but the show was a great success. At one stage Phil took over as lead singer and Peter played the drums – a long cherished ambition finally fulfilled. Even Steve Hackett, long since departed from Genesis, turned up to play on 'I Know What I Like' and 'The Knife'.

Peter's financial future was saved and now he was determined to press on with his innovative ideas, often in the teeth of resistance and abuse. Yet this was the man American record company mogul David Geffen, who signed Peter in 1982, would call: "One of the world's major talents". During the Eighties Peter Gabriel would himself become a 'world musician' whose influences became ever more diverse. His travels would take him across the continents in search of new ideas as well as new audiences.

Reflected Peter: "On my passport it says 'musician'. I would have preferred 'humanist'. I'm not happy with the description because I'm not a very good musician. Lots of people suffer from being put into little boxes or compartments in terms of careers and people psychologically allow themselves to be restricted by the categories they put themselves into. So – I'm a humanist."

VII

A Song For Rosanna

ROCK'N'ROLL MYTHOLOGY DEMANDS that its stars and icons lead a life of non-stop anarchic hedonism. At least that was the perception when rock was young and both artists and their fans saw their role in terms of revolutionary, anti-establishment escapism. The concept of turning such activity into a lifelong career, with all its attendant demands on both the intellect and character, were slow to take root. The Sixties were a non-stop party for most of its heedless participants; certainly among the ravers of the pop scene, a characteristic of each new generation, who in turn thought theirs was the first to embrace this novel concept.

During the Seventies however, rock and pop, the great twin obsessions of the carefree and free-spending teenager, became a vast business, sucking in and spitting out its prey with ruthless efficiency. Peter Gabriel was determined not to become another of its victims. He would use the best of what commercial success had to offer and hopefully hang on to a normal life in the process. But as a self-proclaimed humanist he was prone to all the foibles and temptations that humans suffer. The highs and lows, the pain and pleasure would ultimately be reflected in his music. But even when undergoing enormous personal pressure, Gabriel the driven man would achieve much in the practical and physical sense – turning what many saw as flights of fancy into an extraordinary but very real world of his own creation.

The all important women in his life had to learn to find a role in that expanding Gabriel universe or find themselves mere orbiting satellites, providing heat and light, but never making full contact.

At the start of the Eighties Peter Gabriel seemed both happy, reasonably prosperous, and content while safely ensconced at

123

home in Bath with Jill and daughter Anna Marie and their latest addition Melanie. With his own small studio in a nearby cottage, Peter was able to keep close to both family and business. As his fortunes improved so the studio would move to a new location, and become one of the biggest and best in the country.

Apart from the occasional tour, he could stay close to the children, watch them grow up and share their fun, while satisfying his creative needs in the studio. Peter told journalist Ray Coleman in 1981: "For me family life is tremendously important. A lot of rock people become absent parents and I don't want to be one of those. It's important for the children to have a visible father." This may have been true, but it was around this time that Gabriel family life became more difficult as Peter and Jill found themselves drifting apart.

When Peter had lived in London he had to put up with neighbours complaining about the noise of his piano practice. Out in the country there were no such problems and he could when necessary get back into the thick of the music business by spending time in New York, his favourite city. Country living still meant he was cut off from lots of his old London based acquaintances. "My friendships have suffered. I lead an erratic life and there has been less socialising. But then I don't enjoy crowds or parties."

Needing more space for tape boxes, flasks of helium and disused fox heads, the 'idyllic' cottage in Bath became too confined for comfort. Peter decided to buy a large Victorian house near Solsbury Hill to increase the area available for both family and musical activities. The only problem was his wife Jill didn't like the new home. In fact she announced quite firmly that she hated it.

The vast echoing house was devoid of furniture and devoid of Peter most of the time, as he was away recording. Jill decided to move in with Gabriel at the studios where he was busy working away at the next album. She planned a role as a head cook and bottle washer for the crew and musicians. It was an attempt to improve their relations. While Peter presented a stable and ordered existence to the press, his personal life was actually beset with problems. His obsession with work, which after all depended on contracts being signed and deadlines met, resulted in him neglecting Jill. She in turn felt unable to cope with either Gabriel 'the star' (a role he had tried to banish during the post-*Lamb* period) or Gabriel the studio recluse. She tried to attract his attention by being omnipresent. But even this tactic didn't seem to work. They had known each other for so many years, since they were teenagers in fact, they became like an elderly couple, taking each other for granted, while gradually drifting apart.

Peter was aware of the situation that was developing and realised he had many lessons to learn. A marriage needs constant work to sustain it. Husbandry like gardening relies on tender loving care. As he would say later: "There is no such thing as neutral in a relationship. You're either in forward gear or reverse."

Alas it seemed the damage had already been done, thanks to trips abroad and long hours in the studio. When Peter flew off to America with the tapes of his new album to deliver to the Geffen label, he left behind a tangled situation. Jill was embarking on an affair with Peter's producer David Lord, who had worked as an engineer at Crescent Studios in Bath. During 1980 he began working as Peter's in-house sound engineer. Jill felt isolated by Peter's departure to New York and turned to David for company during her husband's continued absence. She found him fun to be with and their relationship continued all through the period Peter was engrossed in the WOMAD festival. He only learned about it after returning from another trip abroad.

As has since been revealed, he was extremely hurt on discovering of this liaison which inevitably led to a row between Lord and Gabriel. The tense atmosphere resulted in Jill leaving both men, and she took the children to a haven of peace in the Lake District, vowed to live there on her own, free of all entanglements. In time Peter would visit his family and they could at least speak to each other again. But instead of patching things up they only made more discoveries about apparent infidelities.

It transpired that Peter had formed a friendship with beautiful and feisty young American actress Rosanna Arquette, who specialised in *'femme fatale'* roles. She appeared in the motion picture triumph *Desperately Seeking Susan*, which introduced a bejewelled Madonna to the world, and would later achieve fame for her roles as 'Jodie' in *Pulp Fiction* and 'Gabrielle' in *Crash*.

In the resulting fire storm of emotions, guilt, shame and anger, that resulted from her discoveries, Jill gave way to thoughts of suicide and drove her car towards Solsbury Hill – the place that had meant so much to her and Peter in happier times, apparently intending to take an overdose. In the end her mission was thwarted by a road block. It was ironic. Peter's hit song had brought so much publicity and attention to the place, the local authorities had erected a barrier of clay to prevent a feared invasion of hippies for a rock festival. Jill came to her senses and later confirmed: "It was my first and last thought of suicide."

The conflicting sway of emotions and shifting loyalties continued through most of the decade. Jill and Peter would stay together until the autumn of 1987 when they finally separated and Peter once again began seeing Rosanna Arquette, until that relationship also foundered.

The impact of Arquette on Gabriel was profound. In many ways it appeared a hopeless match, and yet the huge differences in their personalities seemed to make Rosanna all the more attractive. The actress had worked with director Martin Scorsese, whom Peter had met in 1983 when they discussed the possibility of Gabriel writing film music for his movie project *The Last Temptation Of Christ*. Rosanna had appeared in Scorsese's section of the film *New York Stories* and later in his 1985 movie *After Hours*. She was outgoing, uninhibited and represented the sort of liberated values that Peter as a "tight assed Englishman" (to quote his own description) found appealing.

Her real name was Rosanna Lauren and she was born on August 10, 1959 in New York City, one of a family of five children. At age six she was going to anti-war rallies with her activist mother Mardi. Her father Lewis was an actor and director. At eight Rosanna appeared in her father's children's productions. She began her professional acting career as a teenager with bit parts in various TV shows and movies. Her sister Patricia Arquette, also an actress, developed her own career and most notably appeared with Johnny Depp in *Ed Wood*. As an avowed political activist and fundraiser, Rosanna's lifestyle was clearly influenced by her hippie childhood experiences. As a result of her wild attitudes and actions, she was dismissed by some movie business moguls as 'a flake' an expression she found highly offensive. But Rosanna would turn down plum roles in blockbuster movies, in order to appear in more artistic productions. It was a brave stance but she admitted it might have damaged her career. Meanwhile she cheerfully became known as 'The Queen of the Independent Scene'.

Rosanna had been involved in rock long before she met Peter Gabriel. She was dating Steve Pocaro, keyboard player with Toto, and such was her personal impact on the band they dedicated a song called simply 'Rosanna' to the actress. It was a big hit, won an award and got to Number 2 in the US *Billboard* chart in May, 1982.

During the early Eighties Arquette grew disenchanted with Hollywood and moved to Europe where she lived and worked in both Paris and London for a couple of years which gave her ample opportunity to see her new friend Peter Gabriel.

In 1983 Peter went on holiday to Antigua with Rosanna but continued to stay in contact with Jill and their children, unable to contemplate the idea of divorce. In 1984 Jill took their daughters to join her parents in Scotland, while Peter went to New York to see Rosanna. He was determined to make up his mind about who would be the main person in his life. On his return he told Jill he had decided to stay at home with her and they managed to patch things up. In 1985 Peter tried to pour oil on troubled waters by flying Jill to New York to meet Rosanna in the hope that they could all at least become friends. It was not a great success and Jill felt intimidated by the boisterous Rosanna. Then came a new twist: Rosanna found a new man, record producer and composer James Newton-Howard whom she later married. Still attempting rapprochement, Peter invited all four parties to lunch. Jill said later that the meeting had "intensely hysterical memories for me".

The pressure was too much and Peter and Jill finally separated in 1987 even after undergoing therapy and marriage guidance. Peter made contact with Rosanna again, who had in turn separated from Newton-Howard. During these difficult periods Peter slept on the floor of his office until he could find a new home. At least while he was alone he could lead a safe and commendably monastic existence.

His renewed liaison with Rosanna seemed to offer peace and fulfilment but instead proved fraught with yet more difficulties. She and Peter broke up again in 1992 after they had both been angered and embarrassed by some nude pictures of Arquette that had appeared in *Playboy* magazine in 1991. Rosanna indignantly told *USA Today*: "Those pictures were never meant for *Playboy*. They were extremely innocent and were never intended to be in a magazine. They were sold without my permission. I felt like I'd been raped." The pictures showed Rosanna frolicking in the sea. "I had people saying: 'Why did you take your clothes off?' I was just swimming!"

When she returned to America, having divorced her previous husband, she met and married Jon Sidell, a Geffen records A&R man. They now have a daughter Zoë Blue. Rosanna gave her acting career a kick start and in 1994 was cast as the tattooed and pierced bunny Jody in *Pulp Fiction* directed by Quentin Tarantino. Director David Cronenberg also cast her as Gabrielle the sexual adventurer in the controversial movie *Crash*. She plunged into work and vowed that her new baby was the most important event in her life.

Arquette finds it difficult now to talk about her years with Peter Gabriel but has described their relationship as "unstable". She claims to have left him because she felt the need to focus on her own work and career. Said Rosanna in 1997: "Peter and I had a very big affair for many years and it was very painful for a lot of people – including his wife. We lived together for three years in England. The most important thing was him – his life, his world. We had a misunderstanding and a falling out. We moved in different directions and lost touch for a while, but it healed and cleared up."

Rosanna obliquely referred to Gabriel when in an interview she was asked what drove her most crazy about men. "Emotional distance and workaholism. I'm not saying work isn't a good thing, but I hate when it takes the place of being emotionally there for somebody. A real relationship is not about dancing in the sunset – it's about moving through shit with each other. That's reality. It's sometimes so hard to let go of the fantasy, because we all really want that. I want both."

Peter himself made few public pronouncements on these

traumas but these relationships were the subject of many of his future songs. Like Phil Collins who also underwent the agony of broken marriage and divorce, Peter would find the best therapy in music. "Well I guess relationships are the one part of my life that is more of a struggle than most," he said in 1992. "I think that many things go extremely well for me, work and that area. Relationships have room for improvement. I came out of a broken marriage and then went into another intense relationship with Rosanna and that broke up as well. Therapy, which I'd started when the marriage went wrong, was something that I did for five years, initially as a couples group and then afterwards for three years as a singles group. That for me was enormously important and made me look at stuff within me that I particularly did not want to acknowledge. There was some anger and aggression in there that I hadn't fully owned up to."

Peter described therapy as enormously helpful, even though he initially found it hard to get accustomed to the idea. The hardest part was getting up in the morning for a 7.40 a.m. session – difficult for a musician used to staying up all hours. "I had the typical English reaction towards getting help of any sort. Any sort of therapy, baring your soul, admitting sickness, I have a natural fear and anxiety about doing anything like that and yet it's been enormously important to me and really enabled me to get out to the other side. I still carry a lot of the same stuff, but I'm much better equipped to handle things."

Added Peter: "Therapy is like car maintenance. Send yourself in to be serviced every few thousand miles and with any luck it stops major problems developing. It's much better than waiting for a smash and then trying to put the pieces together."

VIII

SECURITY

THE EIGHTIES WOULD prove to be an decade of challenge and change for Gabriel. The flower child of the Seventies, who cared more about people than politics, found himself afloat in the age of Thatcher, the Falklands War and inner city riots. The pleasant Victorian image of a dreamlike England reflected by those early Genesis albums became an increasingly distant memory amidst all the turmoil. As the Yuppie replaced the Punk as a dominant social figure, there was also an air of brash reality abroad. But Gabriel the dreamer was able to adapt and fit in with all these changes. Curiously enough Gabriel thrived in edgy, tense, confrontational situations. It may have been uncomfortable but it was just like his schooldays and latter-day experiences with Genesis. Adversity only seemed to increase his power and strength as he reacted sharply to outside stimuli.

Gabriel the artist, husband and lover tried to keep his mind on his work, balancing ambitions and desires with the need to pay bills. Fortunately he was able to call upon a life giving flow of royalties from past Genesis albums for support. But he would need to achieve even greater success if he was to finance grander, more visionary schemes. This would involve taking on the record business and turning its ways to his advantage. He was still wary about playing this particular game but less so as he grew older and longer in the tooth.

Fresh opportunities beckoned and Peter recalled: "I had the dilemma of knowing how to react to the prospect of record deals. It did disturb me a little. I didn't want to be hypocritical about it, but when you are not used to having money and suddenly face the prospect of having some, it requires some thought. Fame is fun and I sort of enjoy it at times, but I can't ever take it seriously. There's a part of rock that is based on mythology. Ego drives most of us but I like to keep that aspect of my personality in check. Ego problems can mess people up."

Most observers still categorised Peter Gabriel as a 'star' but as a maker of hit records he seemed to lack guile or even a clearly defined strategy. Gabriel's greatest hits were sometimes tracks chosen for him by wiser counsels at the record company, who could best hear what was marketable. "There are some tunes which are good singles like 'Games Without Frontiers'," he allowed. "But I don't steer myself that way. The single hits just happen. I could never say, 'I'm gong to sit down and write myself a hit song.' I do have pictures of where I want to go with my music but it takes a long time. I am a very slow worker."

He explained how he assembled his music – almost on an intuitive rather than a calculated basis – creating a collage of sounds and rhythms. On his last album he had begun writing with a different technique – using rhythm as a starting point. "That was because I'd been given some rhythm boxes to play with and they weren't programmable. You could put in your own patterns and that allowed me to put the African rhythms into 'Biko'."

Quite early into his solo career Peter had begun listening to African, Aboriginal and Balinese music with fresh ears. He was open to ideas and any intriguing new rhythms from the Third World, in particular, would be adapted to his own recordings. He'd make cassettes of sounds that interested him, put on the rhythm machine and start composing themes around them.

The simplicity of this approach, novel in 1982, would soon be emulated by a whole generation of bedroom recording engineers and cottage industry hit makers. It might be an overstatement to suggest that the new dance culture was directly inspired by Gabriel's example, but history clearly shows the hit makers of the new decade were only following in the footsteps of pioneers like Gabriel, who had seen what could be done with new technology.

Said Peter prophetically at the start of the decade: "I can hear in my head now a sort of music which involves a lot of percussion, very little regular drum kit and a lot of electronics, leaving the guitar and piano more naked. This is my ultimate direction. In 1975 my view was that I should get out of performing music but I drifted back in. I had nothing in my head about which route I was going to take. What has happened to me as a solo performer has happened completely naturally as I began writing. I thought I might simply write songs for a living, but ended up thinking I was the best person to perform my own work. And that's what happened."

Peter Gabriel's solo career might have been a lost cause had it not been for this overwhelming need to hear his ideas expressed in his own inimitable way and to flesh out the schemes that were the product of a highly developed imagination. Otherwise he might have preferred to rest and recuperate and for the rest of his natural days enjoy the solitude of stress-free life in the countryside.

That would have been unworthy of him and a waste of intellectual capacity. He had to rejoin the treadmill of recording and touring if only to help further his wider ambitions. It was a process that would lead to the creation of Gabriel's empire of sound, as altruistic but more ultimately productive than The Beatles' Apple organisation. It would also lead to the conclusion of his ultimate quest – unconsciously begun way back in the earliest days of Genesis and achieved in the teeth of adversity.

Peter recalls his mood during the immediate post-Genesis period: "For the first 18 months after leaving I wasn't thinking of functioning as a solo artist. It's my incredible method of writing that holds up my career. Sometimes I feel I am going round in circles, chasing my own tail. Being given the boot by Atlantic Records in America didn't help my reputation at that time. They just didn't rate my record's commercial chances. But when Mercury got hold of the record and worked really hard, suddenly I was an OK name and the third album outsold the first two by a long way."

It was ironic that some critics still pigeonholed Gabriel among the so-called elitists of rock and felt uncomfortable with his subject matter for songs, often deriding him as a calculating and self-indulgent poseur. It was hurtful, particularly to an artist for whom songwriting was an act of faith, not to mention a much needed catharsis and form of therapy that helped him express repressed feelings. Any one less inhuman, less calculating than Peter Gabriel would be hard to find, despite his paradoxical love of technology.

A good example of that overriding need for human contact lies with his practice of entering a theatre from the back of the stalls rather than from the stage. "Part of the reason for walking through the audience at the start of a show is to get eyeball to eyeball with everyone. They can clock me over the head as I'm going through to the stage if they want to, but often they don't realise it's me. Personally I don't believe in a sort of elite reserve of people who can make music which separates them from those who can't. Making music is no big deal really."

In September 1982 Charisma released the fourth album entitled simply *Peter Gabriel* which contained his first big American hit 'Shock The Monkey'. Released on the Geffen label in the States the single got to Number 29 in *Billboard*. The album tracks included 'The Rhythm Of The Heat', 'San Jacinto', 'I Have The Touch', 'The Family And The Fishing Net', 'Shock The Monkey', 'Lay Your Hands On Me', 'Wallflower' and 'Kiss Of Life'. Known as *Security* in America, it was first released for Geffen in the US. The label were unhappy about following in the *Peter Gabriel* album tradition and so were allowed to put *Security* stickers on the cover. Recorded at Crescent Studios in Bath it was produced by Gabriel in conjunction with David Lord. The musicians included Jerry Marotta, Tony Levin, Larry Fast, David Rhodes and Morris Pert. Peter also recorded a special German language version of the album.

The results of this collaboration were showcased on an hour long special edition of ITV's *The South Bank Show*, a popular arts programme which offered considerable insight into Gabriel's recording techniques and love for ethnic music. In the process Peter juxtaposed computerised techno ideas with rhythms from around the world, creating a riveting, at times hypnotic, if somewhat oppressive effect. This resulted in rather mixed reviews and some thought the album less appealing than previous works. It failed to get a very high chart rating on release, but 'Shock The Monkey', the first single culled from the album, helped to perk things up and was also nominated for a Grammy. It was also Peter's first single to do better in the States than in England. The follow up 'I Have The Touch' was coupled with non-album track 'Across The River'.

Although the songs all had thought provoking lyrics, Peter's approach to writing still seemed charmingly simplistic. He revealed that at the start of the project he had only an outline sketch for the words to each song. Said Gabriel: "I use odd sounds and noises from the voice, which I call Gabrielese. I think often that the naked sound of the voice is more emotive without lyrics." His intention at this juncture was to use his voice as a sound creator, rather like a human synthesizer. "I think we all make noises and particularly when we get involved or emotional about something, the colours and the tones of those noises change."

He told *Trouser Press* in 1983: "On this album I tried to create a sound library, mainly working with a Fairlight CMI synthesizer. We went to scrap yards, factories, wind tunnels and university engineering departments. But there is still a lot of stuff on the album played on conventional instruments." At one stage during recording Peter actually visited a junk yard and found a handy drainpipe he could blow into. The resultant sound was recorded onto the Fairlight and then played on a keyboard.

The lyrics to 'Lay Your Hands On Me' proved particularly controversial and some reviewers complained that Peter was displaying "Christ-like tendencies". However, the song was intended to be selfless rather than egotistical and was about the concepts of trust, healing and sacrifice. He explained: "It's been misconstrued with reviews saying that I'm acting like Jesus Christ and that's not what I'm trying to do at all. I am trying to involve the audience emotionally with the music. I feel it's an offering of trust to the audience. What an artist is trying to do is engage the viewer, the audience, the listener. I feel that at times I should be of use to people. What I like in other people's work is things that make me think about what I am doing – that activates my conscience, my imagination or my spirit."

The song 'San Jacinto' also had an interesting origin. It had been sparked by a meeting with an Apache Indian while Peter was in the States. Peter relayed the story while at his 1994 Glastonbury Festival appearance, explaining how he gave the Apache a lift to his apartment – which turned out to be on fire, the sort of situation that only Peter could encounter without seeming greatly surprised. The Indian wasn't too bothered either. Said Gabriel: "He seemed unconcerned with his possession, he was only concerned about his cat."

Peter and the Indian spent the night chatting and it turned out the mysterious stranger had escaped from a "trumped up murder charge". As a child the Indian had been initiated in the mountains by a medicine man armed with a sackload of rattlesnakes. As part of a ceremony the snakes were induced to bite the boy's arm and he was left on the mountainside to experience a vision. "If he got back down at the end of it, he was brave. If not, he was dead. Very simple. This is the story of what he came back to and what America has done to his culture."

The San Jacinto mountains are near Palm Springs in California. During his visit to this American paradise Peter could see the contrast between the expensive resort and the poorer Indian culture that survives close by. The latter proved on closer inspection to be spiritually richer than the world of swimming pools and golf courses. Said Peter: "I was trying to get a picture of the clash of cultures between this artificial white world of swimming pools and the mountains. Just around the corner are the Indian Canyons and the Indian reservations and for them the San Jacinto mountain is holy."

The opening track 'Rhythm Of The Heat' begins with mysterious chants over a hypnotic drone and reaches a climax with a thunder of tribal drumming. The thinking behind this piece is predicated on the African obsessions of Carl Gustav Jung, the noted Swiss psychiatrist (1875-1961). Peter had a strong interest in the works of Jung, a passion he shared with fellow recording artist Sting, and he was especially intrigued to read of Jung's exploits in Kenya where he lived for a while with a tribe of warriors. Taking part in a frenzied ceremony Jung became possessed by a powerful entity or spirit and had to plead with the warrior drummers to stop playing so that he could escape its malevolent grasp. Said Peter: "That was interesting, this great Western mind swept up by his own shadow."

Jung founded the analytical school of psychology and broadened the work of Sigmund Freud on psychoanalysis, interpreting mental and emotional disturbances as an attempt to find personal and spiritual wholeness. As a child he was prone to dreaming and fantasy which influenced his adult work. In that respect there are close parallels to Peter Gabriel's own experiences. Jung's book *Psychology Of The Unconscious* showed a link between ancient myths and psychotic fantasies, surely an appealing idea to the writer of *The Lamb Lies Down On Broadway*.

The hit song 'Shock The Monkey' contained the line 'shock the monkey to life' and some concluded this was about applying shock treatment to apes in cruel experiments. Peter however insisted it was 'a love song'. It was about the condition of jealousy that is often a trigger for man's animal instincts to surface in a relationship. The lyrics went further with the allegory as Peter sang "Fox the fox, rat on the rat . . . darling, don't you monkey with the monkey".

As with most of Peter's songs, the obvious, superficial meaning cloaks a deeper idea. Often the composer himself is still struggling to give space for the germ of an idea to grow and develop. For example the immensely moving 'Wallflower' has been described as Peter's response to the work of Amnesty International, containing his thoughts about political prisoners being confined to mental institutions. But it could be just another love song. Gabriel himself confirmed that the song was a direct reaction to the arrest of Lech Walesa, famed leader of Poland's Solidarity Movement. "They're trying to get you crazy – get you out of your head. They feed you scraps and they feed you lies, to lower your defences, no compromise" sings Peter in a voice filled with pain and grief as he describes the imprisonment of the brave by the cruel. "They put you in a box so you can't get heard, let your spirit stay unbroken, may you not be deterred." These simple heartfelt words have more relevance than acres of rock'n'roll jargon, but clearly mark the line between the young carefree Gabriel who led an altogether different existence, from the older, wiser man beset with the world's cares.

'I Have The Touch' is an examination of the reaction of supposedly reserved English people to close body contact, which he observes is often limited to a formal shaking of hands. Peter's own need to reach out is contrasted with the natural desire for space in a relationship. "The pushing of the people – I like it all so much . . . I move with the movement and have the touch," sings Peter on this pulsating anthem to "wanting contact."

Peter went on an extensive US tour with his band in 1982 to promote the album. Clad in Japanese martial arts outfits, the

band entered each venue from the back of the auditorium playing 'Rhythm Of The Heat' on marching drums, while waving
torches beamed over the audiences. During the show 'Lay Your
Hands On Me' became the basis for an extraordinary display by
Peter, in which he built on his earlier shock tactics of roaming
the audience. Instead of being the remote untouchable figure on
stage bathed in spotlights, Peter dived into the crowd, clutched
onto his fans and clambered over their seats.

Security should have created a sensation. Certainly it did well
enough, but events elsewhere tended to overshadow Gabriel's
efforts. During the early Eighties the pop world was mesmerised by the sudden success of Phil Collins in the wake of his
début solo album *Face Value*. Nobody was more surprised than
his old colleagues from Genesis. "Who could have predicted it
– eh?" was Mike Rutherford's sage comment at the height of
Collins mania.

Phil's decade-long run of hits began in 1981 with 'In The Air
Tonight' which rocketed to Number 2 in the UK, hotly pursued
by 'You Can't Hurry Love', 'I Don't Care Anymore', 'Easy
Lover', 'One More Night' and a host more. His albums stayed
on the charts for months and Phil achieved all his childhood
ambitions, becoming a movie actor, a hugely popular international pop superstar and a multi-millionaire in the process. At
the same time, he held on to his post as lead singer, drummer
and stand-up comic/compere with Genesis. It was an astound-
ing barrage of achievements and a tribute to Phil's bound-
less energy and creative enthusiasm. But where did it leave
the band's old singer, and his somewhat angst ridden songs
about political prisoners and obscure psychologists? Would the
man once hailed as the creative brain behind Genesis and cornerstone of their success take this lying down in his cabbage
patch?

Whatever else might be said about the self-effacing Mr.
Gabriel, he had his pride and competitive spirit. If in the
public's eyes there was to be a battle between Gabriel v. Collins,
then certainly Peter could hit back with his own brand of
commercial blockbuster success. So – it would just take a little
time – that's all.

In the meantime he would entertain the troops with a double
album *Peter Gabriel Plays Live* released in June 1983 and

devised to placate Geffen as an interim measure before the next studio album. It was a welcome set of performances nonetheless, including versions of 'The Rhythm Of The Heat', 'I Have The Touch', 'Not One Of Us', 'Family Snapshot', 'DIY', 'The Family And The Fishing Net', 'Intruder', 'I Go Swimming', 'San Jacinto', 'Solsbury Hill', 'No Self Control', 'I Don't Remember', 'Shock The Monkey', 'Humdrum', 'On The Air' and 'Biko'. The range of material alone served as a reminder of Gabriel's consistently inventive output over the previous eight years.

1983 to 1985 seemed a relatively quiet period in Peter Gabriel's career, at least in musical terms, but the turmoil in his private life reached the point where Jill and Peter sought marital guidance. It seemed to help. Certainly it was Peter's decision to stay together with Jill and look after their two daughters and their period of separation concluded, they bought a new house in Bath in 1985. Rosanna Arquette remained a good friend, although as we have seen it was difficult for Jill to accept her, even when Rosanna found herself a new boyfriend she would eventually marry.

Peter took time out to travel, getting away from these emotional entanglements, and went to Brazil in search of more sources of world music. He became heavily involved in writing film scores, notably the *Birdy* project for Alan Parker. But it wasn't until 1986 that Gabriel finally re-emerged on the rock stage with his biggest and best work thus far. He unleashed an album of such power and quality, it elevated him overnight into the big league that was his right, if not always his sole objective.

The launch of *So* his fifth and most popular album was of vital importance to his career. Even at this crucial time he typically showed more concern about his work for Amnesty International. He cancelled a promotional trip for the album in order to join the Conspiracy Of Hope tour of the US, organised in support of Amnesty. An amazing line-up of stars included U2, Peter Gabriel, Sting, The Police, Bryan Adams, Lou Reed, Joni Mitchell, Miles Davis and Bob Dylan. There was concern at Geffen that a tour before Peter's new album came out would damage sales or at the least upset promotional plans. In the end Peter agreed to do his own promo tour as well. Meanwhile the

Conspiracy Of Hope tour began at the Cow Palace, San Francisco on June 4, 1986.

Peter's band at this time included old colleagues Tony Levin and David Rhodes with the remarkable Manu Katche on drums, Larry Klein (bass) and Ian Stanley (keyboards). During the set they unveiled new songs from *So*, including 'Red Rain' and the all powerful 'Sledgehammer'. They played six dates and Peter's performance of 'Biko' was considered by many to be the linchpin of the whole Amnesty event, which was aimed specifically at raising awareness, getting political prisoners out of jail and recruiting new members to the cause.

The shows were a great success and Peter was greeted with great warmth by a visiting ex-South African political prisoner who had suffered with Steve Biko under the injustice of the Apartheid system. He greatly appreciated the sincerity of Gabriel's musical message. This response must have encouraged Peter, who was sometimes racked by self doubt about his own motives for writing a song like 'Biko' while under attack from press sceptics who thought he was being 'hypocritical'. Yet he had been embarking on charity shows and benefit appearances for many years and always for causes for which he had an instinctive, heartfelt sympathy.

He was particularly moved – and angered – by the plight of some of those former prisoners of conscience he met on the tour, including a Chilean woman, Veronica De-Negri, whose son was killed. "He had gone back home and been burned to death in the street by police – they'd poured petrol over him and set fire to him. I was just churning inside with these different emotions," recalls Peter.

At the end of June, 1986 Peter was back in London playing at an anti-apartheid concert on Clapham Common alongside Boy George, Elvis Costello, Sade, Sting, Billy Bragg and Hugh Masekela. Half a million people came to cheer the stars and once again Gabriel's performance stood out as one of the focal moments of a remarkable event.

This flurry of activity coincided with one of the most positive and productive periods in Peter's career. *So* was finally released in May, 1986, and went straight to Number One in the UK and US album charts. It was his first studio album release in four years and there was a great upsurge of joy and pleasure among

Peter's lifelong supporters who felt this level of success was well overdue.

So achieved many things, either by accident or design. It at last put away any lingering residual associations with Genesis. He was now clearly his own man, just like Sting who had left The Police at the height of their fame. He had also caught up with Phil Collins and taken his own rightful place at the table of the superstars. And he had done it all without compromising his music. While stompers like 'Big Time' reflected the kind of self-mocking humour that had been his forte during the less angst ridden periods of his life, another new song, 'Don't Give Up', showed he had retained his unique ability to explore relationships and human frailties.

One of the finest items on the album and indeed in the body of Peter's work thus far, 'Don't Give Up' proved extraordinarily moving. Kate Bush joined Peter in a duet that moved the hardest of men to tears and certainly struck a chord with many listeners whatever their circumstances. It seemed to affect most strongly musicians and artists of the same generation as Kate and Peter, who would often confide that they found the song almost unbearably relevant to their own circumstances at this time in their lives. Kate sings to Peter tender words of encouragement: "Don't give up – you still have us – you know it's never been easy."

The song was originally inspired by visions of life in the Dust Bowl where the harsh conditions affected farmers during the great American Depression of the Thirties. It also concerned unemployment in general, but it was hard not to equate the song with more personal problems and about keeping relationships together in trying circumstances. Whatever its origins, the sensitive lyrics and gentle melody appealed to folk more than all the angular and neurotic shouting that pervaded some of his previous albums. It was simple, it was meaningful and it worked. Peter told me after the song won an Ivor Novello Award in London: "I get letters from fans and even other musicians who say I brought them to tears with 'Don't Give Up'. But then ... I've always wanted to make the world miserable! I've always liked that in other people's music, when I get weepy or tingles in the spine. Kate Bush had a lot to do with the feeling in that song."

Oddly enough Peter had originally conceived it as a country ballad which at worst would have turned it into a maudlin whine. He explains: "I started off on that song singing both the parts myself but I thought it would work better with a man and a woman singing, so I changed the lyrics around. At one point I tried to work it up into a gospel-country style and there are still echoes of that approach in the piano playing." In its pristine state 'Don't Give Up' got to Number 9 in the UK charts in November, 1986.

The *So* album with its simple cover picture of Peter in a fashionable hairstyle, together with its unpretentious title, all reflected the new intensity and strength of purpose that now seemed to grip the composer. He had dealt with his marriage problems as best he could and during these mid-life years at the height of a hard-nosed decade, he was focused as never before.

There were practical reasons for many of the changes. Says Peter: "When I completed the *Birdy* soundtrack I wanted my focus to shift to songs rather than to remain on rhythm and texture which were dominant on *Gabriel 4*. Having done a complete album of textures and sound with *Birdy*, I'd got that out of my system. I wanted to be more playful, a bit more open, less mysterious . . . it was a dark period for me and one in which I had to become a little more open to the world. Creation as therapy is a thread in the material on *So*."

'Sledgehammer' above all seemed to express Gabriel's new found confidence and virility. Released a month before the album it was a funky exploration of all the composer's fondness for R&B and soul and it won him many new fans. It was a Number One for a week in the States in July, 1986 while a second single from the album 'In Your Eyes' got to Number 26 a few months later. 'Sledgehammer' eventually sold at least a million copies worldwide.

The album and accompanying video won Peter two BPI awards including Best British Male Artist and Best British Music Promo Video. When he was presented with the statuettes for these awards on 'live' TV he grinned and said: "Now I have two of these, I'll investigate the mating potential."

He later received nominations for four Grammy Awards. The sheer scale of the success of *So* seemed like a vindication of all his past decisions and career moves and he was still pushing the technology of the times one step further. The video for 'Sledgehammer' showed a brilliant grasp of animation techniques. Peter had been fascinated by the possibilities of video technology since the mid-Seventies, long before it had become an essential tool of promotion. There had been film clips of pop groups made since the days of The Beatles and The Stones. But in the days when the UK had only three TV channels, tightly under union control, these films remained largely unseen by the public. Peter anticipated that video would help free up directors and allow greater access to inquisitive artists like himself.

He had made a series of surreal videos including 'Shock The Monkey' (1982) and 'I Don't Remember' (1983) which were considered too disturbing to be shown on prime time TV. 'Sledgehammer' was directed by Stephen R. Johnson who had previously worked with David Byrne of Talking Heads. He used a technique of 'pixellation' shooting a sequence of frames which, when projected up to speed, gave an illusion of human animation. Johnson met Gabriel in Bath and came up with a story idea before commissioning Aardman Animations of Bristol to work on a painstakingly filmed series of scenes involving Peter's head surrounded by flying fruit, plasticine objects and even a model stream train. The use of 'Claymation' techniques took hours of work and cost over a hundred thousand pounds, but it produced a work of genius and helped hammer the single up to Number 4 in the UK chart. Peter also had the satisfaction of seeing 'Sledgehammer' knock the latest Genesis single 'Invisible Touch' off the top spot in the US.

Peter recalls the 'Sledgehammer' video took eight days to shoot. "It was slow work. We had to shoot frame by frame and I had to hold my head still for hours and I got incredible aches and pains in parts of my body I never knew existed. I had a load of fish flying around my head which stank after a while and in the heat became really unpleasant."

The video has since become a classic of the genre. *Rolling Stone* ranked it Number One in their '100 Top Music Videos' (October, 1993), it won nine MTV Awards and the Video Vanguard Award for career achievement in 1987.

Another great new song 'Big Time' clearly mocked at the kind of showbiz success which Peter had achieved with the album. In fact it was a satirical poke at the 'big time operator' and contains the immortal line: "Had my bed made like a mountain range, with a snow white pillow for my big fat head."

Peter tells how his bank account, mouth and belly were all getting bigger in the pursuit of success. "That song was about success as a standard goal, and I see myself in the same situation. The lust for success is something I don't like, and I can see myself doing it. At home I like to bury myself in normal life. But I can enjoy being a pop star in New York! I don't want to spend my whole life touring. There are so many other projects I want to do, like becoming a visual image maker. On the road you don't get the chance to learn and absorb."

As the ultimate Gabriel blockbuster 'Sledgehammer' and its stable mate 'Big Time' certainly helped restore Peter's fortunes. The production by Daniel Lanois of U2 fame was tight with less emphasis on effects and freaky sounds and more on shouting brass sections.

Peter confirmed that 'Sledgehammer' and 'Big Time' were celebrations of the kind of soul music that turned him on as a teenager. There had been a plan to do an entire album of 'covers' but it was decided that a pastiche was a better idea. "This is my contribution to that song writing tradition," he said. "Obviously there was a lot of sexual metaphor in there. I was trying to write in the old blues tradition, much of which is preoccupied with mating activities. The idea was the sledgehammer would bring about a mini-harvest festival."

Peter denied that he had blatantly set out to rival Phil Collins' success. "No, it wasn't deliberate but I knew that by using brass I would invite comparisons with Phil. But ever since I was at school, Atlantic soul and Stax have been a pivotal influence on me, and I've always wanted to emulate them. I'd been considering doing an R&B and soul album which is still on the shelf. I was definitely trying to borrow the style of that period. In fact the leader of the brass section on the track was Wayne Jackson who was one of the famed Memphis Horns. I respect Phil's music and would like my own to reach as large an audience as possible." But Peter was annoyed at repeated suggestions that he was just trying to copy Phil. "That pisses me off because about the time of my third album there were considerable stylistic changes in Phil's music and I feel my influence on him hasn't been fairly acknowledged."

As well as thunderous soul stompers *So* contained many more delicate fragments like 'In Your Eyes', a gentle ballad on which he was backed by the popular Senegalese singer/ songwriter Youssou N'Dour. The piece was inspired by the love songs of Senegal. These can either refer to the love between man and woman or the love between man and God. To Peter this intriguing concept seemed to parallel the Western idea of the sacred versus the profane. Peter and Youssou were interviewed on BBC TV's *Breakfast Time* show about their work together, in which they talked in French, much to the confusion of the presenter.

"For me there is a real joy with 'In Your Eyes'. I think some of that comes through to an audience. If you really want to beam in to anyone – who they are or what they are – you can do so through their eyes. This song acknowledges that. But I am not trying to put myself over as a preacher. In fact 'In Your Eyes' had to be edited and I think it lost quite a bit as a result."

'Red Rain' the opening piece, has Peter singing in a strained, hoarse style that has characterised much of his more recent work: "I am standing up at the water's edge in my dream. I cannot make a single sound as you scream . . . red rain is coming down."

Daniel Lanois played guitar on the track with David Rhodes, Peter played piano while drums and percussion were added by Jerry Marotta and Stewart Copeland. The song was based on a recurring dream in which Peter found himself swimming in a swirling sea of red and black which eventually parts into two white walls. The scene becomes a story in which the red sea and red rain represent thoughts and feelings denied in normal human society. The red rain is the blood that is shed if feelings of pain and anger are allowed to fester within the human psyche and are not safely vented away. 'Red Rain' was one of several ideas Peter had conceived for his *Mozo* project last heard of in the Seventies. The *Mozo* songs were carefully scattered over his various albums and included the aforementioned 'Here Comes The Flood', 'Down The Dolce Vita', 'On The Air', 'Exposure', 'Red Rain' and 'That Voice Again'.

The latter track concludes side one of the original vinyl album. 'That Voice Again' is one of Peter's personal favourites and is about judgement and the admonishment "Let he who is without sin cast the first stone". Sings Peter: "I'm hearing right and wrong so clearly there must be more than this . . . it's only in uncertainty that we're naked and alive."

The song was going to be called 'First Stone' but Peter then dropped the more obvious Biblical allusions. He actually wrote three sets of different lyrics before finally collaborating with David Rhodes on the final version.

'Mercy Street' is about the idea of writing as therapy which in some ways underpins the entire *So* exercise. Peter had heard about a book of poetry and an unpublished play called *Mercy Street* by Anne Sexton, an American housewife. She had written a collection of work called 'To Bedlam And Par Way Back' after a doctor at a mental hospital suggested she start to write to help her own condition. Peter found that 'Mercy Street' was full of images of dreams and a constant search for a suitable father figure, whether it was a doctor, priest or God.

"That search kept her alive longer than many around her and gave her life meaning, and now her work gives hope to others," says Gabriel.

" 'Big Time' is a satirical story about a basic human urge. A small man from a small town achieves all his ambitions, with all parts of life, personality and anatomy growing larger than life and consequently, very heavy. In America, which is still a vigorous and enthusiastic nation, success has reached religious significance. This drive for success is a basic part of human nature – and my nature."

His drive was finally rewarded when 'Big Time' peaked at Number 8 in the US *Billboard* chart in January, 1987.

'We Do What We're Told', sub-titled 'Milgram's 37', is a strange, inconclusive piece inspired by accounts of American experiments in which students were ordered to inflict pain on patients in a laboratory. The students were told it was all part of a legitimate process and thus they failed to halt electric shock treatment, even when it was apparently causing 'victims' maximum pain. In fact the students themselves were part of the experiment, as the 'victims' were actors feigning agony. The man in charge Professor Stanley Milgram was trying to see how far men would go in obeying orders, an obvious parallel situation to prison camp guards in wartime.

The words to Gabriel's piece are minimal. After repeating the cry of "We do what we're told" the song is resolved with the lines "One doubt, one voice, one war, one truth one dream."

Peter had been mulling over the idea for some years and he told *Spin* magazine in 1986: "I knew why I took so long to record it. I think I had to wrestle with the subject matter until I could find an interpretation that identified with the heartening side of the story, but that also had the ring of objective reality." He added: "It's what I would call a 'dark corner' and it's perhaps the only track that rests on texture and atmosphere as its key components. Most of the others are songs you could strum along with on a guitar."

Peter conspicuously cleaned up the 1987 MTV Awards with *So* and in February he was presented with his trophies for Best British Male Artist and Best British Music Video for 'Sledgehammer' at the sixth annual Brit Awards. 'Big Time' kept the album bubbling in the charts but a five track 'Big Time' CD was withdrawn by Virgin because it was too long to be categorised as a single! It was later re-issued and has since become a collector's item.

Once he'd cleared the decks of Amnesty shows and other benefits, Gabriel assembled a fine band for his own 'This Way Up' tour, which began in November, 1986 in Rochester, Illinois and finished six weeks later in Los Angeles, Cal. The line-up included Manu Katche on drums, David Sancious on key-boards and old hands Tony Levin and David Rhodes. It was the first solo tour by Peter in three years and he played most of the material from *So* to packed houses. A duet with Youssou N'Dour on 'In Your Eyes' provided an excellent encore number when the troupe played to 20,000 fans at New York's Madison Square Garden.

Leaping backwards into the crowds for 'Lay Your Hands On Me' and working with special light effects, Peter once again combined personal contact with the big rock show that made his performances such memorable experiences. Peter's return to the big time climaxed when he played two nights at the Giants Stadium at Meadowlands, New Jersey in July 1987 in front of 50,000 fans.

Cheering crowds, royalties and accolades pouring in . . . Peter Gabriel had at last achieved all the goals the schoolboy had dreamt of when he jumped on the classroom desk to sing soul songs "out of character". But how could he top *So* and would he even want to try? Instead of simply rushing to bring out a *So* Mk. II he went back to plan, to scheme and come up with something new. Although there would be multifarious Gabriel activities along the way, it would be a long wait before he came back to face the public with his next epic album.

1987 represented a year of triumph for Peter, but it was also marked with sadness. Just as Gabriel was winning awards and selling albums by the truckload, he lost his first great champion and mentor, Tony Stratton-Smith. The founder of Charisma Records who had so much believed in both Gabriel and Genesis, was taken ill during a trip to Jersey in the Channel Island. He was suffering from a perforated ulcer but it transpired during surgery that he also had incurable cancer. He died at the age of 53 on March, 19, 1987. Peter Gabriel, along with his fellow Charisma artists as well as many from the world of sport, mourned the loss of 'Strat'. Peter paid a moving tribute in *The Times* of London, calling his old manager "a man of passion and a crusader".

Wrote Peter: "Despite the competitive nature of the business, he cared more for the quality of the work than the quantity sold, always preferring the difficult challenge of backing outsiders. His artists were supported as family. His favourite occupations he listed as writing, talking and drinking and in each he could compete with the best. Strat earned himself a unique place in the world of entertainment and sport, a big man with a big heart. I will miss him."

Stratton-Smith had sold Charisma Records to Virgin boss Richard Branson in 1985 so that he could concentrate on film projects and later moved to a house on Las Palmas. He was in Jersey to visit an old friend Vera Brampton when he fell ill and died. At least he had lived to see one of his most cherished artists achieve the kind of success that he felt was so richly deserved.

IX

COME TALK TO ME

AS ROCK STARS began to enjoy the money that poured in during the boom years of the Seventies, many were tempted to squander their new found wealth. Often from poor backgrounds, ill educated and with little common sense, they would pour their royalties not into pensions, shares or offshore accounts, but into drugs, booze and women of ill repute. Some collected arsenals of weapons or bought cars, clothes and castles. Eventually when the machine guns, hot rods and gold lamé underpants lost their allure – and resale value – the erstwhile stars simply rotted in sloth and idleness, until they ended up in worse circumstances than when they had started out on the road to fame.

Not so Peter Gabriel. He would be one of the few visionaries who would not only invest in himself, but in the musical future of others. He put a tremendous amount back into the music industry that had spawned him and left it a better, more productive place. Rather than waste money on selfish pleasures, he set it to work and utilised his cash for creative projects that were ultimately far more satisfying than feeding a hedonistic lifestyle.

When Peter recorded *So* he used the old barn studio, but the success of the album allowed him to greatly expand his working environment. He decided to create a new studio complex based around an old water mill, situated on the edge of the village of Box, a few miles east of Bath in the beautiful English countryside of Wiltshire.

This area is certainly conducive to creative and imaginative work. It is surrounded by prehistoric sites, burial mounds, ley lines and ancient earthworks. Glastonbury and Stonehenge are not far away and the place is a hotbed for flying saucer sightings

148

and the appearance of mysterious crop circles, not to mention a veritable plague of ghosts. No wonder Peter enjoyed the ambience.

Unfortunately the site he chose for his great scheme was close to a river (as one would expect at a water mill), and although this ultimately provided an attractive feature it was the cause of frequent and expensive inundations, leading to panic-stricken cries of "Here comes the flood!"

As well as a river, there is also a railway. The main line between London and Bath and Bristol is nearby which means that Inter City express trains roar past every hour heading for the Brunel Tunnel, named incidentally in honour of the man who created the Great Western Railway, the great Isambard Kingdom Brunel. Not so bad if you were a train enthusiast like Peter, but the vibrations played hell with the recording equipment. A special pit had to be excavated and filled with concrete to stabilise the foundations. Construction began in October, 1986 and was still continuing when the Gabriel band arrived to rehearse for the next US tour.

A plague of break-ins by mindless thieves also contributed to constant delays. The 200-year-old building had previously been a flour mill, a girls' school and even at one stage a semolina factory. The studio and ancillary facilities were built around this set of Victorian buildings, which included barns and a moat. When completed it was called the 'Real World' a symbol of Peter's ideas made flesh.

Despite the occasional setbacks it was clear to Gabriel's friends and fellow musicians that this elaborate studio complex now represented Peter's future. Touring would become less important and studio work would be the fulcrum of his activities. Peter wanted all the latest available technology to be installed once the studio buildings were complete but even the royalties from *So*, which sold three million copies in the US alone, were insufficient to finance all his plans. When Peter left Genesis he was far from being a rich man. He recalled in 1986: "When I left we still hadn't made any money, even though everyone assumed we were millionaires. We'd accumulated huge debts, which was one of the reasons why I had a lot of pressure to stay in the band at that point. The last time I toured was the first time I went into profit. Until then I'd always made a loss on tours."

Now that he was finally making money he was happy to invest it in the studio, even if at one stage it looked like the budget would soar to five million pounds and a certain amount of trimming was required.

The overall design was the outcome of an architectural competition and the winning plan included half burying the main control and recording room into the landscaping to reduce its visual impact and dampen those bad vibrations. Water surrounded the remainder of the main room and flowed beneath glass panels in the stone recording area while the fast flowing stream swept through the landscaped gardens outside. It was wonderful to see a river at the bottom of the garden – even if the garden was sometimes at the bottom of the river.

There were three main control rooms while the Big Room and the Workroom became integrated recording and mixing areas. A special Writing Room, hidden among trees near the mill pool was later extended and is now completely self-contained, a wood and glass structure overhung by sycamore trees, which gives complete privacy to any stray composer desperate for the peace and tranquillity necessary to create his next masterwork. No more neighbours banging on the wall and shouting "Turn that noise down!" Indeed if any neighbours from hell do turn up, intent on planting fast growing conifers or spot welding used cars on the premises, they could always be quietly tipped into the river and no one would be the wiser.

At the centre of the complex, the main studio control room is situated in the 'Big Room'. Here the walls are constructed of glass, metal and ceramics to help muffle the sound. The console faces large picture windows which look out over the mill pond. It has been described as the most beautiful studio room in the world.

The recession of the early Nineties took its toll of commercial studio bookings but many artists now use the studio. Says Peter proudly: "What I've actually created at Real World is very busy and there are a lot of people wanting my time."

As visitors from overseas, armed with Doudouks and Ney Flutes, trudge down the hill in search of fulfilment, accommodation is provided both in the main house and at two cottages on the site. There is even overspill accommodation for programmers and talking drummers at various guest houses and hotels in the village.

Here the development of Real World has provided an unexpected boost to the economy. Shove ha'penny and skittles continues unabated amongst the regulars at the local inn, but even the most absorbed skittler pauses as the sound of a lonely Doudouk echoes eerily across the ley lines and they mutter respectfully: "There goes young master Peter – God bless 'im as a scholar and a gentleman."

The studios became Peter's main base for operations and the home of his own record label Real World. After his separation from Jill, after 18 years of marriage, it also became his main residence. Here a full-time staff help him carry on his business affairs and co-ordinate all their multifarious activities, from benefit concerts to the on-going work of WOMAD. As a constant stream of musicians, artists, producers, A&R men from all over the world pay their respects, so a special catering team provides a diet of suitable dishes. A pleasant contrast to the days when Genesis would have to send out for a bacon sandwich or a packet of crisps while attempting to record 'Supper's Ready'.

Says Peter: "The reason why all of my royalties have tended to go into studios rather than houses around the world is so I'm never separated from my tools and never dependent on record company approval to make the music that I want to make."

In 1991 he invited a host of international artists and producers for a special project with WOMAD and Real World Records known as 'Recording Week' which resulted in a collaboration of musicians from different cultures producing the kind of exciting and daring work that Peter always knew was possible. It had been his dream from the late Seventies, when he first began to realise that basic rock music had become the 'stagnant form' his old chum Steve Hackett had so famously rejected in the days of Genesis.

Said Peter: "I became interested in non-Western music because of my enthusiasm for what I heard in its grooves. It was wonderful and I began to suspect conventional rock rhythms would lead to conventional rock writing. When I first conceived the idea of an event that combined third world music and rock it was from the point of view of a fan. I was convinced there were many people like me who would find non-Western music as exciting as I do. Besides there were an increasing number of rock musicians like me who had their ideas changed by what they'd heard in Africa and elsewhere." Partly through helping to get WOMAD going he felt he was redirecting some of the attention and money back to the source.

"I'm not trying to deliver African pastiches. I'm using the influences as tools to take me to somewhere else within my own music. I think I've done my part in trying to promote the music of other countries so I feel completely comfortable with what I'm doing. The process isn't one way. There are plenty of musicians in third world countries taking from our styles. I can even hear the influence of Genesis in some French African bands."

During 1988 Peter continued to make sporadic appearances and his profile was enhanced by the release of a collection of video hits, called simply *CV* which topped the UK music video charts. In June he appeared at the sixth annual Prince's Trust Rock Gala at the Royal Albert Hall, London and a few days later was a guest on the Nelson Mandela 70th Birthday Party held at Wembley Stadium, London where he performed his anti-apartheid anthem 'Biko'.

In July it was announced that Peter would take part in an Amnesty International World Tour with fellow stars Sting, Youssou N'Dour, Bruce Springsteen, and Tracy Chapman. Called 'Human Rights Now!' the 1988 tour had taken Peter months to organise and get off the ground. Recalled Peter: "What I remembered most was the changing faces. Japanese faces, Indian faces with turbans bobbing up and down, Greek faces, African faces . . . all within a few days. Everyone pulled their weight and the whole tour was a colossal achievement. We travelled together, we plotted together. I got elected to do a few of the dirty jobs. There were lots of little political jobs – lots of political flash fires – a delicate balance of large egos all round. I'm not sure whether I'm good at it, but part of me likes it."

Peter was particularly impressed by the efforts of co-star Bruce Springsteen to come to terms with the situations and environment of each country they visited on this unique tour. "Bruce is Mr. America in many ways and that Coca-Cola culture is incredibly insular, but he was struggling with the languages, listening to the local music and studying the politics of each country as we went along. He's got a real big heart, that was very clear."

As part of his continuing work in the international field Peter also helped establish 'Witness', an organisation which armed activists around the world with handheld video cameras and other communications tools, to record infringements of human rights. It seemed a far more valuable use for camcorder technology than making *You've Been Framed* style comic clips and ephemeral pop videos.

The following month the Martin Scorsese film *The Last Temptation Of Christ* opened in both America and the UK with a Peter Gabriel composed musical score. Geffen released the soundtrack album called *Passion* and sub-titled *Music For The Last Temptation Of Christ*. The album won a Grammy for Best New Age Recording and a nomination for Best Original Score. The award was presented at the 32nd Annual Grammy Awards ceremony, held at the Shrine Auditorium, Los Angeles on February 21, 1990. *Passion* was also the first release on Real World Records, which was launched by Gabriel and WOMAD in 1989. The plan was to record and promote a huge range of artists from around the world, at the Real World studios.

Peter felt he had learnt a lot from the process of writing the soundtrack. "*Passion* taught me a fluidity of sound and instrumentation. I was just coming across sounds that were beautiful to work with, and I wanted to incorporate some of the things I'd learned with the approach that I've used for the last three albums. The film is about the struggle and presenting that was the first goal. The attempts to lift it were really not the subject matter until the very end, the victory."

Gabriel gave a full explanation of his methods on the liner notes. "I was excited to be asked to work on the music. When I first discussed the project with Martin Scorsese in 1983 I wanted to find out how he was intending to film this controversial novel. He wanted to present the struggle between the humanity and divinity of Christ in a powerful and original way and I was convinced by his commitment to the spiritual content and message. He is an excellent and very musical director and working with him has been a great experience."

Scorsese has been described by film aficionados as a 'God

among directors'. He is most famous for such powerful movies as *Taxi Driver, Raging Bull, Goodfellas* and most recently *Kundun* (1998) about the Dalai Lama and the Chinese invasion of Tibet. After they finished mixing the music it seemed to P.G. there were some unfinished ideas that needed developing. And he took some extra time to complete the album. Several pieces were available that were not included in the film and he felt the record should be able to stand as a separate body of work.

Said Peter: "We recorded some of the finest singers and soloists in the field of world music and set the score on a backdrop of traditional North African rhythms and sounds. It was a wonderful experience working with such different and idiosyncratic musicians."

Gabriel recruited players from as far afield as Pakistan, Turkey, India, Ivory Coast, Bahrain, Egypt, New Guinea, Morocco, Senegal and Ghana. "For many of them working with this material was something quite new and they were very enthusiastic. The soundtrack is full of the spirit of their performances."

After this experience Peter was keen to do more work in the movies. "I'm very interested in doing more film music, but there seems to be so little time. Also it can be very difficult to break through into that scene. Basically I've done what has been offered to me and, time permitting, I'd like to do more."

Passion got to Number 29 in the UK album charts and Number 60 in the US in June, 1989. That same year Peter attended the launch of the Greenpeace album *Rainbow Warriors* (Geffen) to which he had contributed the track 'Red Rain'. The event was staged in Moscow and was attended by Annie Lennox, the Thompson Twins and U2. In June that year Peter contributed to a Youssou N'Dour album called *Set* and a single from the album featuring a duet by Peter and Youssou called 'Shaking The Tree' was released as a single, which got to Number 61 in the UK. Once again the song was about understanding problems and trying to do something about them, a familiar *motif* for Peter.

'Shaking The Tree' was co-written with Youssou N'Dour as a critique of predominantly male society and was in praise of women's growing confidence. One surmises it was not a great hit in Afghanistan. The album was produced by George

Acogny, a former New Yorker who moved to Senegal where he began working with Youssou. A close friend of Peter's he introduced Gabriel to brilliant French African drummer Manu Katche who later became an integral member of Gabriel's troupe of performers.

The song also provided the title for a *Greatest Hits* compilation and in December 1990 *Shaking The Tree: Sixteen Golden Greats* got to Number 11 in the UK album charts and was a Top Fifty hit in the States.

Peter continued to make occasional appearances at special events and on April 16, 1990 he guested at 'Nelson Mandela – An International Tribute To A Free South Africa' a concert held at Wembley Stadium, London. Alongside Peter were Bonnie Raitt, Neil Young, Simple Minds and Aswad.

On the 20th anniversary of Steve Biko's death Peter visited South Africa and he was invited to attend a special memorial where 25,000 people gathered to watch the unveiling of a statue to the murdered activist. Peter was asked to sing an unscheduled version of 'Biko' and he bravely had a bash, even though there was no backing band, and only a small PA and tiny stage for him to perform on.

"Someone had brought along a copy of the CD and people hurriedly looked around for a CD player which was hooked up to the PA for me to sing along to," recalled Peter. He found it a very moving occasion. "I met both the Biko family and Nelson Mandela, who was extraordinary."

At another memorable charity show in 1991 he appeared by satellite hook-up from Holland in 'The Simple Truth' concert held in aid of Kurdish refugees at Wembley Arena. This was all very well. Concerts were one thing, but the world was growing impatient for a new Gabriel studio album. They would not have to wait much longer.

In 1992 Peter returned to the fray with *Us*, his first personal, non-soundtrack type album since *So*. Many unfamiliar with Gabriels' working methods wondered why he had taken so long to stage his 'comeback'. He explained he just did not want to rush into making a second version of *So*. That would have been too easy and obvious. *Us* would prove a much more powerful and disturbing album.

He told reporters: "It has been a long time, but not as long as some people made out. Although it was six years from *So* it was only three years from *Passion* and *Passion* for me is every bit as important as any other record I do."

The new work came at a crucial time. Peter had just spent five years undergoing therapy which he felt he needed after the traumatic final break-up of his marriage to Jill in 1987. Said Peter in 1992: "I stopped doing therapy just before Christmas and I suppose that, rather than dealing with allusion and fantasy, I thought it was time to get my hands dirty and deal with the real stuff that was going on and the lyrics were written to reflect that."

The searching self analysis that Peter underwent during his years of therapy were partly designed to explore and bring out the darker side of his personality. Partners are assailed by doubts when they cannot find contentment with each other and are often baffled by the seemingly inexplicable causes.

Explained Peter: "Part of what I discovered through therapy was the bastard in me, if you like and I was trying to get in touch with that and put it in some of the songs. I knew it was there, the lumpy bits which move around on the surface. *Us* was not easy to pen, despite the therapy and there is a certain point where I don't want to write about me all the time. It gets boring when I see it in other artists."

Us was produced by Daniel Lanois and released on the Real World label in September 1992. Having worked on Gabriel's previous three albums, Lanois was the right man for the job – strong-willed but sympathetic. And said Peter about their working relationship: "We have incredibly strong and different opinions – but opinions that are quite frequently reversed."

On the CD notes Peter was able to articulate his feelings about the album: *"Much of this record is about relationships. I am dedicating it to all those who have taught me about loving and being loved. Especially to my parents Ralph and Irene. To Jill for giving so much in all the time we were growing up together. To Rosanna for all your love and support that I didn't properly acknowledge. And to my daughters Anna and Melanie, my pride and joy."*

Although Peter claimed that the CD title was just a nicely shaped word, the *Us* in question was himself, Jill and Rosanna. The songs were about their entangled lives and the therapy programme he had undergone to help him find himself and enable him to reveal his feelings to others, thus unshackling the iron mask of self-imposed emotional restraint.

But how did the subjects of his tormented inner soul themselves feel about being publicly celebrated in song? Rosanna Arquette seemed both quietly amused and impatient. She said in 1994: "I've had enough songs written about me. You can only have so many songs written about you, especially if you're not getting any royalties from them!"

Arquette later said that she was planning a film based on her affair with the man she calls 'Mr. Peter'. "It's about a girl and a rock star. If Peter can write songs about our relationship, I can do a movie."

Gabriel recorded several different versions of the songs he wrote for *Us*, not all of which made it onto the final album. Among those like-minded souls participating in the sessions were Brian Eno, Peter Hammill, John Paul Jones, Manu Katche and Sinead O'Connor. As with *Passion* Peter employed a range of musicians from around the world to provide atmosphere, utilising rare ethnic instruments, brought from Armenia, Turkey, Kenya, Senegal, Moscow and Egypt.

Given the theme and circumstances of the recording, not to mention Peter's mood, it was unsurprising that the general tone was markedly less upbeat than *So*. Nevertheless as with all the known works of Peter Gabriel this one has sustained its appeal and repays constant, careful listening. *Us* contains many flawless gems. Bagpipes herald the haunting and unforgettable opening song 'Come Talk To Me', a tune which once played, tends to stay glued into the subconsciousness for hours.

Peter's affecting cry of "Won't you please talk to me, we can unlock this misery" is accompanied by a rumble of African drums that add supporting strength to Peter's vocals that sometimes seem quite overwhelmed with grief.

Peter told *The Box* in December 1992: " 'Come Talk To Me' is a very emotional track. The song is about the blockage in communication between two people and, in fact, there was initially a block with one of my daughters, which got me going on that lyric. And then I sort of opened up. It has the most dream-like imagery in the verses and this direct 'Come talk to me' in the chorus and so the idea of having a second voice seemed to make a lot of sense."

The same mood pervades the charmingly honest 'Love To Be Loved'. "In this emptiness and fear, I want to be wanted, 'cos I love to be loved."

If this isn't sufficiently moving, he caps this with another delicate and tender piece 'Blood Of Eden' sung with Sinead O'Connor. "I saw the signs of my undoing they had been there from the start and the darkness still has work to do . . ." sings Peter before delivering the beautiful harmonised chorus "In the blood of Eden lies the woman and the man."

It is as heart-rending as his duet with Kate Bush on 'Don't Give Up'– so sweet you wonder they can bear to sing together. Said Peter: "Sinead's both soulful and emotive and what I like about her singing is she gets this beautiful, innocent, airy voice but it comes straight from the gut with no bullshit."

Adding to the atmosphere is the mournful sound of our old friend the Doudouk played by Levon Minassian. It should be explained that the Doudouk is not native to Wiltshire but is an Armenian double-reeded instrument. Its unique tones can be heard interspersed throughout the album. Peter traced the finest exponent to a jeweller's shop in Marseilles, France. Here the owner Mr. Minassian was prevailed upon to shut down the shop for a few days while he came to England for the *Us* recording sessions.

In urgent need of a restorative after 'Blood' the listener is revived with 'Steam' an R&B romp in the tradition of 'Sledgehammer' complete with funky brass section. Metaphorically speaking Peter once again leaps onto the school desktop and shouts: "Give me steam and how you feel can make it real, real as anything you've seen."

Says Peter: " 'Steam' has been described as 'hot, wet and wobbly' and in some ways it was the most 'up' track on the record. It's got all these soul references and comes out of the same family that 'Sledgehammer' grew out of, like Stax, Atlantic and the other music from my early years. Steam itself is hot and wet so I think there was an obvious sexual reference there. There is also a character situation in the song about a relationship between a man and a woman. It's accusatory, but not really autobiographical. I mean there are references but it's not directly addressed to anyone, it's more about having fun. The woman in the song is very bright, sophisticated and cultured.

She knows everything about everything. What he does know is about her. She doesn't really know a lot about herself."

'Steam' was a US top ten hit and the accompanying music video won two MTV Awards and a 1993 Grammy for Best Music video.

'Only Us' is interspersed with strange gurgling noises as it builds up momentum over a wailing Eastern rhythm. Kudsi Erguner adds the attractive Ney flute (not to be confused with the Neigh Flute) and with L. Shankar on violin the World Music atmosphere gives a strangely psychedelic counterpoint to the gloomy prognostications of Western man. "The further on I go, oh the less I know," sings Peter, sounding a little like Syd Barrett in his less lucid Floydian moments. "With 'Only Us' I was using the 'us' in a more general way – us as a species, as a people. It's got some of my favourite sounds and textures and guests."

'Washing Of The Water' has the simplicity of a hymn and Peter sings with all the sorrowful profundity of a lonely child: "River, river carry me high, 'til the washing of the water will make it all alright."

Peter agrees it has a spiritual overtone. "Directly it's a love song about being in a painful place and recognising that. In a sense there is this image of the water from the river and the sea and the washing being healing, cleansing and purifying. I hadn't thought that my work was becoming more spiritual, but as I look at it now, I think very often you need a little distance from what you do, to get a real sense of what it might represent. I think in the desire for the water to wash over me there is a spiritual yearning as a result of emotional pain."

The final moments as he intones in "Bring me something to take this pain away," are almost too sad to bear, without a stiff glass of brandy or at the very least a hot mug of comforting cocoa.

If Peter is sometimes in danger of appearing like a king-sized wimp, he quickly redresses the balance with funky and at times violent tunes. 'Digging In The Dirt' quickly dispels the tender mood created by 'Washing Of The Water'. This song contains his most direct and brutal message. "This time you've gone too far . . . I told you . . . don't talk back, just drive the car, shut your mouth I know what you are."

Peter agrees it is his most angry and abusive song. He

159

explains: "I actually had another project, looking at death row and its inmates and what makes people kill. And it occurred to me that maybe my interest was partly because there were murderous feelings in myself. In relationships I can be both passive and aggressive and I started to recognise some abusive things in me that were hidden. So there are two threads interwoven in the song – the killer and my own personal history." On the evidence of this song, a far cry from 'Don't Give Up' and 'Love To Be Loved', Peter is not an entirely blameless victim. The sudden outburst of violence is all the more shocking coming from someone normally perceived as kind, placid and slow to anger. Here for a moment you could almost be forgiven for imagining him to be a fiend in human shape.

He says, somewhat fiendishly: "I was looking at the darker side of myself. I was also reading books about murder and anger expressed in different ways. One was called 'Our Desire To Kill' about prisoners on death row. I was trying to find the bastard in me, which I can feel and which I now feel much more comfortable with. Musically I wanted something that was quite dark, sticky and steamy. There are lots of layers and the song is all about investigating the layers within yourself, like the layers in an onion. You come across something else each time and you try to peel it back and find out what lies underneath." It has to be said that on past experience, such practices are bound to end in tears.

The song was the first single culled from the album and was the subject of a video made with wildlife film maker John Downer, famed for his use of miniature cameras.

The eighth track 'Fourteen Black Paintings' was directly inspired by a visit Peter made to a chapel in Texas, during an American tour. His guitarist David Rhodes insisted that Peter went to visit the chapel. "When he described it to me it really didn't sound like a place that I would have any interest in at all. But I went there and it was full of these 14 black paintings and it was one of the most spiritual places I have ever been. It was a very powerful experience and the whole place, I discovered, was dedicated to human rights, civil rights and has links with Martin Luther King and Ghandi. It's a multi-denominational chapel, so it's very open from a religious standpoint. That's how the title got locked in, because it felt like a very spiritual track."

The talking drums of Asane Thiam add to the mysterious atmosphere of what is more sound scape than conventional song. Just as the listener's attention span begins to flag, Peter leaps manfully back into the rock pool with 'Kiss That Frog'. Good spirits are duly revived. On what is superficially a fun piece Peter warbles: "Can't you hear beyond the croaking . . . Don't you know that I'm not joking."

Although the middle section does not scan very well, the imagery is striking and the sound of Senegalese shakers is matched by some froggy organ sounds. There are even welcome touches of electric lead guitar, once so common and fast becoming a rarity in pop until the arrival of Oasis only a year or so after this album's release. Interestingly, Peter was contemplating a return to the extensive use of lead guitar on his next album, due for release in 1998.

'Kiss That Frog' became a hugely popular number on Peter's live shows with its irresistible chorus: "Jump in the water, c'mon baby jump in with me."

The theme seems faintly ludicrous until its origins are laid bare by the composer. Says Gabriel: "The lyric idea for 'Kiss That Frog' came out of a book I was reading by Bruno Betelheim called *The Uses Of Enchantment*. I was looking at fairy stories, mainly from a psychological point of view and I found it fascinating. I think he was arguing that in the story of the princess learning to love the frog, in accepting it, the prince would emerge. This was actually a very good analogy for an introduction to sexuality. Beneath the fairy story is the sexual underbelly. Musically it's based on an old groove that I was working with when I was doing the soundtrack for *Birdy*. It's got more references to Latin music than to rock. The lyrics are a bit on the edge, as I wanted them to fall on the sweaty side."

Gabriel felt that in terms of sex education, the very real fear and horror that actually went with young people's first sexual experiences wasn't always addressed and was usually ignored. "Betelheim was arguing that the legend of the princess and the frog was very good, because what sat in the psyche after the story was that something that might at first seem repulsive can turn out to be very pleasant."

The angst of the urban poet, sung in Bruce Springsteen mode, is revealed in the final item called simply 'Secret World'. Says Peter: "It is about the private world that two people occupy and the private worlds that they occupy as individuals within that space, and the overlap of their dreams and desires. It came out of a difficult period, including many years of marriage and then a powerful relationship afterwards. There were some mixed references for me."

'Secret World' with its changes in sound, rhythm and emotion is one of those songs that Peter says represents a journey through different landscapes. It was put together in a style known as 'Songlines' inspired by a book by Bruce Chatwin.

Said Peter: "A lot of the record is very personal and is about the relationship between two people, the good times and the bad. After a particularly bad time I decided I had to look inside myself and find out what was going on and what was going wrong. Group therapy helped to give me more of an 'us' focus. Making music is also a therapeutic process and I think it's one in which you can have control. So in some ways it is safe for an artist to put all of these very personal things into their work, because they are the director, and the editor and the writer. They can play God with things that are actually outside of their work."

During the general progression of his albums there has clearly been a long-term tendency to 'home in' on personal matters. Gabriel realises this can be very self-absorbing but says it is the subject which matters most to him as a composer.

"I feel that it is an area which is very important to me. Us means two people, a relationship, and 'us' as in all of us. I read somewhere that the measure of man's civilisation is where he places the line between 'them' and 'us'. When you put people in the box marked 'them' you can kick them around a lot more easily than you can when they're in the box marked 'us'. So I think it's useful to try and empty the box marked 'them' and fill up the box marked 'us'."

Even though Peter's songs deal with many painful issues and predicaments, his writing is not a cut and dried process, culled from some secret personal diary filled with bizarre entries (*Got up, made breakfast, had really ghastly relationship*). Often the way his songs come together defies logic. He'll use all the available studio technology; call upon an array of gifted musicians and artists, and sift influences from the outside world in his search for creativity and inspiration. Often the songs themselves are fragments of ideas labelled with lugubrious working titles. 'Digging In The Dirt' was known as 'Plod' until it was eventually made whole. Bits of riffs that have been on demo tape for many years are pressed into service, and many different versions of a piece are recorded in different styles, before it becomes, magically, a complete song destined for pride of place on an album.

Although *Us* sold a million copies in America and four million worldwide Peter admitted it was a more 'difficult' record than *So*. "There wasn't a 'Sledgehammer'-type single which made a lot of difference. I was still very pleased with how it did, and as with my third album I think it will stand up better in hindsight than perhaps it does at the time."

And indeed it did. *Us* is an impressive, important, brilliant piece of work which is still giving up its secrets and yielding hidden pleasures.

The success of *Us* and *So* not only enabled Peter Gabriel to expand his Real World empire, he was able to indulge himself a little as well. He was still unlikely to engage in the wild, excessive lifestyle of his rock peers. He has never been one for throwing TV sets out of hotel windows or riding motor cycles up and down corridors, but he has not deprived himself of all stimulants, nor led an entirely monk-like existence either. You can't inhale helium for fun, take out Rosanna Arquette *and* stand accused of being a fuddy duddy.

Yet Peter still keeps his distance from the hurly-burly of rock'n'roll. "I think of myself as a human being rather than a pop star or entertainer. You see so many hollow men walking around the rock circuit and they've spent all their life being marched from stage to hotel to airport and so on. I like functioning in ways that are perhaps a little relevant to people with screaming kids, bills to worry about and all the normal, pre-occupations of real life. All that puts the other stuff in perspective, because it's very easy to get caught up in all the rock thing."

Even so he could not immerse himself entirely in a life of

selfless nappy changing interpolated with angst ridden album making. Disentangled from a permanent relationship perhaps for the first time in his life, he was free to do as he pleased – without the burden of guilt. In one bound Gabriel was free! Free first of worried parents; then of restrictive schooling; of a claustrophobic rock band; of a demanding wife and needful children. Now in mid-life there was no need for a crisis. There were holidays ready for the taking in exotic locales like Africa and South America and the USA.

Peter took up skiing and snowboarding with a passion. The man who professed to be afraid of heights proved fearless on the slopes. During the US winter season he'd spend blissful hours driving a roaring Snowcat across the deep powdery snows of Grand Targhee, Idaho. It was a sport that provided the sense of liberation that pop music once promised that callow, spotty youth who had danced on table tops all those years ago.

If anyone deserved some fun after the traumas of the previous decades it was Peter Gabriel – humanist.

X

SECRET WORLD

WHATEVER HAPPENED TO Peter Gabriel in his personal life during the turbulent years after he left Genesis in 1975, there was no let-up in his energetic pursuit of an ever expanding artistic vision. He alone of all the artists who achieved fame during the early days of British rock music had been truly 'progressive'. His aims were clearly focused – most of the time. And his standards were high – all of the time.

He produced a richly varied body of original work and his greatest records like the third *Peter Gabriel* album, *So*, *Passion* and *Us* have increased in stature with the passing years. His skill in balancing the need to entertain, with his own desire to explore new ideas and technology, has proved almost magically successful. Especially when one considers the opposition and cynicism he has sometimes endured. As the roles he played in Genesis and the achievements of his youth fade in the memory and come to mean less to new generations, he finds it easier to shed the baggage of preconception, those marching columns of suitcases full of opinions and images that have become out of date and irrelevant.

Said Gabriel in 1987: "It's well known that I went to a public school, came from a middle-class background and was with Genesis. All these things go with the package and help determine the way I'm perceived. In many other places they don't know about them and they don't care and I actually feel more comfortable in that situation because I'm being judged on what I'm doing, not on other's perceptions of who I am."

And Peter Gabriel has done rather a lot. He expanded rock's previously limited horizons by championing World Music and its rich diversity of artists hitherto neglected in the West. He revealed an awareness of human and political problems that was not submerged in self interest. He surmounted the down-right hostility of the British music press at the start of the Eighties, who could not accept his right to mature and develop beyond the realms of Genesis. He achieved popular success with scarcely any of the media help often lavished generously on the less talented and least deserving. Somehow, in the teeth of neglect and often amidst personal distress, the singer and composer has never given up, even when close to despair and overwhelmed by events in his public and personal life.

He went on to earn the respect and admiration of a new generation of fans and became an inspiration to his fellow musicians. Something in his attitude, his ongoing struggle, his stubborn determination to stick with his ideas, not only won that respect but endeared him to increasing numbers of people who could identify with his patently honest persona. His fan base is hugely loyal. Visitors travel from all over the world on pilgrimages to his home; many just content to catch a glimpse of their hero, with no wish to intrude.

This is in marked contrast to the photographers that occasion-ally camp out in the bushes to find out who is visiting The Real World studios, hoping to spot those celebrities with whom Peter has been 'romantically linked' in the press. They include Sinead O'Connor and German supermodel Claudia Schiffer. The latter is a blonde-haired beauty from Dusseldorf, who, incidentally, lists her favourite pop singer as 'Phil Collins'. Claudia, one of the top five models in the world, whose clients include Chanel, Versace and Pepsi, was engaged to magician David Copperfield. She has described such celebrities as Gabriel and Prince Albert Of Monaco, as "just good friends". Claudia made her major film début in *Blackout* (1997), and says her favourite film director is none other than Rosanna Arquette's old mate Martin Scorsese, another link with Gabriel. The drug of celebrity has not unhinged Gabriel, as it does so many film actors, models and pop stars. There is of course no escape from the curse of being recognised, but his fans are a special, more understanding and sympathetic breed. On planes he'll be handed personal letters or poems instead of being asked for his autograph. 'Sightings' of Peter Gabriel are reported with all the eagerness once accorded The Beatles or such reclusive legends as Syd Barrett or Peter Green.

Gabriel has never been a total recluse, however much he values his privacy. He handles all the attention with his usual mixture of slight embarrassment, kind consideration and good humour. Although it's hard to imagine him in the role of Playboy of the Western World, he has his moments. Observes Peter wryly on the subject of fame: "I don't think you can achieve fame in any walk of life without being a groupie for it in some way or another. There's part of me that always enjoyed all that and I need to let it out . . . I don't take it too seriously though."

He has been accused of workaholism and too much dedication towards the creation of his own unreal Gabriel fantasy world, often at the expense of love and friendship. But the seemingly relentless drive that spurs him on is a facet of his natural curiosity as well as a form of exorcism. He may well be casting out demons, but there is no master plan for world domination. World understanding is his rather more laudable aim. And he'll try every which way to achieve that goal through his songs and performances.

"I am not afraid of failure," he says. "There is more to learn from failure than success. The best advice I have ever received is 'In every opportunity, danger; in every danger, opportunity.' The last thing man will let go of is his suffering." For Peter the greatest satisfaction still lies in dreaming, the activity that set him apart as a child. Thinking wonderful schemes, wondering how new ideas might work . . . this is the stuff of Gabriel land, not the flow of hits, dollars and headlines. "Most of all I love being around ideas and generating new ones," he says. "We have what we call a dinner club, a sort of loose meeting of minds over a meal and several bottles of wine, and we dream. Brian Eno and I have been involved in it for a couple of years and it's wonderful. *It's like a bath for the imagination.*"

Much has been made of Peter's darker moments (and there *is* a deep underlying sadness, revealed as we have seen in such songs as 'Washing Of The Water' and 'Secret World'). Yet he remains essentially a man blessed with a finely tuned sense of humour. He can smile and laugh at secret jokes and the follies of life.

Above all he can laugh at himself. He is gently amused at the way, for example, machinery tends to malfunction when he is around. For somebody who delights in new technology and whose father was an inventor, he is singularly inept at handling equipment. He says manufacturers refer to him as an RFM – which means "read the fucking manual".

Thinking back to practically every occasion I have met Peter – strange, erratic events inevitably went on in the background. He is a living exponent of the chaos theory. I still fondly remember that afternoon spent with him at his flat in Notting Hill Gate when the rain poured steadily through the hole in the kitchen roof. No attempt was made to stem the flow. Peter simply gazed helplessly at the onrush of waters and gave a wan smile. Now if he could have reversed the rain flow by some sort of *magnetic impulse* – that might have been worth trying.

On another occasion I found him immersed in the effects he was creating using a tape recorder, headphones and a microphone. He had devised a special tape delay. "Put on the headphones and try and speak into the microphone," he instructed. The tape played my voice back into my ears a split second later and completely scrambled the power of speech. It was virtually impossible to talk aloud for more than a few seconds without getting hopelessly confused. My attempts to use this device reduced Peter to fits of laughter. I have no idea what the purpose of this experiment was but it showed in an alarming way just how the senses can be fooled. It was around this time he experimented with the use of helium to raise the pitch of his voice. It was hilarious and apparently quite dangerous. Peter is the sort of chap who would emerge from chemistry lessons with burnt eyebrows and a 'Who me?' expression.

It was well known that when Peter played with Genesis there would be equipment breakdowns. Whether he was in New York, London or Watford Town Hall the mysterious forces of the cosmos worked against him. The blame for this could not be directly placed on the singer, but it did seem a coincidence. In his presence I often felt a mysterious, dark aura, causing reverberations in the atmosphere. Was that the cosmos – or a curry – at work? At any rate when the band wanted to play me their latest album, we had to listen to it on a cassette on a stereo in a Mini car parked outside a studio, because all the professional tape players malfunctioned as soon as they detected his presence.

Some years later when Peter was playing with his own band in Liverpool, we sat in the dressing room of the Empire theatre, and conducted an interview in complete darkness. The power had failed throughout the building during a sound check and all the lights had gone out. There were no windows to let in even the faintest glimmer and all I could hear was a disembodied voice, answering my questions in sepulchral tones. It was eerie. If anyone ever achieves thought transference, levitation or astral projection – I believe it will be Peter Gabriel. Apparently he gets countless fans trying to tune into his brainwaves. I tried it myself – and got the engaged signal.

Perhaps the difference between the Boy Gabriel of the Sixties and the Man Gabriel of the Nineties is that he now seems capable of sharing his powers and influence with others sympathetic to his aims and beliefs.

The 'Secret World' shows he performed in 1993/94 in particular revealed that empathy between himself, his players and their audience. The image he presented on stage at these shows also underlined just how Gabriel had matured and emerged like a chrysalis from the callow youth of yesteryear. It was fortunate that given the ravages of time, he retained his charm and lissom agility on stage. Even more telling however was the quiet, cool confidence, mingled with an easy manner that said: "Relax. Bear with me. All will be revealed."

April 1993 saw the start of the 'Secret World Tour', produced by Peter and the pioneering Canadian director and designer Robert Lepage. The show blended Lepage's own visionary, theatrical style and Peter's personal songs. The tour was a huge success and was seen by over a million fans in five continents as the company toured for 18 months. His double CD *Peter Gabriel: Secret World Live* and the accompanying video made by Francois Girard, was released in August 1994, and helped celebrate and bring to a wider audience these most meaningful and spectacular shows. The video revealed the full extent of Gabriel's personal maturity as a performing artist. Two shows were filmed and recorded at the Palasport Nuovo, Modena, Italy on 16 and 17 November, 1993. The video and CDs contain dynamic versions of the best of his contemporary work. Some 8,000 fans greeted the opener 'Come Talk To Me' with roars and applause and subsequent songs were met with a sizzling display of blazing cigarette lighters, held aloft by the fans in an attempt to provide their own light show.

The tunes included 'Steam', 'Across The River', 'Slow Marimbas', 'Shaking The Tree', 'Red Rain', 'Blood Of Eden', 'San Jacinto', 'Kiss That Frog', 'Washing Of The Water', 'Solsbury Hill', 'Digging In The Dirt', 'Sledgehammer', 'Secret World', 'Don't Give Up' and 'In Your Eyes' – all performed with grace, wit and intensity.

A photograph of a tangle of power and communication cables streaming across the stage, displayed in the CD booklet, illustrated the complexities inherent in putting on such a show. It looked just the sort of spaghetti junction to cause those legendary Gabriel-esque malfunctions. Mercifully Gabriel's control of the elements is now so well developed, glitches have become a thing of the past, a source of relief to his technicians and fellow musicians.

For these shows Peter assembled one of his finest bands. With the slick and dextrous Manu Katche leading from the back on drums, the ensemble included David Rhodes (guitar, vocals), Jean Claude Naimro (keyboards), Shankar (violin), Tony Levin (bass), Levon Minassian (Doudouk) and Paula Cole (vocals). Peter himself revealed a startling if hitherto undetected talent as an excellent blues harmonica player on 'Kiss That Frog'. However, it wasn't just the musicianship that wowed the Italians – always among Peter's most loyal fans. Said Peter: "I was keen to do something different. This was the biggest visual thing I had done for a long time." The show involved a range of brilliant set pieces. A tree that emerged from beneath the stage. A suitcase that swallowed up the musicians and a telephone box with a never ending phone cord. As well as these effects the show was presented on two special stages.

Explained Gabriel: "The album *Us* was about relationships but rather than just personal relationships we looked at polarities. Town and country, synthetic and organic, male and female. The masculine and feminine relationship is represented by square and round stages. My favourite part of the show was when we moved from the masculine stage to the feminine stage. It was designed in such a way as to have narrative running though it from start to finish."

As a public display of Gabriel power 'The Secret World Live'

revealed some of the singer's own 'secrets' – notably the importance he places on empathy with his fellow creative artists. The
show was the result of years of work, but in a trice it explained
once and for all just why the singer had to leave his old band. In
the past he had been engaged in a struggle to get across ideas
that fermented in his imagination. To the men of Genesis his use
of costumes and bizarre lyrics at best seemed like a tolerable
way of gaining publicity. At worst however they were perceived
as a side show – an irrelevant irritation. The competition for
space with the band was ultimately counterproductive. Certainly in the heat of the moment, brilliance flared, but it was
often in danger of being strangled at birth. Nobody was to
blame for that situation. There were mistakes all round and
nobody can fairly claim the benefit of hindsight. No man is an
island entire of itself. Never send to know for whom the bell
tolls; it tolls for thee.

What Gabriel had achieved by 1993 was a perfectly balanced
environment in which the artists could clearly be seen working
together in a common cause and with mutual respect. There
have doubtless been occasions when even the best trained
Doudouk player has thrown a 'wobbly'– slamming his instrument into its case and announcing sharply "I'm leaving the
group!" But in general the video evidence from Peter's 'Secret
World' gives a picture of a new found serenity. Good music can
be produced without the necessity for constant internecine
strife.

The show conceived by Gabriel and Lepage opens with the
centre stage dominated by a red telephone box of traditional
British design. Inside is Gabriel, wrestling with a difficult call
as he sings 'Come Talk To Me' and wrestling with an even
more difficult telephone lead. As he struggles to get out of the
box the lead is stretched across the stage but eventually drags
him back inside. It is a Luis Buñuel influenced surrealism that
the Spanish film director might have used to depict the burdens
of respectable conformity, but in this case represents the English
man's eternal struggle to communicate.

'Steam' the *Us* album's bow to soul, has the band rocking out
with ill concealed pleasure. Peter clad in black tights engages in
the kind of sexy dancing only the middle aged can do without
self-conscious shame. "Give me steam!" he cries as clouds of

hot vapour jets upwards from recesses in the stage. In 'Across The River' Peter can be seen in close up, revealing a trimmed moustache and beard that serves to distract from the hairline beginning to recede from a furrowed brow.

"This song was written 12 years ago for WOMAD Festival," says the composer in a terse and serious introduction that bears little relation to the verbose and fanciful story telling of yesteryear.

But there is no need for extraneous verbiage on a song as exquisite as this. Spectral sounds emit from Shankar's weird violin then Peter smiles as he pounds huge, earth moving chords from his keyboard, before picking up an oar (if you'll pardon the phrase) and paddling across an imaginary river Styx. 'Shaking The Tree' sees a leafy tree emerge from beneath the stage to become a symbolic centre piece. Tony Levin, Peter's long-term and brilliant shaven-headed bass player, clad for the occasion in what look like bizarre shorts, joins in the communal dancing. A special feature of the whole performance is the way the band are choreographed. Gabriel's dances with David Rhodes are a weird kind of video re-wind motion.

Indeed the body language between all the players and dancers is very telling. The occasional smile, the shared glance, the encouraging nod, all speak of a commune in action, where support is freely given and Gabriel their titular head offers the kind of respect to his followers that he expects for himself. The artists who have taken part in the musical adventure Peter Gabriel has offered over the years are very privileged. Few 'rock bands' can offer the same kind of rewards in terms of musical fulfilment combined with such well intentioned artistic discipline and integrity. That is what makes Gabriel's work and presence unique in the Nineties. He is a leader in the best sense.

Frank Zappa was a great catalyst, who could bring out the best in his cohorts – even if they didn't always enjoy the experience and could be heard grumbling about the money and the conditions. Gabriel is both understanding and a generous provider – as can be seen from the looks on the faces of those whose job is to interpret his visions. They tend to smile a lot.

As one of his first drummers Jerry Marotta once said: "For the first few years of working with him, there wasn't a single person from the road crew that wouldn't have gone out on a tour for no money at all, just to be involved with this guy and his calibre of music and professionalism."

As the 'Secret World' show progresses 'Blood Of Eden' showcases not only Peter's most heartbreaking, throat cracking vocal style, but introduces the beautiful Paula Cole taking the Sinead O'Connor role, just as she later takes over the Kate Bush tradition on 'Don't Give Up'. (Paula's subsequent career was greatly helped by these appearances on the second leg of the 'Secret World' tour.)

The mood is energised with a witty interpretation of 'Kiss That Frog' with more smiles from Paula. Peter's forehead is etched with worry lines as he sings 'Washing Of The Water' and utters the final lines "Take this pain away" with the utmost despair. Some have asked how Peter can sing such deeply personal lines night after night in the hurly-burly of a 'live' performance. But as he explained to Robin Denselow in a penetrating *Guardian* interview: "Once it's written it's in a controlled environment, so I don't feel difficult about performing it. When it's buried and not exposed to the world, that's the difficult part. Coming to terms with buried emotions and bringing them out is a difficult process. It comes out in writing or therapy, but the therapy for me was more of a challenge because I wasn't able to control and manipulate it the way I can with my music."

Peter describes the act of writing songs as providing a resonating chamber for the emotions. "But it's a packaged emotion in a way. It sounds derogatory but it isn't. If it is put in a song or a book or a painting it's made safe. It's got a wrapping around it to make it more comfortable than in a directly confrontational situation."

The joy of performing must alleviate some of the pain inherent in performing his more personal, soul searching songs. 'Solsbury Hill' is a case where the cool, casual yet spirited dancing becomes an integral part of the musical experience, expressing the mood perhaps more strongly than the lyrics.

Even more expressive is Peter's face, seen in extraordinary close-up on 'Digging In The Dirt'. A special camera probes and exaggerates his bulging eyes and huge nose and projects his image on a giant screen. He looks truly evil as he snarls "This time you've gone too far!" Peter used a head camera focused on his face and the results are bizarre, providing a distorted view of his performance. Explained Gabriel: "The song 'Digging In The Dirt' is about anger and rage. It shouldn't be beautiful and pretty. This technique allowed me to film from my perspective. I have never seen this – as a performer – before."

'Sledgehammer' is greeted with whistles and claps as Peter joins Levin and Rhodes in a curious creep across the stage until the time honoured cry of "One, two – three!" signals an explosion of activity. Peter runs down the length of the stage to dance and sing with the aid of a radio mike around his neck. As Manu Katche sets up a funky beat Paula Cole and Peter present a latter-day Fred Astaire and Ginger Rogers as they dance cheek by jowl. As the stomping, exuberant sledgehammer beat grips both audience and performers, Gabriel, Rhodes and Levin march in unison. Here is a clear demonstration of the Gabriel Principle in action. No lead singer shall strut his stuff with his back to the band. In a complete reversal of usual rock practice the star is part of a team effort where everyone is expected to actively contribute, not just to the music, but to the spectacle. Rhythm guitarists and bass players were once content to stand in the shadows, looking sour faced, miserable and immobile. In Gabriel's World such self distancing is verboten. You have to get involved and the results are a kind of new order in the structure of rock music performance, which is marvellous to behold.

"Sometimes when you look around everything seems still and calm on the surface. And then you detect a little disturbance and you know for sure that underneath the surface lies some other secret world." Peter introduces 'Secret World' with this video insert, and as he refers to "a slight disturbance" his image ripples like water and begins to blur – an eerie and disturbing effect. Meanwhile, back at the concert the song becomes the basis for one of the most effective and amusing stage sequences that Gabriel has thus far devised. The band delivers the song with terrific power, enhanced by flashing strobe lights and the kind of spinning dance steps seen at London's hippie clubs of the Sixties.

Even the huge projection screen above their heads begins to spin. After Peter has sung "Shaking it up, making it up, in our secret world," he reverts to the piano to play a few dramatic chords as the mood changes and silence falls. But this is only a teasing pause, for the beat returns more insistent than ever. Manu Katche rocks out on his drums with masterful timing and feeling for a groove. His robotic rhythm accompanies the appearance of a conveyor belt load of battered old suitcases which roll across the stage, recreating the scurrying activity of a busy airport terminal – where musicians spend many hours of their lives.

One big case stops in front of the band. Peter puts on a long black coat (becoming fleetingly Mozo the mysterious stranger), and picks up the case. After carrying it across the stage he opens the lid and, arms folded, ushers into the seemingly bottomless bag, each member of the band. First to descend into the darkness is David Rhodes, followed by Manu Katche, Paula and finally Tony Levin, who pops up again to loud cheers, only to be gently but firmly pushed back into the all-encompassing luggage. Peter then drags the case away as the audience screams its approval. A drum machine has kept the rhythm flowing but as Peter looks up, a huge dome descends over the stage like a gigantic flying saucer. As it hits the deck the music stops and the crowd explodes.

It would be hard to top this moment. But Peter and the band return to perform 'Don't Give Up' on which Paula Cole gives a wonderfully sympathetic support to Gabriel at his most downcast and traumatised. It may just be a song, but they live out the parts with an intensity that is heartbreaking.

Sings Peter: "I was taught to fight – taught to win. I never thought I could fail . . . no one wants you when you lose." As he sits despondently on the stage Paula brings hope with her gentle entreaty . . . "Don't give up" . . . made more poignant by a sombre piano chord that heralds her entrance. Always a well structured piece this 'live' version only serves to emphasise its underlying strength and outstanding beauty. However, there is a surprise in store when Peter smiles, grasps Paula's hand and leads her into a spirited reggae reprise of the song. They wipe away their tears and break the tension.

The final number 'In Your Eyes' sees the dome rising and the band returning to their stations. This time the entire ensemble is drawn into a kind of dancing fever, similar to the one that spread across Europe in the 13th Century. Only this time there is an African element to the chanting and singing. The choreographer clearly worked overtime on this production in which Peter jumps and dances with selected members of the cast before joining in a grand finale. Everyone circles the stage in a ring o' poses. "It's in your eyes," states Peter having the last word, before Levon Minassian's haunting Doudouk closes a magnificent show.

Deservedly Peter's 'Secret World Live' video won the Best Music Video, Long Form at the Grammy Awards ceremony on February 28, 1996.

In the wake of the success of *Us* some old Gabriel hands feared Peter might fade once more from public view, retreating into his secret world perhaps to practise the flute, levitation and astral projection.

But the older, more practical and organised Gabriel kept both feet firmly on the ground. He embarked on a fever pitch of activity, branching out into different territories, actively developing new technologies and making yet more 'live' appearances. Peter had predicted as far back as 1979: "Technology is the revolution in the sense that it will change people's lives more than any other single thing in the next 50 years, much more than Marx – or Hitler."

In 1993, as part of his commitment to technology he took two 'Mind Blender' trailers around America which had cost one million pounds to develop. 'The Mindblender' was hailed as the world's first motion video ride and was developed in the US. Each trailer held 30 people who sat in devices somewhat akin to flight simulators and they watched computer graphics on laser disc videos via a 16 foot, high definition screen displaying his single 'Kiss That Frog'. It was produced by Brett Leonard, director of *The Lawnmower Man*. The effect was described by Peter as "heightened reality with music" rather than virtual reality. "It was the first music video ride with the seats programmed to dance. All the seats moved with the film. As you dive or swoop your brain tells you you're inside the environment, not separate from it." The trailers travelled from Toronto to Detroit, and from San Diego to far flung Los Angeles on their strange odyssey.

Also during 1993 he embarked on a tour of the US Southern

States, heading on out from Dallas to Miami, taking with him his multi-media stage show, in which he acted out the songs from *Us* with the miniature camera strapped firmly on his head. During this frantically busy period he brought his band back to England to appear at WOMAD'S 'A World In The Park Festival' in Bath, not far from his home, playing alongside those world music artists from Colombia, Jamaica and Zaire, he had so assiduously helped and promoted.

Just two days after this event Peter was back in the US for another stint with the trailers and then went to Cornwall, England, in August for yet another WOMAD event. Soon after he returned to America for the US launch of WOMAD and a series of ten shows at which he appeared alongside artists from Jamaica, Uganda and India. These shows also included some advanced technological ideas. Said Peter: "The idea was to throw in a bit of modern with the ancient."

It seemed like Gabriel was working himself to the point of exhaustion and those who admired him were concerned at this punishing schedule. He has admitted he sometimes takes on more than one man can be expected to handle. "I do feel that sometimes I take too much on my shoulders and don't leave myself enough time to make records. The problem is that I love everything that I do and I need it because it makes me feel alive and keeps me interested. I need to take risks. I don't like to say 'No'. I am good at getting things started, at kicking them off, but I'm weak at following through."

In 1994 he was scheduled to perform at Norway's Kalvoya Festival, a non-profit orientated event sponsored that year by Digital Music Express. DMX was a multi-channel system of bringing music into homes by cable, something that clearly intrigued the son of the inventor of Dial-A-Programme.

The same year he played at Glastonbury Festival in England where he performed using electricity generated only by wind power, in an attempt to combine music with environmental awareness. Apart from his interest in DMX the development of CD ROM ('ROM' means read only memory) presented Peter with yet more exciting possibilities. By the mid Eighties vinyl LPs and singles which had dominated the record market for decades were suddenly phased out with almost indecent haste.

The compact discs which replaced them were only a halfway

house in some eyes. The discs had the capacity to store vast amounts of information, far more than was needed for 25 minutes worth of music. Peter could see that the CD itself would one day be superseded by CD ROM, although there would be a few glitches along the road to achieving this latest revolution.

On February 1, 1994 Peter launched *Xplora 1 – Peter Gabriel's Secret World* on CD ROM. Co-produced by his newly formed Real World Multi Media company and Steve Nelson of the US based company Brilliant Media, *Xplora* was the first product of its kind in the world. It was originally designed for use on Macintosh computers and then given the Windows 95 treatment for PCs. Intended to be the first of a series, this début product provided a fascinating journey through Peter's world. Gabriel himself appeared on a screen guiding the user on a trip to see how his album *Us* was put together and also to gain access to top music events like the Grammies, the Brits and even a WOMAD festival. This one, incidentally, was based on a San Francisco WOMAD festival which had attracted 100,000 fans. The interactive CD ROM also went into the many other areas that Gabriel and Real World took on board from art, video and human rights issues to gardening (back to the cabbages) and even train spotting. It had over 100 minutes worth of video, 30 minutes worth of audio and more than 100 still images and a whole book's worth of text. Although it was a new concept for music fans, *Xplora 1*, which cost $250,000 to make, became the year's biggest selling music-based CD ROM, and won multimedia awards around the world, including the 1994 BIMA Award, and the Sparky from the Interactive Media Festival. It also carried off four prizes at the Digital Media Awards.

Peter had taken a businesslike stance by setting up Real World Multimedia, bringing together artists and technologists with the aim of developing, producing and publishing new multimedia titles. Said the Grand Vizier of vision: "We wanted to call the CD ROM *Xplora* because we are trying to create an environment in which people can have adventures. In the past we've had a linear journey from one point to another but now we are providing the material and a little world in which people can make their own journeys and their own decisions. Eventually the artist will not just provide a particular piece of work to be heard, seen and enjoyed in one way, but provide a collage of materials for people to play with, explore and create something for themselves."

The first Gabriel CD ROM was packed with ideas and said Peter: "I was very keen to try and get people into the creative process. For instance we had one track 'Digging In The Dirt' where people would be able to do their own mix. It's limited in the sense that we have four tracks only available, but that still gives you quite a good feel for some of the work that is done in the studio."

Peter loves working with strange instruments from around the world and through WOMAD and Real World Records, he had come across all sorts of interesting music and some remarkable players. "It is fun to be able to click on these different instruments on the CD ROM and hear what they sound like and hear how they can compete very effectively with others."

The interactive studio tour available on *Xplora* was a source of quiet joy to Peter who could only dream about such things in the days of Dansette Record players and black and white TV. With his CD ROM people got a chance to go into one of the rooms at his studio to try mixing a track. "They can see us involved in writing and building up a song or go in another room where I normally work and find Brian Eno with a group of musicians from different countries and see how they might interact together in different jam sessions."

It took hours of work to design *Xplora* and Peter set out to avoid what he thought was "cold, sci-fi and a little dehumanising" on some other CD ROMs he'd seen. "We very much wanted something that was personal and warm and had some natural references so you would see water, leaves, rocks, flowers and grass. It is these types of elements as back drops which I think helped give our disc its character. I also appear as an agent to help guide users through different places and I make suggestions if nothing is happening and give the viewer a gentle kick. In many of the screens there is a marriage of high-tech and handmade which is part of the aesthetic philosophy for much of what we do. We wanted to get under the skin. This is all new territory, not only for us but I think for everyone and we worked on it for a year trying a lot of different ideas to entertain people."

The *Xplora* CD ROM was divided into four sections. The first related to the *Us* album and videos and had the directors talking as well as showing some of the ideas behind the videos. There were also a series of images with 11 different artists to accompany the songs. The artists talked about their reactions to the music and what led them to create the images used on the art work. A world music section allowed the user to explore all sorts of musical traditions from around the world.

Said Peter: "The Real World Records section was a real source of pleasure enabling me to work with a lot of wonderful artists from different countries. You can click on any one of their album sleeves, listen to a little of their music and get some background material or see some videos of the different artists involved. There is also a means of stopping the world spinning for a moment and visiting any one of the countries on the surface of the planet, seeing what sort of musical noises emerge out of that country." There was also a visit to a WOMAD festival. "This particular section allows you to explore a festival site, see what's happening on the different stages, check out different artists and what's happening backstage."

On *Xplora 1* there was even a personal file in which the users come across the top drawer of a big trunk. Here they can rummage around and find lots of different things to play with, including an interactive passport and an old photo book which allows the viewer to discover some of Peter's home movies and videos. There's another section which deals with his records, which are ready for exploring. There is also more information on some of the organisations which Peter has been involved with like Amnesty and Witness. This 'behind the scenes' section was very popular.

Says Peter: "One of the most coveted items of any gig is the pass, the highest and most important of which is the laminate, so we have a tray full of laminates that will let you backstage at some of the award shows such as the Brits and the Grammies and also enables you to take the interactive studio tour."

CD ROM was really just waiting for Peter to discover. "For years I had wanted to be an experience designer rather than just a musician and this new technology is one of the things which allows artists to take a step in that direction."

Certainly it was a lot more convenient and cheaper than

building a theme park. "This is in no way a peripheral activity for me. I think that this type of media is going to be at the very centre of what I do in the future and it's great fun to get to play with it. These new medias are coming at us very fast and they're going to confront the world in which we live. They're going to transform the music business. A lot of us that have an affinity towards visual things, with pictures, film and video, are going to fall into experience design and this is where I want the centre of my work to be in the future."

Peter felt excited about being an artist working in the mid-Nineties when so many new ideas were coming on stream. "There is a fundamental revolution happening in the way that media are getting mixed together. We're getting information, education, entertainment and communications all being thrown together in one big soup. It provides us with all sorts of possibilities as artists and as individuals. I think it will change the way that we communicate with each other. Obviously to be there at the birth of a new medium and have a chance to explore different things and putting them together in different ways is very exciting. I think there's all sorts of possibilities now that I and a lot of others can't wait to get into."

Peter believed that the way people interact with all the new technology would change the way they lived and the way they thought. "This particular medium will allow us to interact for real time and build new multi-media environments and communications as we go. There are some parallels with what's happening with sampling technology, which is still fairly new to us. Musicians are suddenly able to grab any sounds, rhythms, colours, textures and noises and start throwing them together in different ways, even in their bedrooms. It doesn't necessarily mean that because you have 500 colours on your palate that you are going to make better paintings. Content is still everything. But it does provide people with a lot more tools. I think it empowers people because it will give them access to so much."

He felt that people wouldn't need to acquire great skill levels in each field to use what the new facilities had to offer. "But you can use other people's skills to help create something of your own." Gabriel saw it all as a fundamental cultural shift.

Even so it did not take into account the phenomenon of the couch potato, that person who would still sooner sit with a can of beer watching *EastEnders* or the *Teletubbies* on TV rather than busily interact with the latest CD ROM in the search for creative fulfilment. Peter has an answer for this assumption. "This sort of TV computer technology which still is for most people a fairly passive relationship, is suddenly going to be something that can really activate us. There are times I am sure that people will want to be a vegetable and just sit back and absorb. That's how I use TV sometimes, just to switch off and become a zombie. But it is also going to be able to be flipped around to become a creative catalyst to fire us, charge us and accelerate us down the routes that excite us."

Peter found the whole digital revolution, which he had been talking about and pioneering for so many years, incredibly exciting. "I believe that the technology could transform a lot of the world both socially and politically. I know that sometimes people think it is arrogant and elitist for a rich westerner to be talking about the joys of computers and technology, when in many parts of the world people are struggling to stay alive or to feed themselves and I certainly accept that. However if you look at the history of technology and the way that prices decrease, you will see transistor radios, televisions, fax machines or telephones that we now take as everyday items were once all luxury, elitist items and I'm sure the price of this technology will come right down. The satellite communications systems that we are now developing and telephone companies going global will mean that any village on the surface of the planet could have a small information kit, which would allow them to satellite up link and down link. They could have it solar powered and with a few low cost PCs they could become information processors."

Gabriel feels that all that is needed is for costs to come down and this will allow third world countries to become information economies as powerful as countries in the Western world.

Said Peter: "A lot of aid projects at the moment are very hampered because you get these huge packages of money which sometimes don't get distributed properly, due to corruption. This technology could enable these small mobile units to reach the people directly and they can then communicate without having to go through the government communications systems. They can power their systems without having to be dependent on their own countries' power supplies. I am sure that it is going to be harder to control and censor information. It is going to be impossible to stop, just as the Soviet Union at one time tried to stop the introduction of fax machines, which they also found impossible. To me it is a great source of joy that this sort of networking is going to happen, whether governments want it or not and there is a real chance of the technology empowering the people."

Gabriel's next CD ROM project called *Eve* and released in 1996, allowed the user to mix and create his own version of Peter's songs. The CD ROM was a technical and artistic triumph and won the prestigious Milia D'Or Award.

"This type of work is really the most exciting thing that is going on at the moment and I think it is going to become a centre of my work as an artist and also what we do at Real World as a publisher. In a sense it's a move from being a record company into becoming a sort of interactive creator and experience design label, which is the name I prefer. It really feels as if we are on the edge of a revolution."

As an artist of international prestige and distinction Peter was called upon to sing on many different soundtrack and tribute albums over the next few years, which he thoroughly enjoyed as a different kind of challenge.

He sang a new song called 'Partyman' with The Worldbeaters on the MCA soundtrack album for the Paramount movie *Virtuosity* released in August, 1995. In September Peter performed Leonard Cohen's 'Suzanne' on A&M's tribute album to Cohen. He even sang the difficult and demanding standard 'Summertime' on another tribute album called *The Glory Of Gershwin*. And he collaborated with Nusrat Fateh Ali Khan on 'Taboo' on the soundtrack to *Natural Born Killers*. It proved to be the last such collaboration. Nusrat died aged 49 on August 16, 1997 at a London hospital after a cardiac arrest. One of Pakistan's most popular artists and a noted singer of Qawwli devotional songs favoured by Islamic mystics, he had performed on Peter's *Passion* CD and had released several albums on the Real World label.

In April 1996 the music TV network VH1 held their 'WH1 Honours' show at the Universal Amphitheatre in Los Angeles where Peter was given a special award. He managed to get

VH1 to donate all the proceeds to the Lawyer's Committee for Human Rights' part of the Witness project that he founded in 1992 in conjunction with the Reebok Foundation. Over the years they supplied hundreds of video cameras to activists in over fifty countries, as well as fax machines and other communications tools.

The tragic death of Diana, Princess Of Wales in September, 1997 provoked a strong response from the musical community and Richard Branson of the Virgin business empire initiated a special tribute album project, calling on many international artists to participate. Peter Gabriel contributed 'In The Sun', a cover of a beautiful Joseph Arthur song that appeared on *Diana, Princess Of Wales: Tribute* a 36 track double compilation CD released on December 1, 1997. Peter's performance was singled out for praise by the critics and said *The Independent*: "Of all the new material, Peter Gabriel's 'In The Sun' is by far the most impressive, a version of a Joseph Arthur song marked by Gabriel's usual taste and sensitivity." *The Times* called it 'a stark, achingly beautiful song.'

He also gave a version of his 'Love To Be Loved' to the Huckleberry House 30th Anniversary Jam with proceeds going to the Huckleberry Youth House project.

Peter was also featured on an album of songs from the film City Of Angels, released in March 1998. The movie, a story of romance and desire starring Nicolas Cage and Meg Ryan opened in April. As well as tracks by Alanis Morissette, US, Eric Clapton and the Goo Goo Dolls, the soundtrack featured Gabriel singing 'I Grieve' the first new solo recording from Peter since 1994. The same month that the soundtrack appeared Peter attended the 10th Annual Reebok Human Rights Awards ceremony in New York to honour young activists who had campaigned against violence around the world.

Amidst this endless round of recording, filming and composing, Peter Gabriel still had time to dream. His most celebrated long term project has been the creation of a Real World Experience theme park. He has been dreaming about the idea for many years. Said Peter in 1992: "The Real World Experience Park is the ambition that I still have to fulfil."

At one time it looked like it might come to fruition when a site became available in Sydney, Australia. Although Peter was impressed by Disney World, he wanted to build something less commercial, that would be more interactive, challenging and perhaps educational for visitors. He heard from a friend about a plan to develop a two acre site in Sydney near the sea and suggested Peter put forward a proposal. He commissioned a British architect, Will Alsop, to submit plans. It needed at least £30 million to get the scheme off the ground and Peter was encouraged when Richard Branson of the Virgin Group expressed an interest in supporting the idea. However, despite all their plans and promises of assistance, in the end their idea was rejected by the Australian Ministry of Silly Walks – that is to say Works. A year later Alsop's plans for Peter's theme park were revived when another site became available in Cologne, Germany. This time the projected cost of building the park was expected to be £150 million. In the meantime Euro Disney was built near Paris, France. Even the experience and expertise of Disney could not prevent that project from losing money during its first years but Peter remained convinced there could be a viable alternative. "The ideology and aesthetics of the amusement park were established in the Forties and Fifties and I strongly believe that the creative minds of today could come up with much more interesting experiences than has usually been the case," said Peter. "With interactive technology you could have events and experiences that would respond to the visitor so it would be a truly participatory process."

Peter continued working on the project with Brian Eno and Laurie Anderson. By 1992 the plan was to build the park in Barcelona, Spain. Here artists, musicians, film makers, psychologists, architects and scientists would work together to create new forms of interactive experiences and high tech multimedia rides. Said Peter: "It would be like a little laboratory that people don't go into for research, but fun, pleasure and profit and creative satisfaction. To me the marriage seems very natural. It combines my personal interests and I've always worked on the theory that if something really excites me there's a good chance it will work for other people."

Interestingly when the British Labour Government committed themselves to creating a Millennium Dome experience in Greenwich, England, the organisers invited Peter to write some music for the event, which in some ways paralleled his own ambitions. It remains to be seen how tangible and successful these visions become.

Peter described his vision for his own theme park as a place to have fun. "You couldn't survive without fun. If it was just serious and a place where you were challenged then it would be too much. Maybe it could involve a regular funfair as well. I picture a lot of places in the future that will be a combination of holiday camp, university and art gallery. It's the way things must go. With mass unemployment, it seems there are only three solutions to the prospect of massive riots – education, entertainment and conscription. And the first two are preferable to conscription."

By 1998 more than a decade had gone by and the idea of the Real World Theme Park still seemed like a pipe dream. But in the early months of the year Peter was in contact with the mayor of Barcelona who sent his chief city planner to England to discuss a proposal for a new site. The new theme park would differ greatly from that originally discussed by Peter, Brian Eno, Laurie Anderson and Robert Lepage. After all technology had taken many steps forward and some of their ideas had been overtaken by events. In it's original form it might have been a bit like one of those World Fair Visions of the Future staged in the Thirties which depicted a world full of flying cars and moving pavements. The new idea was to create a 'Magic Garden' rather than a mega park.

Just when it seemed that Peter Gabriel was firmly established as a man of the late 20th Century, a figure who bestrode the Nineties with calm authority, without let or hindrance, there arose a disturbing echo from the past. It concerned a certain pop group he had once been involved with – in the dim and distant past.

Genesis had marched on to glory in the intervening years and reached new peaks of success with their albums *Invisible Touch* (1986) and *We Can't Dance* (1991). Despite the fact they could still easily sell out concerts and tours around the world, one of their number had grown restless. Although they still produced high quality commercial music, the special magic that been there during the Gabriel years had long deserted them. Phil Collins had presided over the move from long, rhapsodic themes that typified their early work, towards tighter, punchier and more soulful pop songs. It worked but his own material often seemed to overlap and in any case his dual role as solo artist and Genesis front man meant double the work, not always welcome when he was looking to settle down and take life at a slightly less hectic pace.

And so Phil announced his departure from the band during 1996 with the intention of concentrating on his own career. In fact Phil had been hinting that he would leave as far back as 1993. He told me that it increasingly seemed like he was just acting out his role on stage with the group. Finally it was announced that Genesis were without their lead singer – and drummer. It may not have been such dramatic, headline stuff but, just as when Gabriel left them two decades earlier, it was predicted that the band and its honourable tradition of music making must finally be over.

But founder members Tony Banks and Mike Rutherford were made of sterner stuff. They resolutely carried on, recruiting 28-year-old Scottish singer Ray Wilson. He had previously fronted a band called Stiltskin who had a Number One single with 'Inside'. Genesis also brought in a new drummer known as Nir Z. They recorded a new 11 track album called *Calling All Stations*, released in September, 1997, their first studio effort since 1991's *We Can't Dance*. The band's first single off the album was 'Congo' and they commenced a European tour in January 1998 which included UK concerts at the NEC Birmingham (February 25, 26), London's Earls Court (27), and shows in Glasgow, Newcastle, Cardiff and Manchester during March. Those who went enjoyed the shows but some were under the illusion that Phil Collins was still in the band while others thought Peter Gabriel might turn up. It was a tough job for the relatively unknown singer, but he had the right kind of positive attitude, which he cheerfully displayed to the world on his press and TV interviews. Having to learn five hours of complex Genesis material for the shows was tough enough but he also had to follow in the footsteps of two of the rock world's biggest stars. It was a hard couple of acts to follow. He acquitted himself well but must have suffered extra butterflies, or pangs of annoyance, when there was speculation that Peter Gabriel might consider rejoining the band to replace Phil Collins. Although it seemed an absurd idea in view of all that had happened, as Sean Connery once said: "Never say never again."

My own view is that one day in the distant future all the ex-Genesis members will appear together at a charity show on some vast, slowly revolving stage to perform the whole of *The Lamb Lies Down On Broadway*. During this momentous performance a huge row will develop resulting in everybody biffing each other on the nose and shouting "And another thing!" After which they will weep, laugh and then play the most thunderous version of 'Watcher Of The Skies' since 1973.

Peter had not sung in public with his old mates Genesis since the 1982 reunion show at Milton Keynes. However, he did record some new vocal tracks for some rare 'live' *Lamb Lies Down On Broadway* material intended for a Genesis boxed set. Indeed several Genesis box sets are planned. The first will cover the Peter Gabriel years up to 1975 and include 4 CDs and a 72 page booklet. Two of the CDs will include a whole concert from *The Lamb Lies Down On Broadway* tour and another CD should cover the *Selling England By The Pound* era, with 'live' material and 'B' sides.

In 1997 Peter and Phil Collins went back into the studios with Mike Rutherford and Tony Banks to record a new version of 'The Carpet Crawl' to be released as a single prior to the box set. It features Peter on vocals and Phil on drums. The project was scheduled for autumn, 1998 release. CD 1 & 2 features *The Lamb* and CD 3 has 'live' versions of 'Dancing With The Moonlit Knight', 'Firth Of Fifth', 'Supper's Ready', 'I Know What I Like' and 'Stagnation' (a BBC 'live' recording), 'Twilight Alehouse' (B side of a 1973 single), 'Happy The Man' and 'Watcher Of The Skies' (unreleased single version, 1972).

The digitally remastered tracks on CD 4 will include 'In The Wilderness' – a rough mix without strings from 1968; and 1970 recordings from the BBC *Nightride* show including 'Shepherd', 'Pacidy', 'Let Us Now Make Love' and 'Going Out To Get You' demo (1969), 'Dusk' demo (1969), 'Build Me A Mountain' – rough mix (1968); and a series of 1968 demo tracks including 'One Day', 'Where The Sour Turns To Sweet', 'In The Beginning', 'The Magic Of Time', 'Hey!', 'Hidden In The World Of Dawn', 'Sea Bee', 'The Mystery Of The Flannan Isle Lighthouse', 'Hair On The Arms And Legs' and 'She Is Beautiful' demo 1967 (early version of 'The Serpent'); 'Image Blown

Our' demo 1967, 'Try A Little Sadness' – demo 1967 and 'Patricia' demo 1968 (early version of 'In Hiding').

A further volume is proposed to be released in the autumn of 1999 covering the period from 1975 to 1980 and Volume 3 should be out in the autumn of the year 2000 covering the years from 1981 onwards.

Much of this old material had never been released before and Peter had been helping with what proved a fascinating project. His task was to replace some old vocal tracks, where the huge costumes he had worn during the Genesis *Lamb* shows had masked not just his face, but the sound as well. It was the covert operations involving Peter that fuelled the rumours. Gabriel's organisation emphasised: "Although Peter remains a good friend of the members of Genesis, he will not be rejoining them, nor will he be touring with them, despite rumours."

As 1998 dawned speculation and excitement continued to rise about the eagerly awaited new Peter Gabriel album. If it was anything like *So* or *Us* then it would have to be one of the finest works of the decade. In the event it seemed it would be nothing like those albums.

PG had been working on it for many months and although he was 'off the road' he was expected to return to touring in time for the album's release towards the end of the year. Certainly he planned to be singing at a show to commemorate the 50th Anniversary of Amnesty International, scheduled for December 10, 1998.

Originally it had been hoped to release the new work during the autumn of 1997 but it had been delayed in order to avoid clashing with the release of the new Genesis album and to allow the work to be finished to everyone's satisfaction. At any rate the production team of Gabriel, Dickie Chappell and Meabh Flynn had spent months piecing together samples and sounds from recording sessions held during the summer. The idea was to build them into what Real World sources described as "the extravagant audio collage that would be Peter's next album". Peter had some working titles for the songs ready at the start of 1998. He had written and recorded about 40 songs and the best would be selected for the album. Among the finished items due for inclusion were 'Signal To Noise', 'Children', 'While Earth Sleeps' (from the film *Strange Days*, co-written with Deep

Forest), 'Seven Zero' (an instrumental), 'Lovetown' and 'Party-man' (from the film *Virtuosity* co-written by Tori Amos and George Acogny).

There had been some input from Björk collaborator Marcus Dravs, but the musicians mainly involved included the nucleus of the Peter Gabriel band. Meabh has been in charge of sorting through many thousands of sequences to make what were raw recordings, described by some as "extraordinary", into something that would ultimately sound even more revolutionary. He built an entire percussive sample library that would allow Peter to play samples directly from the keyboard. The intention was to make a record unlike any previous Peter Gabriel album. One significant departure would be the absence of an outside producer. There would be no one blowing whistles or attempting to lock the composer in a closet. Mr. Gabriel himself would take charge of that department – and devil take the hindmost.

One major surprise in store was that Peter intended to play guitar on an album for the first time. Peter had picked up the instrument not long before starting to write his new songs. Said a colleague: "Peter has taken to it like a duck to water. Some of the album has been written on guitar, which can only mean a real sea-change in his writing style."

Undoubtedly the instruments Gabriel used on previous albums affected the way he conceived and structured songs. On the first solo album he mainly used the piano. On the second he was involved with the newly developed Linn drum. On his third album he utilised the Prophet and on *Peter Gabriel 4* it was the Fairlight, while on *So* he relied heavily on computer technology.

Said Peter: "A lot of things have come out of playing around with rhythm, machines, synths, effects and computers in ways that were not intended. Boredom and fatigue are also great creative tools; sometimes you have to kill ideas off in order for new ones to emerge!"

"The new album's material will clearly bear the mark of the guitar as a principle writing weapon," said Real World. "It's different," said his engineer Dickie Chappell, before the album was released. "Melody is the key thing. There's lots of strong melodic stuff in the vocal lines and the arrangements. I think people are going to be surprised."

Talking about his creative processes, Peter added: "Sometimes writing a song is like scaling a mountain. You think you're at the top but there's still more to climb. Then you look down and you know you've reached the goal. I once read that Chilean farmers put up nets to collect morning dew to get fresh water and for me the creative process is like this – misty ideas floating in the air which you work to catch and collect until they have enough mass and momentum to survive on their own."

Throughout his career Peter has relied on those sudden notions and bursts of inspiration which have guided rather more than any hard nosed business plan or strategy. Everything he has done, from his days with Genesis, through the early solo albums and onto WOMAD, World Music and the creation of his Secret World has been born out of these magical moments.

"When I was growing up on my dad's farm, we would go out to get the cows in for milking. We walked around the perimeter of the fields and herded the cows together towards the gate. Many artists have the target in mind and go straight at it, but I come from the edges and circle in toward the centre. When I'm working on one thing, something magical will mysteriously arise and I'll feel the urge to follow it. I'm great at diversions!"

Hair has long been a crucial ingredient in the creation of pop music. From Bill Haley's kiss curl to The Beatles mop tops, and from the green spikes of punk to the Mancunian fringes of Oasis, hairstyles have been a badge of honour. So there is nothing worse for any musician than loss of hair, which can only mean – loss of face.

When Peter shaved the front of his head way back in the early Seventies, he was amused at the reaction of the press and public to this simple gesture. Later he cropped his hair skinhead style during a period of personal angst and conflict. However in recent years there has been no need to take such drastic measures. The once beautiful, hairy youth of the hippie era has had to accept that styling of any kind is no longer an option. If there is a long hair revival in the wake of the success of such bands as Radiohead, then Peter Gabriel will not be able to join in the celebrations. His flowing locks are no more. They are defunct, shorn away and short to the point of baldness.

The warning signs had been there as far back as 1989 when Peter admitted: "In my twenties I would have been shocked to think that I would worry about a receding hairline. I thought I was above that. Bullshit! It's still somehow tied up with fears about sexual potency. I get it. I tried treating it with Minoxidil, but it doesn't seem to do much good."

By 1992 he was greying at the temples and the hairline was receding still further. By 1998 poor Peter had given up the struggle. Fans were shocked to see Peter appearing at public functions wearing glasses and completely bald. The years of battling against hair loss had ended in failure. Peter claims this previous self-imposed baldness, partially so in Genesis and total in the late Seventies had "prepared me for the worst". But now he had no choice. "It's just a case of doing less with less," he said sadly. It seemed he woke up one morning during the summer of 1997 and decided the remaining tufts of long hair were just emphasising the patches, so he cut them all off. Finally he gave in to nature's way and had the lot removed. At the same time he allowed himself to change his mind about one previously held conviction. "Bald men are more sexy," he announced defiantly.

It would have been a shame if this follicle failure had thwarted Peter's career ambitions, making him depressed or unwilling to face the public. But there is much more for the 'humanist' to do as he faces the year 2000. There is the theme park to bring to life, more technology to explore, more publishing, more writing, more recording – more of everything. As Peter says: "If you can make sounds that are interesting, you should continue until you are seventy years old."

Perhaps the underlying motivation for all Peter's activities has been the idea of transformation. He achieved it during his performances with Genesis, reaching a peak with the costumes and complex story lines he devised for *The Lamb Lies Down On Broadway*. He went on to reinvent himself both visually and musically during his early solo albums and with the 'Secret World' tour of the early Nineties his transformation as a person seemed complete, in a way that was perhaps all the more shocking and effective for those who still retained such strong memories of Gabriel past.

It is even more intriguing to consider that while Peter has put so much effort into making his musical career a success, he might have taken an entirely different path. It was something that occurred to him when he was at his lowest ebb after his split from Genesis. "At one point I thought I had the choice between being a musician and being a farmer. I am a mixture of both personalities. A more introverted person who loves solitude, nature, ideas. And then there's the other part of me that loves attention, loves being a performer, loves the excitement and cut and thrust of competition in the music business, the whole capitalist circus. So I'm torn between the two and the only way I can resolve it is by trying to get a good heap of both in my life."

The 'new' Gabriel of the Nineties was no overnight trans-mogrification. It was the result of years of accumulated experiences, including everything from acute stress to acute happiness, which now told in every line on his face and every last shaven hair that fell from his head.

Is the new Gabriel happier or more fulfilled? He is certainly more confident and commanding, helped no doubt by sessions of mind control EST training. He has said that selfishness is his most unpleasant characteristic. "I'd say that was at the top of the list" and adds that 'Fear is my greatest fear." The years of therapy, counselling and courses in greater self awareness have all played their part in sublimating his negative characteristics and bringing out the stronger man within. It was after the success of *So* that Peter left his old manager Gail Colson to take greater responsibility for his own affairs. It was something of a traumatic split after their years of work together, but it freed up Gail to embark on new challenges and Peter took on a new manager to run his business affairs. Gabriel the strong, had to cut loose from past ties, perhaps to prove to himself he could be the master of his own destiny.

The broad and cheerful smile as he triumphantly holds some new music business award or trophy aloft tells the story of a man who has ferried himself across the river and come back – to tell more tales and sing us more songs. He was Harold The Barrel, he was the man in the cardboard mask; he was Rael and he was Mozo. He is a man constantly reborn. The next layer of the onion is about to be peeled away. In truth the Peter Gabriel Story starts here. . . .

DISCOGRAPHY

7″ SINGLES

Peter Gabriel with Genesis

The Silent Sun/That's Me
Decca F 12735
Feb 1968

A Winter's Tale/One-Eyed Hound
Decca F 12775
May 1968

Where The Sour Turns To Sweet/In Hiding
Decca F 12949
June 1969

The Knife (Part 1)/The Knife (Part 2)
Charisma CB 152
1971

Happy The Man/Seven Stones
Charisma CB 181
May 1972

Watcher Of The Skies (withdrawn)/Willow Farm
Charisma CB 199

I Know What I Like (In Your Wardrobe)/Twilight Alehouse
Charisma CB 224
March 1974

Counting Out Time/Riding The Scree
Charisma CB 238
November 1974

The Carpet Crawlers/The Waiting Room (Evil Jam)
    Charisma CB 251
    April 1975

7″ SINGLES

Peter Gabriel – Solo

Solsbury Hill/Moribund The Bürgermeister
    Charisma CB 301
    March 1977

Solsbury Hill/Solsbury Hill (demo)
    Charisma CB301DJ
    March 1977

Modern Love/Slow Burn (picture label)
    Charisma CB 302
    June 1977

Modern Love/Slow Burn (silver label)
    Charisma CB 302
    June 1977

DIY/Perspective
    Charisma CB 311
    May 1978

DIY (re-mix)/Mother Of Violence/Me And My Teddy Bear
    Charisma CB 319
    September 1978

Solsbury Hill (live) (flexi disc)
    Sound for Industry SFI 381
    December 1978

Games Without Frontiers/The Start/I Don't Remember
    Charisma CB 354
    January 1980

No Self Control/Lead A Normal Life
    Charisma CB 360
    May 1980

Biko/Shosholoza/Jetzt Kommt Die Flut
    Charisma CB 370
    August 1980

Biko (promo edited version)/Shosholoza
   Charisma CBDJ 370
   August 1980

Shock The Monkey/Soft Dog
   Charisma Shock 1
   September 1982

Shock The Monkey (DJ version)
   Charisma Shock 350DJ
   September 1982

Shock The Monkey/Soft Dog (picture disc)
   Charisma Shock 122
   September 1982

I Have The Touch/Across The River
   Charisma CB 405
   December 1982

Solsbury Hill/Games Without Frontiers
   Old Gold Series OG 9265
   January 1983

I Don't Remember (live re-mix)/Solsbury Hill (live)
   Virgin GAB 1
   June 1983

Walk Through The Fire/The Race (by Larry Carlton)
   Virgin VS 689
   May 1984

Sledgehammer/Don't Break This Rhythm
   Virgin PGS 1
   April 1986

Don't Give Up (duet with Kate Bush)/In Your Eyes (African mix)
   Virgin PGS 2
   September 1986

Don't Give Up (with video-still poster)/In Your Eyes
   Virgin PGSP-2
   September 1986

Don't Give Up (DJ version)
   Virgin PGSDJ2
   September 1986

Big Time Curtains
  Virgin PGS 3
  March 1987

Red Rain/Ga Ga
  Virgin PGS 4
  June 1987

Biko (live)/No More Apartheid (extended)
  Virgin PGS 6
  January 1988

12″ SINGLES

Peter Gabriel – Solo

Biko/Shosholoza/Jetzt Kommt Die Flut
  Charisma CB370-12
  August 1980

Shock The Monkey/Soft Dog
  Charisma Shock 12
  September 1982

Shock The Monkey/Shock The Monkey (vocal/instrumental)
  Charisma Shock 343
  September 1982

I Go Swimming/Solsbury Hill/Shock The Monkey
  Charisma REP1 420
  May 1983

I Don't Remember (special DJ selection)/Solsbury Hill/
Humdrum/On The Air
  Charisma RAD 10
  May 1983

I Don't Remember/Solsbury Hill/ Kiss Of Life (live)
  Virgin GAB 12
  June 1983

Games Without Frontiers (live)/
Schnappschuss (white label limited edition)
  Virgin GAB 122
  June 1983

Discography

Walk Through The Fire/The Race/ I Have The Touch
   Virgin VS68912
   May 1984

Sledgehammer/Don't Break This Rhythm/
I Have The Touch (1985 re-mix)
   Virgin PGS 112
   April 1986

Sledgehammer (dance mix) (cassingle)/Don't Break This Rhythm/
Biko/I Have The Touch
   Virgin PGT 112
   May 1986

Sledgehammer (dance mix)/ Don't Break This Rhythm/
Biko/I Have The Touch (1985 re-mix)
   Virgin PGS 113
   May 1986

Don't Give Up/In Your Eyes (special mix)/ This Is The Picture
   Virgin PGS 212
   September 1986

Big Time (dance mix)/Big Time (7″ mix, extended version)/Curtains
   Virgin PGS 312
   March 1987

Big Time (extended) (cassingle)/Curtains/No Self Control/
Across the River
   Virgin PGT 312
   March 1987

Big Time (white label pre-release DJ copy)
   Virgin PG2312DJ
   March 1987

Red Rain/Ga Ga/Walk Through The Fire
   Virgin PGS 412
   June 1987

Red Rain (cassingle)/Ga Ga /Walk Through The Fire
   Virgin PGT 412
   June 1987

Biko(live)/No More Apartheid (extended)
   Virgin PGS 612
   January 1988

Peter Gabriel

CD SINGLES

Peter Gabriel – Solo

Big Time (extended version)/Curtains/No Self Control/
Across The River/Big Time (7″ mix)
    Virgin GAIL 312
    March 1987

Biko (live)/No More Apartheid/I Have The Touch ('85 remix)/
Jetzt Kommt Die Flut
    Virgin CDPGS 612
    January 1988

Solsbury Hill/Shaking The Tree/Moribund The Bürgermeister/
Solsbury Hill (live)/Games Without Frontiers
    Virgin CDT 33
    1988

Sledgehammer/John Has A Headache/Don't Break This Rhythm/
I Have The Touch/Sledgehammer(dance mix)/Biko (extended)
    Virgin CDT 4
    1988

Shaking The Tree (Peter Gabriel & Youssou N'Dour)/Old Tucson/
Sweeping The Leaves
    Virgin VSCD 1167
    May 1989

Solsbury Hill/Shaking The Tree/Moribund The Bürgermeister/
Solsbury Hill/Games Without Frontiers
    Virgin VSCDT 1322
    December 1990

Digging In The Dirt/Quiet Steam
    Charisma PGSDG 7
    July 1992

Steam
Steam (mixes)
    Realworld PGSDX8, PGSDG8
    January 1993

Blood Of Eden/Mercy Street/Blood Of Eden (mixes)/Sledgehammer
    Realworld PGSDX9
    March 1993

Blood Of Eden/Mercy Street/Blood Of Eden (mixes)
  Realworld PGSDG9
  March 1993

ALBUMS – VINYL

Peter Gabriel with Genesis

From Genesis To Revelation
  Where The Sour Turns To Sweet/In The Beginning/ Fireside Song/
  The Serpent/Am I Very Wrong/In The Wilderness/The
  Conqueror/In Hiding/One Day/Window/In Limbo/Silent Sun/
  A Place To Call My Own
  Decca SKL 4990
  March 1969

Trespass
  Looking For Someone/White Mountain/Visions Of Angels/
  Stagnation/Dusk/The Knife
  Charisma CAS 1020
  October 1970

Nursery Cryme
  The Musical Box/For Absent Friends/The Return Of The Giant
  Hogweed/Seven Stones/Harold The Barrel/Harlequin/
  The Fountain Of Salmacis
  Charisma CAS 1052
  November 1971

Foxtrot
  Watcher Of The Skies/Time Table/Get 'Em Out By Friday/
  Can-Utility And The Coastliners/Horizons/ Supper's Ready/
  i Lover's Leap, ii The Guaranteed Eternal Sanctuary Man,
  iii Ikhnaton And Itsacon And Their Band Of Merry Men,
  iv How Dare I Be So Beautiful? v Willow Farm,
  vi Apocalypse in 9/8 (Co-starring The Delicious Talents Of Gabble
  Ratchet), vii As Sure As Eggs Is Eggs (Aching Men's Feet)
  Charisma CAS 1058
  October 1972

Genesis Live
  Watcher Of The Skies/Get 'Em Out By Friday/
  The Return Of The Giant Hogweed/The Musical Box/The Knife
  Charisma CLASS 1
  August 1973

Selling England By The Pound
> Dancing With The Moonlit Knight/I Know What I Like (In Your
> Wardrobe)/Firth Of Fifth/More Fool Me/The Battle Of Epping
> Forest/After The Ordeal/The Cinema Show/Aisle Of Plenty
> Charisma CAS 1074
> October 1973

In The Beginning
> (1st album retitled)
> Same tracks as 'From Genesis To Revelation'
> Decca SKL 4990
> September 1974

The Lamb Lies Down On Broadway
> The Lamb Lies Down On Broadway/Fly On A Windshield/
> Broadway Melody Of 1974/Cuckoo Cocoon/In The Cage/
> The Grand Parade Of Lifeless Packaging/Back in NYC/Hairless
> Heart/Counting Out Time/The Carpet Crawlers/The Chamber Of
> 32 Doors/ Lillywhite Lilith/The Waiting Room/ Anyway/
> Here Comes The Supernatural Anaesthetist/The Lamia/
> Silent Sorrow In Empty Boats/The Colony Of Slippermen
> (The Arrival, A Visit To The Doktor, The Raven)/Ravine/
> The Light Dies Down On Broadway/Riding The Scree/
> In The Rapids/It
> Charisma CAS 101
> November 1974

Genesis Collection
> Volume One and Volume Two
> Boxed set Volume One
> Trespass/Nursery Cryme (double repackage)
> Charisma CGS 102
> April 1975

Volume Two
> Foxtrot/Selling England By The Pound (double repackage)
> Charisma CGS 103
> April 1975

Genesis R-O-C-K Roots
> Re-issue of 'From Genesis To Revelation' plus early singles
> Silent Sun/That's Me and
> A Winter's Tale/One-Eyed Hound
> Decca ROOTS 1
> May 1976

Where The Sour Turns To Sweet
    Where The Sour Turns To Sweet/In The Beginning/ Fireside
    Song/The Serpent/Am I Very Wrong/In The Wilderness/
    The Conqueror/In Hiding/One Day/Window/In Limbo/Silent Sun/
    A Place To Call My Own
    Rock Machine MACHM4
    1986

ALBUMS – VINYL

Peter Gabriel – Solo

Peter Gabriel 1
    Moribund The Bürgermeister/Solsbury Hill/Modern Love/
    Excuse Me/Humdrum/Slowburn/Waiting For The Big One/
    Down The Dolce Vita/Here Comes The Flood
    Charisma CDS 4006
    February 1977

Peter Gabriel 2
    On The Air/Do It Yourself/Mother Of Violence/A Wonderful Day
    In A One Way World/White Shadow/Indigo/Animal Magic/
    Exposure/Flotsam & Jetsam/Perspective/Home Sweet Home
    Charisma CDS 4013
    June 1978

Peter Gabriel 3
    Intruder/No Self Control/The Start/I Don't Remember/
    Family Snapshot/And Through The Wire/Games Without
    Frontiers/Not One Of Us/Lead A Normal Life/Biko
    Charisma CDS 4019
    May 1980

Peter Gabriel 4
    The Rhythm Of The Heat/San Jacinto/I Have The Touch/
    The Family And The Fishing Net/Shock The Monkey/
    Lay Your Hands On Me/Wallflower/Kiss Of Life
    Charisma PG4
    September 1982

Peter Gabriel Plays Live
>The Rhythm Of The Heat/I Have The Touch/Not One Of Us/
>Family Snapshot/DIY/The Family And The Fishing Net/ Intruder/
>I Go Swimming/San Jacinto/Solsbury Hill/No Self Control/I Don't
>Remember/Shock The Monkey/Humdrum/
>On The Air/Biko
>Charisma PGDL 1
>May 1983

Birdy – Music From The Film, by Peter Gabriel
>At Night/Floating Dogs/Quiet And Alone/Close-Up (from 'Family
>Snapshot')/Slow Water/Dressing The Wound/Birdy's Flight (from
>'Not One Of Us') /Slow Marimbas/The Heat (from 'The Rhythm
>Of The Heat')/Sketchpad With Trumpet and Voice/Under Lock
>And Key (from 'Wallflower')/Powerhouse At The Foot Of The
>Mountain (from 'San Jacinto')
>Charisma/Virgin CAS 1167
>March 1985

So
>Red Rain/Sledgehammer/Don't Give Up/That Voice Again/
>In Your Eyes/Mercy Street (for Anne Sexton)/Big Time (success)/
>We Do What We're Told (Milgram's 37)
>Charisma/Virgin PG 5
>May 1986

ALBUMS – CD

Peter Gabriel with Genesis

Nursery Cryme
>The Musical Box/For Absent Friends/The Return Of The Giant
>Hogweed/Seven Stones/Harold The Barrel/Harlequin/
>The Fountain Of Salmacis
>Charisma CASCD 1052
>September 1985

Genesis Live
>Watcher Of The Skies/Get 'Em Out By Friday/The Return Of The
>Giant Hogweed/The Musical Box/The Knife
>Charisma CLACD 1
>October 1985

Selling England By The Pound
Dancing With The Moonlit Knight/I Know What I Like (In Your
Wardrobe)/Firth Of Fifth/More Fool Me/The Battle Of Epping
Forest/After The Ordeal/The Cinema Show/Aisle Of Plenty
Charisma CASCD 1074
February 1986

The Lamb Lies Down On Broadway
The Lamb Lies Down On Broadway/Fly On A Windshield/
Broadway Melody Of 1974/Cuckoo Cocoon/In The Cage/
The Grand Parade Of Lifeless Packaging/Back in NYC/
Hairless Heart/Counting Out Time/The Carpet Crawlers/
The Chamber Of 32 Doors/ Lillywhite Lilith/The Waiting Room/
Anyway/Here Comes The Supernatural Anaesthetist/
The Lamia/Silent Sorrow In Empty Boats/
The Colony Of Slippermen (The Arrival, A Visit To The Doktor,
The Raven)/Ravine/The Light Dies Down On Broadway/
Riding The Scree/In The Rapids/It
Charisma CGSCD 1
1986

(As Above Virgin CGSCD X1)

Foxtrot
Watcher Of The Skies/Time Table/Get 'Em Out By Friday/
Can-Utility And The Coastliners/Horizons/ Supper's Ready/
i Lover's Leap, ii The Guaranteed Eternal Sanctuary Man,
iii Ikhnaton And Itsacon And Their Band Of Merry Men,
iv How Dare I Be So Beautiful? v Willow Farm,
vi Apocalypse in 9/8 (Co-starring The Delicious Talents of
Gabble Ratchet), vii As Sure As Eggs Is Eggs
(Aching Men's Feet)
Charisma CASCD 1058
July 1986

From Genesis To Revelation
Where The Sour Turns To Sweet/In The Beginning/ Fireside Song/
The Serpent/Am I Very Wrong/In The Wilderness/The Conqueror/
In Hiding/One Day/Window/In Limbo/Silent Sun/A Place To Call
My Own
Razor MACHK 11
1988

Trespass
>Looking For Someone/White Mountain/Visions Of Angels/
>Stagnation/Dusk/The Knife
>Charisma CASCD 1020
>June 1988

Trespass/Nursery Cryme/Foxtrot boxed CD set
>Virgin TPAK 1
>October 1990

1/2/3 boxed CD set
>Virgin TPAK 9
>October 1990

Sour Turns To Sweet
>Where The Sour Turns To Sweet/In The Beginning/ Fireside Song/
>The Serpent/Am I Very Wrong/In The Wilderness/The Conqueror/
>In Hiding/One Day/Window/In Limbo/Silent Sun/
>A Place To Call My Own
>Razor MACD 4
>July 1991

From Genesis To Revelation
>Where The Sour Turns To Sweet/In The Beginning/ Fireside Song/
>The Serpent/Am I Very Wrong/In The Wilderness/The Conqueror/
>In Hiding/One Day/Window/In Limbo/Silent Sun/
>A Place To Call My Own
>Music Club MCCD 132
>1993

ALBUMS – CD

Peter Gabriel – Solo

Peter Gabriel 1
>(reissue) Moribund The Bürgermeister/Solsbury Hill/
>Modern Love/Excuse Me/Humdrum/Slowburn/Waiting For The
>Big One/Down The Dolce Vita/Here Comes The Flood
>Charisma CD8000 912
>May 1983

Birdy – Music From The Film
    At Night/Floating Dogs/Quiet And Alone/Close-Up (from 'Family
    Snapshot')/Slow Water/Dressing The Wound/Birdy's Flight (from
    'Not One Of Us') /Slow Marimbas/The Heat (from 'The Rhythm
    Of The Heat')/Sketchpad With Trumpet and Voice/Under Lock
    And Key (from 'Wallflower')/Powerhouse At The Foot Of The
    Mountain (from 'San Jacinto')
    Virgin CASCD1167
    March 1985

Peter Gabriel Plays Live (edited down to 1 CD)
    San Jacinto/Solsbury Hill/No Self Control/Shock The Monkey/
    I Don't Remember/Humdrum/On The Air/Biko/The Rhythm Of
    The Heat/I Have The Touch/Not One Of Us/Family Snapshot/DIY/
    The Family And The Fishing Net/Intruder/I Go Swimming
    Virgin PGDLCD 1
    June 1985

So
    Red Rain/Sledgehammer/Don't Give Up/That Voice Again/
    In Your Eyes/Mercy Street/Big Time/We Do What We're Told
    (Milgram's 37)/This Is The Picture (excellent birds)
    Virgin PGCD 5
    May 1986

Peter Gabriel 4 reissue
    The Rhythm Of The Heat/San Jacinto/I Have The Touch/
    The Family And The Fishing Net/Shock The Monkey/
    Lay Your Hands On Me/Wallflower/Kiss Of Life
    Charisma PGCD4
    November 1986

Peter Gabriel 1 reissue As above
    Charisma PGCD1
    May 1987

Peter Gabriel 2
    (reissue) On The Air/Do It Yourself/Mother Of Violence/
    A Wonderful Day In A One Way World/White Shadow/Indigo/
    Animal Magic/Exposure/Flotsam & Jetsam/Perspective/
    Home Sweet Home
    Charisma PGCD2
    May 1987

Peter Gabriel 3
> (reissue) Intruder/No Self Control/The Start/I Don't Remember/
> Family Snapshot/And Through The Wire/Games Without
> Frontiers/Not One Of Us/Lead A Normal Life/Biko
> Charisma PGCD3
> May 1987

Peter Gabriel Plays Live (reissue) As Above
> Virgin CDPGD 100
> May 1988

So (P. Disc) As Above
> Charisma PGCDP 5
> December 1988

Shaking The Tree
> Solsbury Hill/I Don't Remember/ Sledgehammer/Family Snapshot/
> Mercy Street/Shaking The Tree/Don't Give Up/Here Comes The
> Flood/Games Without Frontiers/Shock The Monkey/Big Time/
> Biko/San Jacinto/Zaar/Red Rain/I Have The Touch
> Virgin PGTVD 6
> November 1990

Us
> Come Talk To Me/Love To Be Loved/Blood Of Eden/Steam/
> Only Us/Washing Of The Water/Digging In The Dirt/Fourteen
> Black Paintings/Kiss That Frog/Secret World
> Realworld PGCD 7
> September 1992